Here's What Seasoned Sailors are Saying About "The Essential Galley Companion"

"Amanda Swan Neal has cooked under every condition imaginable and her book is full of tips on how to turn onboard cuisine from a simple fare to a pleasurable experience. Her favorite ingredients are a good dose of common sense with a pinch of subtle humor."

Jimmy Cornell, author of *World Cruising Routes.*

"Chock full of sea-tested recipes based on ingredients available worldwide, this book also includes invaluable advice for the ocean epicure from filleting a tuna to managing waste. Amanda has brought to bear all of her 345,000 miles of offshore experience to create a useful and useable reference for anyone whose kitchen moves from place to place, and then added her wit and wisdom in the form of anecdotes from her days of Whitbread racing and world cruising. This book will be aboard wherever I cruise from now on."

Beth Leonard, author of *The Voyagers Handbook*

"*The Essential Galley Companion* is a breath of fresh air. Compiled and written by someone who knows how to provide good food in often impossible circumstances, it is packed full of essential practical advice."

Tracy Edwards, MBE, skipper of *Maiden*, 1989-90 Whitbread Race

"Amanda's spirit and wide range of experience shows through on these pages."

Dawn Riley, watch leader on *Maiden,* CEO *America True* and executive director Oakcliff Sailing Center

"This is a seagoing *Joy of Cooking,* but with a difference; laced throughout the quite simple and savory recipes are vignettes that serve as windows into worlds that most of us may never see – a farmer's market in the Chilean channels; an anchorage near Cape Horn; a rough watch on a Whitbread boat, or the embrace of a devoted New Zealand family. *The Essential Galley Companion* is the first truly unusual offshore-sailing cookbook to come along in our memory."

Nim Marsh, editor *Blue Water Sailing*

"I love to cook but I'm not creative in the galley. So, I really need a book like Amanda's to provide the impetus for me to try new things. *The Essential Galley Companion* provides a well thought out guide to menu planning and that is the heart of galley success and the most difficult aspect to manage."

Robert Perry, yacht designer

THE ESSENTIAL GALLEY COMPANION

SECOND EDITION

Recipes and Provisioning Advice
for Your Boating Adventures

To Wendy & Peter
Aloha Amanda

AMANDA SWAN NEAL

MAHINA
OFFSHORE SERVICES

Library of Congress Catalog Card Number: 2020911029
Swan Neal, Amanda 1964-
The Essential Galley Companion: recipes and provisioning advice for your
boating adventures / Amanda Swan Neal.

ISBN 978-0-9676904-2-1
Second Edition

Printed by Kindle Direct Publishing
Cover design by W. Bruce Conway
Book illustrations by Ron Wilson
Back cover yacht image by Tor Johnson
Cover dress by Pacific Island Arts

P.O Box 1596, Friday Harbor, WA 98250, USA
phone 360.378.6161   sailing@mahina.com
www.mahina.com

Contents

Dedication
To
Mum and Dad,
who gave me the passion to experience life,
my Nana and Poppa,
who gave me the strength and tenacity
to believe in my endeavors,
and to John,
who gives me love, the joy of life, and the
encourgement to share what I've achieved.

Acknowledgements

I thank Ron Wilson for his artwork and Suzy Wilson for her creativity.

I thank Bruce Conway for his technical assistance.

I thank Carol Noel and Molly O'Neil for their enthusiastic input into this book, Lisa Knowles for her adventerous spirit, and my fellow Maidens for proving that dreams do come true.

I thank all the Mahina Expeditions members who were taste testers, vegie choppers and recipe contributers, and thanks too to the fellow boaters and the restaurants who eagerly shared their favorite recipes.

Introduction

The *Essential Galley Companion* has been designed to introduce you to my onboard cooking, both at anchor and underway.

I wrote this book to answer the frequent requests seminar students and expedition members have in wanting to know how to make their lives at sea easier.

I joined John Neal in 1994 aboard *Mahina Tiare II* and began conducting offshore expeditions. While sailing through Patagonia enroute to Antarctica it became evident that a well-provisioned and efficient galley is essential in providing quick, easy, and nutritious meals for a hungry crew.

Material for this book came from discovering terrific recipes while sharing memorable meals with cruising friends, from new friends and local restaurants ashore, and from fellow expedition members, some of who are great cooks and others who needed a helping hand.

The Essential Galley Companion was written in 2000 while underway on an 11,000-mile, six-month series of expeditions from New Zealand to Alaska, ending in our wonderful homeport in the San Juan Islands of Washington.

This revision was completed during COVID-19 while following our governor's proclamation "Stay Home – Stay Healthy". In adding the 40 new recipes I've tried to keep a focus on recipes that are healthy and interesting plus applicable to your boating adventures. They've been tried and tested with 1,000 expeditions members over the past 20 years and 220,000 miles.

I hope that you'll gain as much enjoyment reading and cooking from this book as I have realized in writing it.

AMANDA

Guide On Using the Recipes

For the recipes I've made the assumption that you're familiar with the basics of cooking.

All recipes are designed to serve four people.

Each recipe is streamlined to enable you to quickly determine if the recipe is suitable for your available ingredients, time frame and weather conditions. I want to avoid overloading you with excessive instructions, especially if you're following a recipe while under way and the pages are dancing before your eyes.

The ingredients are listed in order of most required to least required, allowing for a quick scan down the list to determine the required ingredients and the quantity – this also helps you in deciding what ingredient can be substitutued if the listed ingredient is unavailable.

Wherever possible, I've adapted the recipes so that they're applicable to worldwide use; for example in the fish chapter I've not specified a particular variety of fish unless the recipe works only with that type, such as salmon.

You're welcome to vary the vegetables used in most of the recipes as when you're out sailing you sometimes have to make do with what you have or need to consume before it perishes. I didn't consider it necessary to continue mentioning this throughout the book.

Fresh herbs feature frequently in the recipes. When substituting dried herbs for fresh 1 teaspoon of dried herbs is the equivalent of 1 tablespoon of fresh chopped herbs.

Symbols in the Text

Symbols are included to work as a quick guide.

T Tablespoon

t teaspoon

  Pressure-cooker

  A one-dish meal

* Optional addition to a recipe

S&P Salt and Pepper

Weights and Measures

Conversion Chart for Weights and Measures

Kilograms	Ounces	Cups
1kg.	32 oz. (2 lbs.)	4 cups
750g	24 oz. (1 1/2 lbs.)	3 cups
600g	20 oz. (1 lb., 4 oz.)	2 1/2 cups
500g	16 oz. (1 lb.)	2 cups
300g	10 oz.	1 1/4 cups
240g	8 oz.	1 cup
180g	6 oz.	3/4 cup
60g	2 oz.	1/4 cup

Oven Temperatures

Very slow	250°F	120°C
Slow	300°F	150°C
Moderately slow	325°F	160°C
Moderate	375°F	190°C
Hot	400°F	200°C
Very Hot	450°F	230°C

Chapter 1

Outfitting the Galley

Galley Design

The size of your boat will determine the minimum space allocation for the galley area. I've sailed and cooked on many boats; a 28-foot stripped-out race boat cooking on a one-burner camping stove, a 50-foot motor yacht with an electric range, a Whitbread 60 with its ergonomically-designed cook-pod, cruiser/racer yachts that try to emulate the kitchen at home, a 1909 76-foot restored Fife yacht with the galley forward of the mast on a sloping cabin sole and a 175-foot sail-training vessel for 50 crew. The lesson I take away from these experiences is that more important than size is a layout that takes many critical factors into consideration.

Layout

Personally, I like a U-shaped galley that enables you to brace your bottom allowing you to perform simple galley tasks without worrying about what the boat is doing and which way youre heeling. The other option is a long fore-and-aft galley running along the hull, though this takes up a lot of space in what is traditionally the main saloon area. On larger yachts the galley is often located beside the cockpit in the walkway through to the aft cabin as on Oyster Yachts. With a long galley you need some means of keeping yourself in place and a strap that sits across your bottom is the common solution, though this doesn't allow a quick means of escape to dodge a flying pot. On our 46-foot Hallberg-Rassy, with its U-shaped galley, I'm right in front of the stove but can easily escape missiles.

On a motor yacht space is less at a premium because of the increased volume. Most often the galley is equipped as it would be at home with electrical appliances including stove and refrigerator, large counter space, pressure water, and adequate stowage facilities. As there often is far less motion on a motor yacht than on a sailboat it's not as critical to design the galley area as if it were a continual moving platform.

Sinks

❖ A **deep sink** is my paramount choice for the galley. It doesn't have to be extremely large just big enough to be able to comfortably hold large dinner plates.

❖ If space allows, a **double-sink** arrangement works best. The sinks on *Mahina Tiare III* are 12" x 12" and 12" x 9", and both are 8" deep.

❖ Installing the sink relatively **close to centerline** will allow it to drain on all angles of heel.

❖ If your sinks are positioned **close to the waterline** or against the hull you'll need either a manual or electric pump to drain away the water – or at least an easily accessible ball valve to shut off the salt water which gurgles up the drain when heeled over.

Soap Dispenser

We've installed **two soap dispensers** in our galley. One is for antibacterial hand soap and the other is for dish soap. I've since found a product available in gallon jugs from Costco and Walmart that does both these jobs, so in hind sight I could've installed just one pump.

Water Pumps

❖ Having a **manual freshwater foot pump** instead of a hand pump allows you to use both hands while working in the galley.

❖ Most boats on which I've sailed also have a **saltwater galley pump** to help reduce water consumption.

❖ When we purchased our current boat I was surprised to discover that there was **no saltwater pump** in the galley. John assured me that as we've large water tanks and a high output watermaker we have adequate water to be able to wash the dishes without using salt water. For the first few months of cruising I felt extremely guilty every time I used freshwater for a job where I'd have previously used salt water. After a while I realized that the dish towels stayed fresher and that none of my galley utensils were rusting as they usually did.

❖ A **pressurized water system** with the added convenience of hot water makes the galley area feel more like home.

Counter Space

❖ Counter space is **often limited** and when the boat is underway items can't be put down unattended.

Outfitting the Galley

❖ At sea I place **Scoot-Gard** or a similar nonskid material on the countertop to prevent objects from moving when I set them down.

❖ You need to train yourself to **be a tidy cook**, cleaning up as you progress though a meal, not only in stowing away equipment used but also staying on top of the dishes.

❖ A **fiddle** should surround the countertop to stop articles sliding off, and on our yacht these have slots cut into them for handholds.

❖ Having a **chopping board** custom made for your sink or stovetop will increase counter space.

❖ Our chopping board is **a pullout block** like a drawer that can also serve as additional counter space.

❖ I have been on a few cruising yachts that have an **extra countertop** that swings up and is propped open with a leg.

Storage Lockers

❖ You want to **utilize the space** you have available for the items you use frequently while cooking. Give careful consideration to each item you place in a prime, easy-to-reach location and check that nothing sits dormant in a location that could be otherwise occupied by a more frequently used item.

❖ **Transfer large containers** of food such as oil, jelly, mayonnaise, honey, mustard, salt, cereal and rice into small containers that fit your galley space. Before each ocean passage, top up the containers so you don't have to do it the first week at sea.

❖ **Always return items** to their stowage space; it's frustrating to have to search around in lockers looking for a rearranged or misplaced item.

❖ **You need patience** for finding and stowing gear; it's not easy, and often you have to move two objects out of the way to reach the item you require.

❖ R u b b e r m a i d manufactures an extensive range of **plastic draw- er-dividers** that allow you to sep- arate and organize items.

❖ Use **Scoot-Gard** to prevent items from sliding around in lockers and drawers.

❖ Ensure that your drawers have a **sturdy locking catch** and a stop that prevents the drawer from totally sliding out.

❖ To **organize and divide lockers** use baskets, wooden/plexiglass dividers or install adjustable pegs into the base of the cupboard.

Ventilation

❖ Generally the galley is situated **near the companionway** ensuring plenty of fresh air and easy access to the cockpit, although alternative ventilation is required when the main hatch is closed. One or more of the following would be helpful.

❖ A **dorade vent** placed above the galley helps supply ventilation.

❖ The addition of a **small electric fan** – such as a Hella Turbo – greatly aids in cooling down the cook in the tropics and in heavy weather or rain when hatches and ports are closed.

❖ An **opening port** above my stove is a quick solution for fresh air but it requires constant monitoring for spray, waves or rain.

Stove Installation

To save galley space when building our second family cruising boat my dad decided not to gimbal our kerosene stove. His reasoning was that we'd have big deep pots to keep the food inside and strong adjustable arms on the stovetop to prevent the pots from jumping off as the boat heeled. When the sea conditions were calm enough my dad would let my brother and I bake a cake. Once in the oven the initial baking process required constant monitoring, turning the cake this way and that to ensure the cake didn't develop an uneven tilt. Our cakes inevitably had a lopsided appearance and we'd name it either a port or starboard tack cake depending on its resulting angle.

❖ A **stainless steel grab-bar** should be mounted across the front of the stovetop to prevent people falling on the elements or grabbing the stove for support when the boat rocks.

❖ Stoves are generally mounted **fore and aft** against the hull.

❖ Check that your stove **gimbals with ease** and has no erratic movement. You may need to add more weight down low to dampen its movement.

❖ A gimbaled stove requires a **locking catch** to secure the gimbals when not needed. I always lock the gimbals before opening the oven door on my Force 10 stove as the open door causes the oven to tilt drastically.

❖ A stove top needs a high fiddle, an even grill surface on which different-sized pots can sit flat and adjustable **pan-locking arms** or **pot-holders** to keep pots positioned over the burners.

❖ A stove that is mounted **athwartship**, against a bulkhead, won't be able to utilize gimbals, but is considered safer by some people as it does not rock and lurch with the boat's movement.

Fire Safety

❖ In the event of a galley fire, a **fire extinguisher** should be readily accessible.

❖ A **fire blanket** mounted near the galley can be used to quickly snuff out grease and alcohol fires.

Treating Minor Burns

In my first restaurant kitchen job, I received a nasty burn when I picked up a hot frying pan that the cook had tossed into the sink. I instantly placed butter on it which I quickly learned was a myth, as butter fat stays hot adding heat to the burn. Thank goodness another chef noticed my lack of knowledge and administered the correct treatment, saving me more pain.

❖ **Immerse burns** immediately in cold water.

❖ **Clean seawater** or salt solution is preferable with ice or chemical cold packs added. Soak until the heat dissipates, at least half an hour.

❖ Apply **Silvadene ointment** (Silver-sulfadiazine) thickly to the burned area and cover with clean gauze (somewhat loosely so as not to constrict blood flow). If two burned surfaces are touching each other, between the fingers for example, place sterile gauze between them.

❖ Several times a day, **soak burns** in a sterile container of salt water and reapply Silvadene ointment and gauze. Silvadene is an anti-bacterial agent that prevents infection of burns far more effectively than any other antibiotic cream.

Equipping the Galley

Short~Handled Utensils

Bottle opener with corkscrew
Can opener x 2
Garlic crusher
Knife sharpener
Measuring spoons
Measuring cups
Scissors
Vegetable knife
Vegetable peeler

Long~Handled Utensils

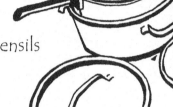

Barbecue tongs
Bread knife
Fish slice
Fish filleting knife
Gas stove lighter x2
Grater
Knife – large
Rubber Spatula
Salad tongs
Serving spoon
Slotted spoon – large
Skewers – for barbecues
Whisk

Galley Helpers

Funnel x 3 – assorted sizes
Measuring cup – mine is like a saucepan, and I use it to melt
    butter or toast small amounts
Mortar and pestle – not necessary, but handy for mixing spices
Rolling pin – I use a wine bottle instead of a rolling pin
Sieve/strainer
Sprouting jar with stainless steel mesh lid
Wooden chopping board x2 – 1 large and 1 small
Yogurt maker or large-mouth thermos
Coffee grinder

Pots and Pans

Revere stainless steel tea kettle with whistle
6-quart Cuisinart pressure cooker
3 nesting Magma stainless steel pots with 2 removable handles
    and one shared lid
5-quart Magma soup pot with lid and steamer basket
8" Teflon sautéing pan
11" high-sided Teflon frying pan with lid or cast-iron skillet
Wok (if you enjoy Asian cooking)
8 x 12 Pyrex baking dish
11 x 14 Pyrex casserole dish
Bread pans – x2 stainless steel
Cookie tray
Muffin tray
2.3-quart stainless steel Thermos pump pot. Ours is installed
    on the galley counter top and is used for hot water.

Electrical Appliances

Blender/food processor
Bread machine
Cake mixer
Coffeemaker
Coffee grinder – also used for spices
Crock pot
Hand blender and chopper

Galley Supplies

Aluminum foil
Apron
Assorted plastic storage containers for leftovers and food storage
Dish towels
Garbage bags – large and small – I recycle my plastic supermarket
    bags so sometimes use these
Hand towel
Hot pads – for placing hot dishes on the table
Paper bags – 5" x 10" brown paper for organic waste
    disposal at sea
Paper napkins – might work out cheaper to use than paper towels
    when purchased in bulk
Paper plates – for barbecues ashore and potlucks

Paper towels – I cut the roll in half to make it last longer
Plastic wrap – I rarely use it
Plastic cups, forks and knives – for barbecues and potluck
  dinners ashore
Tea towels
Ziploc bags – freezer bags are the sturdiest; carry various sizes
Nonskid Scoot-Gard matting to stop objects sliding
Oven mitts

Tips on Cookware

❖ **Pyrex baking dishes** are great onboard, they're extremely sturdy, cook evenly and are easy to clean.

❖ **Teflon-coated baking pans** may rust out in a couple of years.

❖ We have a **Teflon-coated frying pan** that we replace every two years as the Teflon coating wears off.

❖ My mum has a **cast-iron frying pan**. It needs to be seasoned by hot heat and wiped with oil so it won't rust.

Wok Cooking

❖ A steel wok will need to be **seasoned** by wiping it with oil and baking it in a hot oven three or four times before using it. Once seasoned correctly it will be sealed and won't tend to rust as quickly. My mum's wok is so seasoned from her Chinese cooking that when she heats it up it smells divine. The only trouble is that when she uses her wok to make any other ethnic dish – such as an Italian tomato – it ends up with a hint of Asian flavoring.

❖ The **secret to wok cooking** is to keep the heat hot and the food sliced evenly so that it cooks at the same rate. Another option is to add the food at different times, ending with an item such as cabbage that requires the least amount of cooking.

❖ To **clean and care** for your wok after cooking rinse it out with soapy water and place it back on a hot flame to dry it out. If your wok starts to rust just season it again.

Bread Machine

❖ It's **not necessary** to have a bread machine but in the many years I've been cruising with ours I've really enjoyed it.

❖ Our bread machine bakes a **two-pound** conventional horizontal loaf. Its power draw through the inverter is modest as the heating element cycles while the bread is baking. We generally use it when we have the engine on to charge the batteries or are motoring.

Pressure Cookers

My first offshore passage as a child was extremely rough. I have memories of my mum making banana custard using milk powder and the whole dish having a burnt flavor to it. I was rather excited by the prospect of having pudding at all.

Visions of that same passage feature mum struggling, strapped in at galley, while wrestling all sorts of wholesome food into the pressure cooker. Patiently she lights the kerosene stove and sits down wearily to observe its progress. Five minutes later when the cooker is in full pressure and hissing steadily an extra large wave throws the entire pot off the stove and onto the floor. It continued to move, bouncing around the cabin and venting even more steam like some demented giant beach ball with a hole in it. I thought my whole world would explode and soon send me out into the dark blue ocean. Mum started laughing then calmly stood up, scooped up the pot, still hissing away, and placed it gently back on the stove.

❖ Pressure cooking is a **quick efficient one-pot method** for preparing meals, casseroles, soups, stews, and baking.

❖ Pressure cooking reduces conventional **cooking time** by up to 70%.

❖ **In the tropics**, the shorter cooking time of pressure cooking results in reduced cabin heat.

❖ With the lid locked down it **prevents food from sloshing** over the top of the pot in rough weather.

❖ Carefully **read the instruction booklet** that comes with the cooker.

❖ **Brown meats** to seal their flavor and simmer the meal for a few minutes to even out the heat before locking on the lid.

❖ Never fill the pot over **2/3 full** in case the food or liquid blocks the vent.

❖ Always **use plenty of liquid** to avoid the contents drying out and burning.

❖ When the **cooker reaches pressure** it's time to monitor the cooking period.

❖ Don't use **high heat,** just enough to sustain the pressure.

❖ Never remove the lid until **all the pressure** has been released from the cooker.

❖ Once your timing has finished, **cool the pot** by placing it under a cold water tap.

❖ It's best to **season** your cooking after pressurizing as flavors tend to become concentrated while under pressure.

To Use Pressure Cooker as a Mini Oven

1. Remove the rubber-sealing gasket in the lid so it won't dry out.
2. Place a metal trivet on the bottom of the pot (an empty tuna can with the bottom and top removed works well). This trivet acts as a spacer and should be at least 1/2" high.
3. Inside the pressure cooker to allow even distribution of heat place a metal pan so that it provides a 1/2" space between its sides and the cooker
4. Be sure to use a low heat or the bottom of your baking will burn. A flame-tamer on top of the burner helps to evenly distribute heat.
5. When baking bread, grease and coat the inside baking dish with flour.
6. Don't remove the lid until you are sure the baking is cooked, as the heat escapes.

❖ Foods cooked under pressure, then left sealed inside with the pressure cap still on, **remain sterile** for a couple of days without refrigeration. Re-pressurizing before eating kills most organisms. This process works well for meats or if you catch a large fish and don't have refrigeration.

❖ **Food that doesn't pressure cook well**: milk products, eggs, and pasta, as it tends to froth.

❖ *Cooking Under Pressure* by Lorna Sass is a great book for pressure cooking advice and recipes.

Romantic and Guest Entertaining

Remember that the boat is now your home – so there's no need to feel as though you're forever camping out.

On our first offshore cruise in 1977, Mum outfitted our galley with plastic bowls and plates. This was a decision she regretted because the plastic soon scratched and she missed her china dinnerware. When we built our second boat in 1980 Mum purchased two identical dinner sets (one as a spare) and had dad build them into their own storage locker in the galley. She never regretted the extra expense and rarely did we break a dish – even with my brother and I handling them.

My first date with John transpired when he asked me out for dinner while I was working on his rigging. I was rather shell shocked that he asked. I hadn't even noticed that he was even remotely keen on me, especially since we had only met while I was in my work mode. He gave me a choice of a restaurant meal or dinner on his boat. I'd not seen his boat and it occurred to me that I might have to sit through a restaurant meal knowing that I'd still be given the standard chat-up line, "Do you want to come see my boat?" I decided to have dinner onboard, where I could be assured of an easy getaway if I felt uncomfortable with the situation.

Arriving down at the boat after dark, nervously clutching a bottle of wine, I gingerly knocked on the hull. A smiling face appeared out of the hatch and called, "Come on down!" As I stepped down the companionway, I was impressed. *Mahina Tiare's II* interior had a tropical flare, small lamps draped with flower leis lighted the corners and soft Hawaiian music quietly played. In the center of the table set for two sat a bottle of my favorite wine, perfectly chilled. John set to in the galley adding the finishing touches to chicken fettuccine and a tossed salad that brightly contrasted with a tidy bench top. I sat down with a sigh and thought to myself that I'd sail anywhere in the world with this guy.

If you don't picture yourself as the perfect dinner host, perhaps invite friends over for sunset drinks rather than for dinner. Sharing a cool drink and munching snacks while watching the sun go down is nice way to end the day, and it certainly takes the pressure off the cook.

The cruising lifestyle lends itself well to entertaining and a few treasured items help create a special event. Here's

Outfitting the Galley

my list of items I use when we entertain or have a romantic dinners and although these items are not a necessity both John and I receive a lot of pleasure when using them:

Attractive salt and pepper grinders
Candles and candle holder
Cheese board and knife
Crystal wine glasses
Flower vase for fresh flowers
Interesting dishes for serving appetizers – carved wooden bowl, woven bread basket, colored glass dishes
Napkins – cloth and paper
Place mats
Table cloth

Cooking Appliances

Propane Stoves

Propane is the cooking fuel most commonly used on cruising boats as it provides instant and easy heat simply by lighting the gas burner.

Propane Installation

❖ The **hazard with propane** is that it's heavier than air. If a leak occurs the gas will collect in lowest point where even the smallest spark can cause an explosion.

❖ Most boats have a **built-in propane locker** with a drain hole in the bottom that leads directly overboard.

❖ **Aluminum propane cylinders** are double the price of steel propane cylinders but are maintenance-free and lightweight. We carry two 20-lb. tanks and with 8 people onboard a tank lasts 6 weeks. A full tank weighs 30 lbs. so I use our Ruxxac folding dock cart to transport it.

❖ You need to keep **steel cylinders** painted to prevent rust. White is the best color.

❖ An electric **solenoid valve** should be installed immediately after the tank with a remote control switch near the stove. A Xintex propane monitor and control not only turns the gas on and off but also monitors the system for leaks, in which event it automatically shuts off the flow and sounds an alarm.

Outfitting the Galley

❖ Propane or butane is **available worldwide**, though quality differs in from country to country.

❖ Many countries use **different pipe threads** for their tanks which might not be compatible with your tank. When filling our propane tanks in different countries we've found that most refill stations have an assortment of adapters to fit most pipe fittings.

❖ Some countries such as Chile, Iceland and Marquesas can only legally **exchange propane tanks** rather that refill them.

❖ If it's not possible to get your tanks filled at refill station you may have to do so by gravity. It's impossible to completely fill a tank using this method but sometimes it's the only option.

Filling a Propane Tank by Gravity
1. Connect the two tanks.
2. Place the full tank higher than your tank.
3. Turn the full tank upside-down or on it's side and open the bleed valve on your tank.
4. The liquid gas will slowly flow into your tank.

Kerosene Stoves

Kerosene used to be the fuel of choice for cruising in isolated places but now with propane more readily available kerosene stoves are less common on cruising boats.

Advantages: Kerosene is cheap, nonexplosive and produces the most heat per volume of any fuel.

Disadvantages: It requires priming with alcohol and periodic de-carbonizing of the burners, which is a nasty job.

Microwave Ovens

When outfitting our new boat a microwave was on the option list but I didn't give it a second thought. I'd rather have the storage space and I realized that I'm not a microwave cook at home, only using it for reheating leftovers, drinks and making popcorn. Microwaves are common on liveaboard dockside boats but I see few long-distance cruisers using them.

Many large, modern yachts are fitted with microwaves. Steve and Linda Dashew aboard their 78-foot *Beowulf* enjoy theirs, especially in the tropics as it produces less heat below than a conventional oven and in rough weather it quickly heats precooked meals.

Electric Stoves

Requiring a generator to operate, electric stoves are fitted on power yachts and very large sailboats but are uncommon on cruising sailboats.

Advantages: No chance of explosion from propane or additional fuel system. Simple and safe for dockside living.

Disadvantage: Generator needs to be running when stove is in operation.

Diesel Stoves

More common in high-latitude cruisers because, when operating, the entire range serves as a heater.

Advantages: Diesel fuel is cheap; stove is used as a heater and to supplement the waterheater. Stove removes moisture from the cabin.

Disadvantages: In warmer climates the radiant heat is hard to bear. Consideration should be taken when stove is on to avoid unnecessary contact, especially while under way, as the entire unit is very hot. Attention needs to be given to the exhaust to ensure that nothing is in the way. Can't be gimbaled. Combustion process often results in sooty decks and sail covers. Strong winds may create back drafts, resulting in smoke in the cabin, particularly if the chimney isn't long enough. Can only be used when the boat is not heeling much.

Alcohol Stoves

I have not recently met a cruising yacht using alcohol, and personally I don't recommend it for long-distance cruising.

Advantages: Alcohol fuel burns clean, and is safe as it evaporates when spilled. Fire can be extinguished with water.

Disadvantages: Alcohol fuel is expensive and hard to find worldwide. Burns at a low temperature, so you need to allow 15% more time to cooking.

Camping Stove

Carry a multi-purpose camping stove as a backup for your main stove. I also use ours when we go on extended hiking adventures.

Barbecues

The first time I became aware of marine barbecues was when my parents were outfitting to go cruising from New Zealand in 1993 and my dad asked me to purchase a charcoal barbecue from the marine store on my way home. Looking at its size in the shop, I was surprised that my parents were willing to carry such a large item, plus the charcoal, aboard their 36-foot yacht but they've had many years of dining pleasure with it. They'd considered gas but having experienced a few windy potluck evenings when the flame keep blowing out they thought they'd try their luck with charcoal.

I was undecided as to whether or not I wanted to have a barbecue when we were outfitting *Mahina Tiare III*. Visions of half-cooked meals instantly came to mind but John assured me that the large Force 10 gas barbecue would make barbecuing quick and easy.

It certainly is large and on passages we don't want it hanging off the aft rail getting in the way. We stow it inside its cardboard box in the cockpit locker when we go to sea and its 10-lb. propane tank in the side deck gas locker. We've enjoyed many barbecue meals and it's certainly fun and easy for entertaining. Barbecuing on deck helps decrease the smell and heat from the galley area, especially in the tropics.

I've discovered that barbecuing is a "guy kind of thing," so I'll often be quick to suggest a barbecue meal as I know it's one less thing for me to do in the galley. I've noticed that few Europeans have barbecues but for many Kiwis, Aussies and North Americans, a "barbie and cold beer" are the essence of cruising.

Barbecue Do's

- ❖ Choose a **marine barbecue** constructed of stainless steel so to avoid corrosion.
- ❖ **Stow your barbecue** when making passages to avoid complications in heavy weather, while sailing and when docking.
- ❖ Consider a **canvas cover** for your barbecue when in port, as even marine brands don't hold their lovely shine for long.

- ❖ Take care to **avoid sparks** when it's lit.
- ❖ Plan on using your barbecue as an **alternative cooking source** if your main stove fails.
- ❖ **Take your barbecue ashore**, as it's fun to use for picnics and potlucks. Both Force 10 and Magma have optional dock stand brackets.
- ❖ For shoreside barbecues I generally use **paper plates** to save washing up when back on board.
- ❖ **Be careful when flipping your cooking**. A number of chefs have lost precious morsels to the sharks. Perhaps it's a substitute for feeding Rover at the table.

Barbecue Don'ts

- ❖ Never mount your barbecue near your outboard **fuel tank** or anything flammable.

Gas Barbecue

- ❖ Quick **easy lighting** system.
- ❖ Choice of **two gas options:**
  - ❖ Disposable high-pressure 1-lb. LPG cylinder. Approximately 2.5 hours cooking.
  - ❖ Adapt the barbecue for use with your onboard low pressure system.
- ❖ **Be aware of the hazards** of using propane.
- ❖ Option of purchasing a model that has a **radiant burner plate** for use as a stovetop, oven, or barbecue.

Charcoal Barbecue

- ❖ Prevent **spontaneous combustion** by keeping the charcoal dry in a safe place.
- ❖ Don't use **stale charcoal** as it takes forever to light and maintain its heat.
- ❖ **Cheaper to purchase than gas**, with no complicated systems.
- ❖ A trick of Dad's to obtain **three meals from one set of coals:** when a meal has finished cooking place the lid on the barbecue to starve the air and stop the coals from burning.

Cleaning the Barbecue

Gas and charcoal barbecues are not the easiest item to clean. You need to take your barbecue ashore, spray it well with oven cleaner, scrub it with a metal brush, and wash and wipe it down well.

Beach Barbecue Grill

Several friends we've met cruising carry stainless oven grates or metal grills that they prop over a fire on the beach for cooking. If you're on a budget, this is a no-fuss and easy to stow option to purchasing a proper charcoal or gas barbecue – and the food is just as tasty!

Refrigeration

It's not necessary to cruise with refrigeration but in the tropics I rarely meet a yacht that doesn't have a small fridge. Refrigeration gives you a healthier diet, more meal options and reduces waste since produce doesn't spoil as quickly.

Refrigeration Systems

Evaporator: Similar to a household refrigerator, the compressor is controlled by a thermostat and runs on a continual power supply cycling on and off 24 hours a day. Cold gas runs through the plates, cooling the surrounding air, which is called cold-air evaporation.

Holding plate: Used if you don't have a continual power supply. The compressor cools a solution in the plates, which retain the cold, which in turn cools the air, hence the name *holding*. You need to visually monitor the temperature controlling it by turning on the compressor. The compressor is either driven by an electric motor or a belt-drive off the engine and is run for a period of time, usually a minimum of 1 to 2 hours a day when the engine is on. Maintaining constant fridge temperature can be difficult as you tend to freeze the lettuce when the engine is running and melt the ice cream if left to long between operating time.

Icebox

An option to running refrigeration on its power supply is to utilize the fridge compartment as an ice box. If the boat is hauled out or has inefficient or broken refrigeration, just place large blocks of ice in the insulated fridge box. Some cruisers frequently do this in port to avoid running their engine.

Galley Rules

❖ **Wash hands** after using the toilet, before preparing food, and after touching raw meat, for a minimum of 30 seconds with plenty of friction between the hands.

❖ **Crew with infected hand sores**, strep infections, or diarrhea should not prepare food for others.

❖ Use **clean towels** for drying, and change them frequently as they harbor bacteria. Another option is to air-dry dishes.

❖ **Clean cutting boards** and knives thoroughly after preparing raw meat, poultry and seafood. Do not place cooked meat back on a cutting board until after it has been thoroughly washed.

❖ Cook meat to a temperature of about **170° F** (77° C) internally.

❖ Use a **meat thermometer** for roasts, or dice meat into small pieces to assure thorough cooking.

❖ **Refrigerate leftovers** promptly and heat thoroughly to kill bacteria that grow after an hour or more of room temperature incubation.

Chapter 2

PROVISIONING

Galley Provisions

Dry Stores

Baking powder
Baking soda
Cake mixes
Cereals – breakfast
Chocolate – drinking, eating and cooking
Cocoa
Coconut – desiccated
Coffee
Cookies
Cornmeal
Cornstarch
Couscous
Flour – self rising and whole wheat
Grains – barley, buckwheat, faro, quinoa and wheat
Legumes – chickpeas, sprouts, lentils and kidney beans,
  navy beans etc.
Nuts – almonds, hazelnuts, pecans, peanuts, pine nuts and walnuts
Oats – rolled
Pasta – various
Popcorn
Powdered milk
Rice – brown, white and wild
Salt and Pepper
Seeds – chia, flax, hemp, pumpkin, poppy, sesame and sunflower
Sugar – brown, white and confectioners
Tea
Yeast
2-minute noodles

Condiments

❖ **Chutney** includes many varieties from smooth to spicy. Generally
   made with fruit and virtually any fruit, fresh or dried can be used.
   Specific for Indian dishes and great added to dressings, sauces,
   marinades, chicken salad, sandwiches, fruit salad and to accompany
   chicken and fish.

❖ **Dill Pickles** are tangy additions to salads and sandwiches.

❖ **Fermented Black Beans** are used with garlic, ginger, sugar, and rice wine to create Chinese sauces and stir-fries. Black beans have a distinctive bold pungency and need to be used sparingly. Stored in an airtight container and kept cool they will keep indefinitely.

❖ **Fish Sauce** is a robust liquid resulting from the fermentation of anchovies and salt. Used in curries, stir-frys, dips and sauces, it's the salt of Asian cooking.

❖ **Ketchup** lasts well in the tropics. American brand names are expensive outside U.S. and locally produced ketchup may have a different flavor and is often sweeter.

❖ **Honey** I prefer a runny honey which I keep in a squeeze bottle so it's easier use and saves dirtying utensils.

❖ **Jelly** is best purchased in small containers as it spoils quickly in the tropics once opened unless refrigerated.

❖ **Maple Syrup** can be rather expensive but it's a delightful indulgence on pancakes and French toast. Golden syrup is often used outside of North America.

❖ **Mayonnaise** is best purchased in one-quart containers. I then transfer some of the mayonnaise into a small squeeze bottle and thin it out with cider vinegar to make it more squeezable. The squeeze bottle takes up less space in the cupboard and doesn't require refrigeration as it has not been contaminated.

❖ **Miso** is a Japanese culinary staple of fermented soybean paste. High in protein and rich in vitamins and minerals miso goes well in soups, salad dressing, and marinades.

❖ **Olives** are great additions to salads, pastas and Mediterranean cooking.

❖ **Peanut Butter** is every galley's heavy weather standby. Also handy for Asian peanut sauces, baking and protein shakes.

❖ **Sambal-Oelek** is a hot chili paste from Indonesia made from red chilies, salt, vinegar and garlic. Both the paste and the oil are useful together or separately for marinades, sauces and dressings. Found in Asian Markets. You can substitute chili sauce and add extra garlic.

❖ **Soy Sauce** is excellent for sushi and sashimi. Good substitute for salt in oriental dishes even

when not called for. Use in marinades (it's a natural meat tenderizer), dressings and sauces.

❖ **Sweet Chili Sauce** is a poplular dipping condiment that also goes well in sauces, stirfries and salad dressings.

❖ **Tabasco** is a hot chili sauce.

❖ **Tahini** is a toasted sesame seed butter of Middle Eastern origin. It has a mild delicate flavor and is used in sauces, spreads, and dressings. Two popular spreads using tahini are hummus, made with chickpeas, and baba ghanoush, made with smoked eggplant.

❖ **Wasabi**, a hot Japanese horse radish sauce, is essential for sushi and sashimi. It's also marvelous in dressings and sauces. Available in plastic tubes that last a long time or in powered form that you mix with water.

❖ **Worcestershire Sauce** is a rich spicy sauce of vinegar, molasses, anchovies, garlic, tamarind and spices. Used in meat dishes, marinades and soups.

Wines

❖ **Red Wine** is a nice addition to hearty meals such as stews and wild game, it gives an added zing to tomato sauces and a rich dimension to red meat marinades.

❖ **White Wine** goes well with fish, seafood and poultry.

❖ **Sherry, Port, Rum, Brandy and Whiskey** give a sweet flavor to sauces and deserts.

Liqueurs

I'm not suggesting that you carry all of these liqueurs but we generally have a bottle of something interesting and I find that it's a nice indulegence to use a dash now and then. This following is a guide to help you add that extra zing.

❖ **Bailey's Irish Cream** is made in Ireland from Irish whiskey flavored with cocoa, vanilla and cream. Use with chocolate, coffee and vanilla flavors. Avoid mixing with citrus.

❖ **Crème De Cacao** is made from cocoa beans and vanilla. Use with chocolate, coffee, mint and orange flavors.

❖ **Drambuie** is made from aged Scottish malt whiskey, herbs, spices and honey. Use with honey, spices, chocolate and dried fruit.

❖ **Grand Marnier** is made in France from cognac and oranges. Used as a flambé in sweet dishes and savory sauces. Great with chocolate and fruit especially citrus and berries.

* **Kahlua** is made in Mexico from a brandy base, flavored with coffee. Use with coffee, vanilla and dried fruit.
* **Midori** is also made in Mexico from honeydew melons. Use with fruit, ice cream, sorbets and sweet sauces.
* **Tia Maria** is made in Jamaica from a rum base with coffee flavor. Use with coffee, chocolate, vanilla flavors and dried fruit.

Oils

* **Olive** oil has a distinct flavor, useful for moderate heat cooking and salad dressings.
* **Vegetable** oil is the most versatile of the oils and can be used interchangeably (corn, soy etc.)
* **Sesame** oil has a strong flavor, a little goes a long way. Used for oriental dishes and salad dressings.
* **Nut** oils include coconut, walnut, almond etc. Excellent novelty for salad dressings with a fruit vinegar.
* **Avocado** oil has little flavour and a high smoking point. Great for stir-frys, roasting, barbecuing, salad dressing and mayonnaise.

Vinegars

* **Red Wine and White Wine** vinegars are extremely versatile. Add a sprig of herbs to the bottle for flavor.
* **Balsamic** vinegar offers a rich sweet flavor for roast vegetables marinades, salad dressings, glazes and reductions.
* **Rice Wine** vinegar is essential for sushi rice, Oriental sauces, marinades, dressings and as a light vinegar for other dishes. If unavailable substitute dry sherry or scotch.
* **Cider and Malt** vinegars are used less often but are equally important in marinades, dressings, sauces, chutney and pickles.
* **Fruit** vinegar is terrific with nut oils for salads and with some vegetables.

Herbs

I find that in most of the countries I've voyaged to the locals grow a variety of specialty herbs that are readily available at local markets.

In some places herbs such as dill, basil, cilantro and mint may even grow wild.

I enjoy cooking and experimenting with fresh herbs so I've incorporated them in many of the recipes realizing that it's not possible to always have access to fresh herbs.

The French are masters at drying herbs, and I urge you to provision with French herbs whenever you can. One of my most precious galley gifts was a small paisley fabric bag of mixed dried herbs from Provence, given to us whilst we were cruising Patagonia. The expedition member who brought us the herbs had just completed a cycling trip through the south of France and every meal that I cooked, using the smallest pinch out of the bag, instantly transported us all to the other side of the world due to the delightful flavors.

Note: *1 t of dried herbs is the equivalent of 1 T of fresh chopped herb.*

❖ **Anise** is the seed of the plant, called aniseed. With a subtle licorice flavor it's used as a condiment and in the preparation of the liqueur anisette. Aniseed has an aromatic, agreeable smell and a warm, sweetish taste due to its oil, called oil of anise.

❖ **Chinese Anise** is also known as star anise from the star like form of its fruit. The qualities of the fruit closely resemble those of the common anise. Used in baking, Indian cooking and pickles.

❖ **Basil** is a versatile sweet herb that improves the flavor of most savory dishes with a wonderful affinity for tomatoes, meat and eggs. Keeps well in the refrigerator, minced and covered in olive oil. Add dried basil towards the end of cooking but well in advance in a salad dressing so the flavor has a chance to develop. Use fresh basil to create pesto and lively basil-garlic vinegar. Historically, basil has been used to induce romantic passions, while in Italy it represents love.

❖ **Bay Leaves** are from the evergreen laurel tree, a native to the Mediterranean. Used in soups and stews, the dish is most often cooked using the whole leaf, which is then removed before serving. Add to par boiled potatoes for added flavor.

- ❖ **Capers** are the green flower buds of the Mediterranean caper bush that taste similar to tiny sharp gherkins. Used for seasoning in tartar sauce, salads, pasta and sandwich mixes. Capers placed in a white wine sauce add a subtle zest to fish.

- ❖ **Caraway Seeds** are spicy, resembling cumin in flavor. They're a wonderful addition to dark breads, cheeses, confectionery and stews. Crush the seeds to release their flavor when adding them to salads and vegetables, especially cabbage (sauerkraut).

- ❖ **Celery Seeds** have a strong flavor and need to be used sparingly. Ground and mixed with salt it's then called celery salt. Can be used whole or powdered in stews, salads, pickles, vegetables and seafood. They're a good substitute for the flavor of celery.

- ❖ **Cilantro** also known as Chinese parsley, is the leaf of the coriander plant. It's often a basic ingredient for Asian, Italian, French and Latin American cooking. Cilantro offers a lemony-fresh flavor for salads, soups, seafood, meats, salsa and guacamole. When fresh, it keeps well in a cool place with its feet in water that should be changed daily. Another option is to keep it packed in an airtight container with a moist paper towel around the roots.

- ❖ **Coriander Seeds** from the cilantro plant are strong smelling. Use in gingerbread, salads, apple pies and as an ingredient for curry. Often used in Middle Eastern and Indian recipes.

- ❖ **Cumin** has a strong and earthy flavor, resembling that of caraway seeds in taste and is popular in Middle Eastern and Latin American, North African and Indian cuisines. Use a 1/8 t in 1 cup of mayonnaise or salad dressing. Use in pea, bean, lentil or chicken soups. Add to bread, cabbage, cheese, tomato sauce, curry dishes, lentils, stews, meat loafs, Mexican-style baked eggs and marinades for shish kebab and wild game. It's the main ingredient in curry.

- ❖ **Dill** has aromatic and mildly bitter leaves and seeds. Used in cabbage dishes, potato salad, sour cream, fish and bean dishes. The seed is good in pickles and vinegar.

- ❖ **Garlic** is a strongly-scented herb of the lily family, the bulb of which is related to the onion. Used freely by garlic lovers, it's the basic ingredient for salad dressings and many hot meals, always going hand in hand with onions. Keeps up to 8 weeks in a dry, dark place.

❖ **Marjoram** ~ see oregano

❖ **Mint** is always an attractive garnish, the main use for mint is as a refreshing flavor. The most common mints are peppermint and spearmint although you may be lucky enough to come across other varieties including orange, pineapple, lemon and apple. Use in fruit punches, coleslaw, peas, new potatoes, lamb, jellies, assorted chocolates, mint sauces and teas.

❖ **Oregano,** also called sweet marjoram, is a perennial while sweet marjoram is an annual, or warm climate perennial. Use in stews, tomato dishes, meats, vegetables, cabbage, eggs, pizza and salads.

❖ **Mustard** is prepared from powdered seeds of either of the two mustard plant species; black mustard and white mustard. The seeds vary from white to yellow to brown. Yellow is the most common for making mustard, though the rare white English seed is superior. Use in cheese, chicken, hot and cold sauces, cold meats, salad dressings and pickles. Mixed with garlic and sage, it's a tasty rub for pork roasts or try it combined with rosemary for lamb roasts.

❖ **Parsley** is renowned for its high vitamin capacity and versatile flavor that mixes well with other herbs. Use in salads, meats, egg dishes and soups. Keep as you would cilantro.

❖ **Rosemary Leaves** have a strong flavor. Use in marinades, on vegetables especially new potatoes, stuffing, meats, seafood and fruits.

❖ **Saffron** produces a bright-yellow flavoring and coloring. Used in cakes, breads, paellas and risottos.

❖ **Sage** is member of the mint family. The leaves are used in stuffing, stews, meat loaf, goulashes and wild game.

❖ **Sesame Seeds** are pearly, nut-flavored seeds favored in Middle Eastern cooking. They're at their best when toasted in a dry pan for a few minutes. Black as well as white sesame seeds are excellent additions for breads, vegetables, salads and pastas and as a substitute for nuts. Crush and mix with chickpeas to make tahini. The oil extracted from sesame seeds is used in marinades, Oriental cooking and salad dressings.

Provisioning

❖ **Tarragon** is an aromatic, bitter, herb. The green parts of the plant are used in mustard, sour cream, tartar sauces, meats, salads, pickles, vegetables and often placed in a bottle of vinegar to season it. Adds savory flavor to chicken salad and green beans.

❖ **Thyme** has a flavor that is milder than sage, with a smoky hint. Leaves are used with meats, stews, stuffing, soups and creoles.

Spices

❖ **Allspice** has a flavor that suggests a blend of cinnamon, cloves, nutmeg and juniper berries. It is both warm and sweet. Use in relishes, soups, vegetables, eggs, French toast, spice cookies and fruit pies. Add to tomatoes, barbecue sauces and meat loafs. In Peru it is used as condiment like black pepper.

❖ **Cardamom** is available in black and green. The fruit is a small capsule with 8 to 16 seeds that are ground to form the spice. Use as the likes of cinnamon and cloves. Goes well with lentils, Indonesian rice, Indian curries, plain cakes, barbecues and pickles.

❖ **Cinnamon** is yellowish brown bark with a distinctive fragrant aroma and a sweetish, pungent taste. Grown in many countries the flavor varies slightly. Use the quills in hot chocolate, mulled wine and pickles and powered cinnamon in curries, baking and desserts. Don't forget a sprinkle on your morning cappuccino.

❖ **Cloves** were once used by Chinese courtiers to keep their breath pleasant when conversing with the emperor. Their sharp bitterness adds a warm rich aroma and flavor to sweet foods such as oranges and ham. Use in stewed fruit, chutneys, pickles and stews.

❖ **Curry** is a composite of various spices and the ingredients vary according to the type of curry. Curry leaves are used in some Indonesian dishes and curry powder can be used as a substitute.

❖ **Ginger** was the first Oriental spice to be consumed worldwide. Available fresh, dried, preserved, ground, pickled, minced and crystallized. Its hot biting flavor is essential to curry powder, yet also contributes to sweet baked goods such as gingerbread and offers excellent results when added to fruit dishes and juices. Ginger was used in the Far East as a digestive aid and helps to allay motion sickness while a small piece of root in hot water is soothing.

❖ **Nutmeg and Mace** are from the same fruit. The apple seed is dried to form nutmeg, while the skin is removed, dried and then ground into a coarse powder that turns a reddish color. Nutmeg is used with eggs and baked goods, it can be kept in a powered form or whole to be grated with a nutmeg grater as required. Excellent with cabbage.

❖ **Pepper** is available in black, green and white and is a basic addition to most recipes and the dinning table.

❖ **Poppy Seeds** of the best flavor have a black/blue color. Add to salads, fruit salads, dressings, French toast, rice, bread, cakes and cookies. For poppy seed cake, add 1/3 cup to a pound cake mix and bake as directed.

❖ **Turmeric** is a yellow color and often used as a food colorant, replacing saffron. With a slightly bitter and acrid flavor it is used in pickles and Indian curries.

❖ **Vanilla** is a climbing orchid native to tropical America and Asia. Vanilla essence is derived from the bean mixed with alcohol. For best flavor add to food when the cooking has finished. Use in baking, deserts, ice cream and as an accompaniment with almonds and chocolate. Vanilla enhances most if not all sweet bakery and egg dishes.

Freeze Dried Food

❖ **Shelf-stable** with locked in freshness, color, flavor, texture, aroma and nutrients.

❖ Excellent in **heavy weather** since complete meals don't require cooking only the addition of hot water.

❖ Great in an **emergency** situation if it's not convenient to prepare a meal in the galley.

❖ Useful on smaller boats with **storage** and weight limitations.

❖ Less packing and expense if purchased in **#10 1 gallon tins**.

❖ Complete meals are available but tend to be **more expensive** than general foods.

Dried Food

❖ Beef and turkey **jerky** keep for an extended period of time when kept dry.

- ❖ **Chicken stock** purchased in powdered form keeps well and saves space.
- ❖ **Dried coconut milk** when mixed with water replaces fresh coconut milk.
- ❖ **Eggs** are available dried as a powder and can be used in baking and omelets.
- ❖ **Dried fruit** makes a good substitute for fresh and is perfect for treats and snacks. Most common dried fruits are raisins, apricots, cranberries, prunes, dates, apples, papaya and pineapple.
- ❖ **Prunes, raisins, and dates** are super options for relieving constipation and helping you stay regular.
- ❖ **Instant dried milk powder** tastes better chilled. Available in whole cream or nonfat outside the U.S.
- ❖ **Dried mushrooms** bring an earthy flavor to stir-frys, soups, stews and rice dishes.
- ❖ **Dried refried beans** reconstitute quickly and taste just like the canned version.
- ❖ **Dried shrimp** go well in rice, curries and soups.
- ❖ **Sun-dried tomatoes** are a tasty addition to salads, quiche, pastas and mixed with olive oil and basil make a great pesto for pasta or a spread for melba toast.

Canned Foods

- ❖ On average in **rough weather,** five cans will be consumed a day for three people.
- ❖ In **mild conditions** can consumption drops as meals are supplemented with longer to prepare items such as beans, eggs, grains, meats and vegetables.
- ❖ Removing **labels and coating** the cans with varnish adds extra protection if you have a leaky boat with wet lockers.
- ❖ Canned **butter, cheese, milk and cream** are more common outside of North America.

Provisioning

Foods Available In Cans

Dairy
Butter
Cheese
Cream
Milk
Sweetened condensed milk

Sauces
Ketchup
Tomato spaghetti sauce
Stir-fry sauces
Chicken stock

Meals
Baked beans
Chili con carne
Spaghetti
Ravioli
Stews

Soups
Black bean
Chicken
Chowder
Mushroom
Minestrone
Pumpkin
Tomato
Vegetable

Meat
Chicken
Frankfurters
Ham
Turkey
Paté
Spam

Fruit
Apples - baking
Apricots
Berries
Cherries - baking
Coconut milk
Lychee
Mandarins
Peaches
Pears
Pineapple
Fruit salad

Vegetables
Artichokes
Asparagus
Beans - kidney, black, white, pinto etc.
Beets
Chili peppers
Chickpeas
Corn
Green beans
Mushrooms
Olives
Peas
Peppers
Pimientos
Tomatoes - whole, puree, paste, sauce

Seafood
Anchovies - garnish
Mixed shellfish
Tuna
Salmon
Sardines
Shrimp
Smoked oysters - appetizers

Lucky Dip

While visiting one of the more remote San Blas Islands a dugout canoe came alongside with two Kuna Indian women and their molas. Each 18" x 16" mola tells a story created from bright layers of cloth with a top fabric cut in a pattern to reveal the colors beneath. The cut edges are carefully folded under and finished with tiny stitches and top embroidery. Mola designs are religion, mythology, animal and plant life or geometric mazes. Sewn by hand they can easily take two months to complete a design, while also performing daily chores.

I'd been advised that it's best to pay cash for molas as this is the main source of income for the Kuna women. We'd visited a few islands and I'd purchased numerous molas from the ladies when they visitied in their canoes and had decided that I'd reached my budget limit.

Then next morning when another canoe came alongside from a distant village I gestured to the old woman that I was not interested in purchasing any more molas. She gave me a near toothess grin and held up and exquisite piece of work. She'd caught my interest but sadly I couldn't afford any more molas. She then placed her hand down inside her blouse, brought out a package and began peeling off papers holding them up for me to look at. After gazing at numerous papers it occurred to me that they were labels from canned goods. I was amazed at the variety of languages and items, and assumed she must of traded molas for the cans. I thought perhaps the labels she was showing me were cans she'd enjoyed and wished to try again. I didn't recognize many of the labels but decided to try my luck.

I went below and selected a dozen assorted cans that we'd had on board for a while and I knew we wouldn't miss. After placing them on the deck the lady eagerly studied each can, gave it a shake and thoughtfully placed it in one of two piles. Then with another big grin she handed me the mola before carefully packing away a pile of selected cans she'd selected into her bucket of molas.

Fresh Fruits That Keep Well

❖ **Apples** varieties that keep the best are Granny Smiths, Braeburn, Gala and

Envy. Wash and stow apples snugly away where they won't get bruised or roll around. Stored in a cool area they should last up to 1 to 2 months.

❖ **Bananas** on a stalk tend to ripen all at once so beware. Wash the stalks thoroughly by immersing in fresh or salt water for a few minutes to dislodge ants, cockroaches and spiders. Cut off the hands and place in a dark cool place to ripen.

Caution: the sticky stalk residue badly stains.

❖ **Citrus Fruits** keep longer in the tropics if refrigerated. If not refrigerated you need to check the fruit every second day.

❖ **Coconuts** are plentiful in most tropical regions, store well if left unhusked and make an excellent thirst quenching drink. Green husks are best for drinking and last several weeks. Brown nuts are older and contain more white meat and less liquid. They're used for making coconut milk by grating the meat and squeezing out the milk through cheesecloth. The nuts last up to a month.

❖ **Fruit Salads** are popular onboard and by adding a can of fruit it's possible to extend your fresh fruit supplies.

❖ **Mangoes** will keep for two weeks before becoming fully ripe if they're picked when hard with a slight hint of ripening yellow.

❖ **Pineapples** are ripe when the center leaf of the stalk pulls away easily. When shopping, I prefer to choose pineapples that are slightly green with the stalk attached and a slight pineapple smell at the base. Stored upright in the dark they'll last over a week or remove the stalk and keep them in the fridge ready to use.

❖ **Watermelons** keep for two weeks. To test for ripeness knock on the watermelon and listen for a drum sound.

Fresh Vegetables That Keep Well

❖ **Cabbage** is the longest lasting of green vegetables, surviving un-refrigerated for several weeks and up to one month in the tropics wrapped in newspaper, kept dry and ventilated. When needed, instead of slicing through the center, peel off and use the outer leaves, as intact heads don't rot as quickly. Have a collection of tasty cabbage recipes to utilize the last of your cabbage at the end of a long passage.

❖ **Celery** will keep for three weeks in the fridge. Use the stalks from the outside of the bunch to the inside. Trim off the tops of the stalks if they start to turn brown or soggy.

- **Carrots** fresh from the ground and unwashed will last several weeks if stored in a cool dark place. Store bought carrots start going limp and developing black spots after a couple of weeks. Spots can be scraped off and the carrots re-hydrated by slicing them thin and soaking them in a salt solution for a few hours.
- **Cucumbers** will last a few weeks in the fridge. If they start to go bad and produce a white slime prolong their life by pickling them.
- **Eggplants** are readily available in many local markets around the world and go well with tomatoes, in pasta sauces or baked in the Greek dish *Moussaka*, that layers the eggplant with a cheese sauce.
- **Garlic** is readily available worldwide and lasts up to two months.
- **Ginger Root** is best and stored in a dark dry place. After a month it becomes a little woody but it's still usable. I find it's easier to grate ginger when it's frozen so I keep my ginger in a container just inside the freezer door.
- **Green Beans** keep up to a week.
- **Mushrooms** don't keep very well so it's best to saute them upon purchase and freeze them until needed.
- **Onions** stowed in a dark, ventilated and dry space will last several months. Choose small to medium-size.
- **Potatoes** are truly versatile, long lasting and are definitely the all time favorite galley companion. Choose new or smooth-skinned washed potatoes. Remove sprouts if they appear.
- **Tomatoes** if purchased firm, greenish pink and unbruised will last several weeks. Store them where they won't roll around and check them every couple of days.
- **Sprouts** grow well on board and you can try your hand sprouting at wide vareity of seeds. It's best to buy fresh seeds in developed countries as there's more options and they're fresher. Commercially grown sprouts keep up to two weeks in the fridge.
- **Winter Squash or Pumpkins** kept cool and dry, will last several months. Choose small ones as once opened they last only a few days.
- **Zucchini** kept in the fridge will last up to two weeks. Use in soups, stir-fries, Mediterrean dishes and pasta sauces.

Memories of Home

My nana Phyllis is someone I always associate with the homey feeling canning creates. Bread-and-butter pickles, tomato relishes, lemon-butter spread, orange-ginger marmalade, and glistening topaz jars of summer peaches always lined her shelves, labeled with her flourished cursive writing. The labels often had a flower decorating the corner, like the ones she doodled when she was on the phone. She was always at the ready with the kettle, offering a cup of tea to go with home made biscuts kept in a well-stocked cake tin. It was impossible to leave her house without a couple of jars tucked under your arm, perhaps one of strawberry jam and the other a chutney; precious mementoes of summer captured in glass.

When we set out to sea from home for exotic ports our lockers contained wrapped jars, farewell presents from Nana to send us on our way. On opening a crimson jar of plums while anchored under the palm trees I would often feel out of place as memories of home came floating out of the jar like a genie from a lamp.

I admit I've only spent a couple of afternoons working away over bubbling pots to create my own canned gems. I'd like to do more as I sometimes picture myself at a future date humming away in a cozy kitchen preparing a seasonal bounty from a local orchard. At present this image doesn't fit into my current galley and packed boating lifestyle but I know that when I place my first canned jar on the shelf it will be in memory of little nana.

In the past ten years I've only encounted six boats that do their own canning. In the Marquesas, I met a young French couple, cruising without refrigeration, who had filled their entire bilge with canned meat, enough to go around the world. Little did they realize that they would not be able to bring this product into New Zealand, one of their planned stops. Annette on the Danish boat *Scafhogg* canned 110 small jars of meat for their passage across the Pacific to New Zealand from Chile. Four jars take three hours to can therefore all 110 jars took two months!

My mum carries six canning jars. If they've an excess of food, such as seasonal fruit or a large fish and no freezer space, she'll then consider canning it. The jars are also a back up incase the freezer breaks as she'll then can what's in it but only if it's not too rough, she claims.

Dee and Marshall Saunders on their 52-foot motor yacht *Penguin* carry a dedicated pressure cooker that holds 16 pint jars on two levels. They're avid fishermen and have canned their caught salmon when cruising the Pacific Northwest while in Central America and French Polynesia they canned tuna. It requires 30 lbs. of fish to fill 16 pint jars, about one good-sized tuna or salmon.

In conjunction with the presure cooker they also carry a one-burner gas stove that they connect to their barbecue tank. The single element allows them to successfully maintain a constant heat which they find hard to achieve on their electric stove. Dee says the gas stove is also terrific for cooking up large pots of crab or lobster as it keeps the smell and heat out of the galley.

Preserving Food

Canning

Canning food in sealed jars prevents harmful organisms from entering the jars, while organisms already present in the food are destroyed in the canning procedure. The process is rather complex and care should be taken to ensure a totally safe product. I recommend that you become familiar with this process at home, before leaving, as you have access to more space and the required equipment. *The Joy of Cooking* cookbook has detailed instructions on canning.

The Two Canning Methods
The boiling water method for acidic fruits and tomatoes

Sterilize the jars before packing them by placing them in boiling water for 15 minutes. The seals and rubber also require sterilizing.

Sealed packed jars are placed in a pot of boiling water with a rack at the base to prevent the heat from cracking the jars. Ensure that the jars don't touch the sides of the pot or each other and that water covers the jars. Process time is about 25 minutes maintaining a steady boil.

Pressure-canning for low acidic fruits and vegetables, meat and fish

Filled sealed jars are placed in a rack inside the pressure cooker that has been filled with 3" of water. Food is processed under 10 lbs. of uninterrupted pressure from 10 to 100 minutes depending on the food. If the pressure drops below 10 lbs. you must start timing again from zero minutes.

Packing Options

❖ In the **raw pack** method, you place the raw meat into a jar and process it.

❖ In the **hot pack** method, you cook the meat (just a little bit) before you pack it into the jars, you then also add some liquid before processing them.

Canning Foods

❖ **Fruit** is generally canned in sterile jars, either in water or in sugar syrup using the water bath method. Syrup gives fruit a better color and flavor. A medium syrup mix is 1 cup of sugar to 2 cups of water. Honey, brown sugar or artificial sweeteners can be used and the syrups flavored with citrus rind or spices according to the fruit.

❖ **Vegetables** are generally pre-cooked for 5 minutes, packed in jars and covered with boiling water. Process time is approximately 50 minutes at 10 lbs. of pressure.

❖ **Meats** are pre-cooked in the oven or stewed, packed in jars and covered with broth or boiling water. Process 75 minutes at 10 lbs. of pressure.

❖ **Fish** are soaked in brine (1/2 t salt per pint) for one hour. Drain well and pack tightly into jars. Process 100 minutes at 10-lbs. pressure.

Packing Canning Jars

❖ **Fruits and vegetables** are packed firmly into jars 1/2 inch from the top and covered with boiling syrup or water.

- ❖ **Meats** should be packed to within 1 inch of the top and covered to 1/2 inch from the lid.
- ❖ **Fish,** it is not necessary to remove skin and bones, just pack the jar with the skin side out,
- ❖ Remove **air bubbles** by placing a knife blade down the side of the jar and slightly moving the contents.
- ❖ **Wipe** the jar rim and secure the lid.

The Canning Process

- ❖ Process jars in pessure canner following the **manufactures instructions.**
- ❖ **Remove** jars and place on a heat-resistant surface. A wooden board works well.
- ❖ Be sure to **cool** jars away from drafts.
- ❖ The lids are **sealed after 12 hours**. The lid curves down and doesn't move when pressed with a finger.
- ❖ If a **lid is not sealed** check the lid and jar edge for any nicks. Change jars and lids an reprocess within 24 hours.
- ❖ To **check a seal,** tap the lid with a spoon. A clear clinking sound denotes a good seal. If the sound is hollow either reprocess or consume the food.

General Canning Information

- ❖ Canning jars are not readily available worldwide, so **stock up** on a size that fits your pressure cooker or preserving pan.
- ❖ If you open a jar and the food **smells bad or bubbles** throw contents away, don't taste it!

Vacuum Packing

Only a small percentage of crusiers vacuum pack items but those who I do are very enthusiastic about it. Dee Saunders on *Penguin* uses her vacuum packer for salmon, crab, chicken breasts, squid, tuna, and choice cuts of meat.

- ❖ **Frozen food** items that have been vacuum packed last longer, don't taint or become icy.
- ❖ A **large vacuum packer** with a broader heat seal is preferable to a smaller one.

❖ If heading offshore take a substanial supply of **vacuum packer sealer bags.**

❖ Vacuum packing **flour and dry goods** reduces the reproduction cycle of weevils in the food.

❖ Vacuum packing is also useful **for other items** that require protection such as spare parts or winter clothes if you're now cruising in the tropics and don't require them.

Refrigerated Food

The following items can be refrigerated:

❖ **Fruit**: apples, oranges, limes, lemons and pineapple.

❖ **Dairy**: butter, cheese, milk and yogurt.

❖ **Meat**: ham, bacon and cold cuts.

❖ **Vegetables**: avocados, bell peppers, cabbage, cauliflower, celery, carrots, lettuce, mushrooms, sprouts, tomatoes and zucchini.

❖ **Condiments**: juice, jelly, butter and mayonnaise.

Frozen Food

The following items can be frozen:

❖ **Bacon** can be packed in areas of the freezer that don't stay totally frozen.

❖ **Bread** will last a few months frozen.

❖ **Butter** makes good use of areas that don't freeze completely.

❖ **Cheese** a mild cheddar gets a little crumbly so choose a sharp (tasty) cheddar, Parmesan or feta. Works great for utilizing the areas in the freezer that don't stay completely frozen.

❖ **Chicken** breasts diced and placed into quart Ziploc bags. One bag of 3 lbs or 1.3kg is enough chicken to feed 8 people when added to a one pot dish.

❖ **Cooked chicken** pieced and frozen in quart Ziploc bags for later use in soups, stir-frys, pastas and salads.

❖ **Frozen chicken pieces;** 5lb. boxes of frozen chicken are imported into many countries from the U.S. The price is generally reasonable but an entire box utilizes a lot of freezer space. I generally slightly thaw the chicken, remove the skin and repack the chicken into meal sized portions in Ziploc bags

❖ **Crab** cooked and vacuum packed keeps frozen for 6 months.

❖ **Ginger** root keeps well stored in a small plastic jar or Ziploc. When needed the ginger easily grates, from frozen, into your cooking.

❖ **Fish;** any firm white fish or smoked fish freezes well, dark oily fish not so well.

❖ **Lunch ham and turkey slices** freeze well along with sliced corned beef and roast beef.

❖ **One pot dishes** can be cook and frozen before a passage e.g. stews, lasagnas and pies, if time permits and freezer space allows.

❖ **Oysters** vacuum-packed, will last for two months.

❖ **Sausages** are aways welcome on the barbeque while chorizo goes great in paella, soup and pasta.

❖ **Shrimp** frozen while raw and packed in ziplocks will keep 1 month. Pre-cooked frozen shrimp are a brilliant as they can be defrosted instantly in warm water for ready use in stir-frys, soups and pastas.

❖ **Steak;** always store meat in Ziplocs or vacuum-packs to avoid freezer burn.

❖ **Vegetables** such as peas, corn, beans and mixed veggies can be used for soups, stews and stir-frys. Frozen spinach goes well in quiche and green curry.

General Food Advice

Bread

❖ Baking bread at sea offers a joyous and medative calmness in the process, it's very tactile commanding your attention primarily when you're kneading the dough.

❖ To prolong the life of bread wipe it with **vinegar** and wrap it in foil. Store in a plastic bag in a dark cool place.

❖ In the tropics, I store bread in the **fridge or freezer** to prolong it's life.

❖ **Bread machines** and **bread mixes** make easy work of a somewhat lengthy process.

- **Melba toast** is created by slicing leftover Italian or French bread into 3/4" slices. Next dry the slices in the oven or in the sun either in the cockpit or under the dodger. When stored in a paper bag it will keep several weeks. Excellent for use as croutons, French toasts or snacks as a substitute for crackers.
- **French baguettes** keep best in plastic bags.
- Plain **cabin biscuits** or **pilot crackers** make a good bread alternative and aid the seasick sailor.

Butter

- **Canned butter** is a readily available in many countries and saves on fridge space. In the U.S. you can find it on the internet.
- I usually keep butter that's in packets at the bottom of the **freezer** in a quart Ziplock bag where it's generally not cold enough for meat to stay frozen.
- I transfer butter, either from cans or packets, into a 2 cup sized **plastic container** for every day use. This also makes it easier to measure for baking.

Cheese

- Keep mold at by on fresh cheese by wrapping the cheese in a **vinegar** soaked cheesecloth or paper towel then placing it in a plastic bag.
- Large blocks of cheddar cheese placed in an airtight container and surrounded with **cooking oil** will last several weeks without refrigeration. We used this method on an equator crossing when our refrigeration broke down but discoverd that the cheese is slippery to handle especially if you want to create slices.
- **Feta and yogurt cheese** in small cubes or balls keeps well in olive oil which you can season with herbs.
- Cheese that is **protected by wax** will keep up to a month without refrigeration.
- **Canned cheese** will last indefinitely stored in a cool place.
- **Processed cheese** such as Velveeta, Laughing Cow, Kraft and Chesdale will last many months unrefrigerated.

    This cheese has a different texture and I once visited a French friend's boat for an impromptu lunch just after they'd made landfall in the Marquesas and completed their first grocery shopping trip. Michelle kept diving into the oven and after the fourth time, 15 minutes later, she had a worried look on her face. I asked what was wrong and she said, "My stove is not working properly, this cheese on toast just won't melt".

"Ah ha." I said, "You have just discovered fromage plastique! (plastic cheese). It's not the cheese of France for it certainly will never melt."

* **Parmesan** is a tasty, long lasting, low-calorie cheese that grates well.

* **Freezing cheese** works to prolong it's life. Choose a hard, sharp cheddar cheese rather than a mild cheddar which tends to crumble when defrosted.

How to Make Ricotta Cheese

2 quarts milk
vinegar or lemon juice

* Heat milk in a pot but do not boil.

* When the milk is hot, slowly start adding the vinegar or lemon juice one spoon at a time, while continually stirring the milk.

* The acid curdles the milk and forms little lumps, keep adding the acid, spoon by spoon while stirring.

* When the whey water becomes greenish-yellow turn off the heat.

* Strain the milk through a muslin cloth or fine strainer, separating the whey from the curd.

* Herbs and spices can be added for variety.

* Fold the cloth over the curd and place a weight on it.

* Let it drain for approximately 40 minutes.

* Refrigerate and cut into cubes to serve in salad, pasta, quiche or on toast.

Coconut Milk

* **Powdered coconut milk** is available from most Asian food stores. Once the package is opened, keep it in an airtight container to prevent it from solidifying. Powered coconut milk is more economical than canned as you can choose the required amount needed.

- **Canned coconut milk** is readily available but it may be hard to use the entire can in one dish. It'll keep refrigerated for four days once opened and placed in a container or it can be frozen.
- To make a **less fattening** coconut milk:

  1 C of non-fat milk

  1/2 C roasted or dried coconut

  Simmer milk and coconut for 20 minutes, then cool and strain out the coconut.

Cured Ham

- Cured hams will last up to **8 months**.
- **Store suspended,** wrapped in paper with plenty of air around it.
- **Slice** several days supply at a time from **the bottom of the ham** and coat the newly exposed meat with salt.
- **Soak** the slices in several changes of fresh water before cooking if a less salty taste is desired.

Eggs – see Chapter 3, Stowage

Fishing

- **Mahi-mahi, tuna, and wahoo** are easily caught off the back of the boat with a hand line and lure at speeds of 4 to 12 knots. Great for sushi, pan frying, baking, smoking and freezing. See Pelagic Fishing Chapter 20.

Fresh Meat and Chicken

- Fresh local meat and chicken are **available** in most major cruising ports but it may be cheaper and healthier to buy imported frozen meat and chicken.
- **Vacuum-packed choice cuts of meat** may also be available. They'll keep for a week without refrigeration, several weeks refrigerated and longer frozen.

Fruit Juice

- **100% fruit juice** is available in tetra packs, cans and botttles in most countries with apple and orange being the most common.
- **100% juice from concentrate** is the most common fruit juice worldwide.

- ❖ **Fruit drinks** and fruit nectar are availabe world wide but these may have less than 25% fruit content and can have added colourants, preservatives and additives.
- ❖ **Frozen concentrated juice** takes up freezer space and is unavailable in many countries.

Salad Dressing

- ❖ **Prepared salad dressings** can be expensive and of a lower quality with less variety outside the U.S. or Europe.
- ❖ Stock up with salad dressing when in **US or European** supplied ports or when you find a brand you like.
- ❖ Get creative and **make your own** oil and vinegar dressings.

Salami

- ❖ Has similar **keeping qualities** to cured ham mentioned above but doesn't need to be soaked or cooked before eating.
- ❖ Store in a **cool dark place**.
- ❖ Best **purchased as a roll**. Peel off the protective wrapping that often molds, before slicing and serving.

Smoked Food

- ❖ Smoking **chicken, shellfish and fish** is a method that can be used to extend the life of food but these days, more often than not, it is used for flavoring.
- ❖ **Smoking is achieved** by placing prepared food in a confined area and smoking it with fragrant sawdust placed on a rack above a low flame. It may take anywhere from 1 hour for a light smoked flavor and a moist meat to three days for a harder smoked meat that is dry and will keep longer.
- ❖ Fish require **salting or brining** before smoking. This provides a good surface texture and retards spoilage.
- ❖ **Barbecue** smoking. Place a tray of sawdust above the flame and cook the meat on the grill using a low flame.
- ❖ The **pressure cooker** can be used for tea smoking:

mix together	1/4 C	black tea
	1/4 C	uncooked rice
	3 T	brown sugar

Provisioning

In the base of the pressure cooker place the mixture in a metal dish.
Position food above on a metal trivet.

Cook on a low to medium heat with no pressure until food is done,
about 1 hour.

Sprouts

❖ To grow sprouts the only equipment you need is a **jar with a mesh lid**, preferably stainless steel, so that it's easier to drain the sprouts after you rinse them.

❖ The most ideal **sprouting temperature is 65°-75°**.

❖ Beans and **seeds may become bitter** if sprouted too long where-as grains become sweeter on the fourth and fifth day of sprouting.

❖ **Soak** measured amount of seeds in ample water following the sprouting guide below.

❖ **Drain** the sprouts and place the jar lid down at a 45° angle for drainage and ventilation. This is rather hard to achieve on a yacht so you need some props to keep it tilted.

❖ **Rinse** the sprouts twice a day, more often in warm climates, with fresh cool water then position the jar to drain.

❖ When the sprouts have matured or taste alright place them in a bowl of water and **skim off the hulls** that float to surface. It's not possible to get all the hulls.

❖ When sprouts such as alfalfa, cabbage, clover, mustard and radish grow leaves place them in **indirect sun light** for two days before using. The light will allow the leaves to produce chlorophyll which will turn them green.

❖ **Store** sprouts in a sealed container in the fridge.

Sprouting Guide

Variety	Soaking Time Hours	Dry Measure for 4 Cups	Days until ready
Alfalfa	5	4 T	4-5
Adzuki	10	1 C	2-4
Chickpea	10	1 C	2-3
Cabbage	8	1/2 C	4-5
Clover	8	2 T	4-5
Fenugreek	8	1/2 C	2-3
Green pea	8	2 C	2-3
Lentils	8	1 C	2-5
Mung bean	8	1/2 C	3-5
Mustard	8	2 T	4-5
Radish	8	4 T	4-5
Rye	7	1 1/2 C	4-6
Sesame	6	1/2 C	2-3
Sunflower	8	3 C	2-3
Triticale	8	1 C	2-3
Wheat	6	2 C	2-3

Yogurt

Yogurt can be easily made by adding freeze dried yogurt culture or plain yogurt culture to reconstituted powdered milk, long-life milk or fresh milk.

❖ **Whole milk powder** makes a thicker yogurt than non-fat.

Yogurt Making Instructions

❖ Boil 1 quart of milk and let it simmer for a minute, allow it to cool to a temperature that stings your little finger when you dip it in.

❖ Whip 2 tablespoons of plain live yogurt and add the warm milk slowly while stirring the yogurt.

❖ Place milk mix in a wide-necked thermos. If you don't have a thermos use a container and wrap it in a towel. Keep mixture away from drafts and if the air temperature is really cold place a hot water bottle with it or keep it in a warm engine room.

Provisioning

❖ Leave for a maximum of 12 hours, no longer as the yogurt becomes acidic.

❖ Save 2 tablespoons of yogurt to start the next batch.

Yogurt Cheese

Yogurt cheese can be made by draining the whey from yogurt. Place the yogurt in a sieve lined with a damp fine cloth and set over a bowl to catch the whey. It will turn to a Middle Eastern style cheese in 8 hours. It can then be rolled into balls and stored covered in olive oil.

Tetra Packs

❖ Tetra Packs are **excellent** packaging as they don't break or rust, they stow safely, quietly, efficiently, don't require refrigeration, and reduce packaging.

❖ **Products** available in tetra packs: fruit juice and concentrate, UHT milk, cream, tomatoes, soups, stocks, tomato sauce, tofu and water.

Cleaning Supplies

Chlorine bleach – used for treating water tanks, disinfectant, bleaching surfaces and removing mold.

Dish washing liquid – always buy a quality brand for better results rather than a cheaper unknown product.

Dish scrubber

Garbage bags

Hand soap

Metal polish

Oven cleaner spray

Pest spray

Roach baits

Sponges – large, high-quality sponges may be more difficult to find in less developed countries.

Scrub brushes

Soft scrub – used for cleaning stainless steel sink and bench top.

Windex – used for cleaning windows, wiping down bulkheads and general head cleaning.

Substitution Table

If You Need	Substitute
Baking powder - 1 t	1/4 t baking soda and 1/2 C yogurt
Butter - 1 C	3/4 C cooking oil
Buttermilk - 1 C	Add 2 T vinegar or lemon juice to 1 C warm milk, let stand 10 min, or 1 C yogurt
Coconut milk	Simmer 1C milk and 1/2 C roasted or dried coconut for 20 min, cool, strain out coconut
Chocolate- unsweetened	3 T cocoa and 1T butter
Egg -1	2 T cooking oil. Baked item won't be light
Herbs - fresh 1 T	1/2 t dried
Lemon juice - 1 T	1/2 T vinegar
Milk, baking - 1 C	1 C water and 1 1/2 t butter
Sour cream - 1 C	1/3 C butter and 3/4 C sour milk or Nestle's reduced milk
Sugar, granulated - 1 C	3/4 honey or maple syrup. Reduce recipe liquid by 1/4 C

Chapter 3

STOWAGE

Stowage

Organizing Stowage Space

❖ Before investing in a range of **storage containers** check that they efficiently utilize the space available.

❖ **Nets** can be used for stowing items but check fruit and vegetables while underway as bruising may occur.

❖ **Avoid using cardboard and paper** for storing food as it can harbor insect eggs and be prone to absorbing moisture and molding. If this isn't possible place the item in a Ziploc.

❖ The **bilge** area is good for storing bulk items that are packaged in sturdy waterproof containers: laundry soap, engine oil, or awkward items such as diving fins and spare parts that don't mind moisture.

❖ Keep **cans** dry and check frequently. Isolate cans from the hull by stowing them in plastic bins.

❖ **Label** and date containers of bulk stores.

❖ **Keep control of inventory** by implementing one of the following methods:

  ❖ Write a **master list** of items and their location.
  ❖ Sketch **a plan of the boat** and stowage lockers and note what goods are stowed where.
  ❖ Keep **lists of what's in each locker taped inside** door or floorboard.

If you are on a small or lightweight boat you may need to be conscious of **weight distribution**. My friend Theresa did her first major provision and stowage on her boat in Mexico in preparation for their passage to Panama and was relieved to have everything organized and securely stowed away before her husband Michael returned from running errands. Michael congratulated Theresa on her efforts but asked that she walk down the dock with him. Looking back at the boat Theresa noticed that it had a 10° list to starboard and quickly realized that all the heavy provisions and cans were on the same side.

Bulk Supply Management

❖ **Bulk stores of flours, grains, cereals and pastas** are best placed in Ziploc bags and kept in large plastic airtight storage bins.

❖ **Transfer dried bulk items** into square-sided containers with screw down lids. Choose a container size big enough for two weeks supply and stow it in an easy to reach location.

❖ **Vacuum-packing items** saves space, aids organization and helps reduce bugs. It prevents goods from being exposed to moisture and thus spoiling and also helps guard against food becoming stale or tainted.

Daily Commodities Organization

❖ Since **packaging** varies in size and quality, choose sturdy small containers for oil, juice, syrup, jam, vinegar, etc. that fit your galley space. Once you've left your major provisioning port, don't be too eager to throw away these storage containers. It's often easier to transfer bulk or new products into handy reliable packaging than discover you're short on space and storage containers.

❖ I transfer as many **liquid food products** (e.g., jelly, mayonnaise, honey, mustard, ketchup and maple syrup) as possible into plastic squeeze or pour containers with flip lids. This reduces washing up as no spoon or knife is required and the squeeze bottle can be used one-handed making life at sea easier.

❖ **Dry products** – such as drink mix, Gatorade, hot chocolate, raisins and sugar – store well in the Rubbermaid quart bottle with flip lids.

Fruit and Vegetable Stowage

❖ To **sterilize fruit and vegetables**, soak them for 15 minutes in 2 tablespoons of chlorine per 2 gallons and dry them in the sun. The chlorine kills and delays mold and bacteria.

❖ Carol on *Elyxir* has used the above method of sterilization numerous times. On her **extended ocean passage** from Chile to the Marquesas she was delighted with the results and later while cruising Fiji during a major drought she sterilized an over abundance of provisions, purchased in the major port, with the intention of giving her surplus away in the other islands she planned to visit. Carol was correct in thinking that the remote islands would not have sufficient water for their food crops.

❖ **Fruits and vegetables** keep best at a cool temperature, in the dark, with plenty of air circulation.

❖ **Apples and citrus** should not be stowed together as the citrus cause the apples to ripen.

❖ **Onions and potatoes** should not be stowed together as the potatoes begin to sprout.

Stowage

❖ **Plastic baskets** in a ventilated cupboard, bilge or deck box work well for fruit and vegetable stowage.

Care and Stowage of Fresh Eggs

❖ **Eggs** may keep up to two months by using one of these methods:

1. Coat each egg completely with a light coating of **Vaseline** (this is the method I use).

2. **Turn eggs** over every week.

3. **Refrigerate** and turn eggs every week.

❖ **Unwashed, unrefrigerated** eggs purchased directly from the farmer will last longer, but in many provisioning stops this may not be a convenient option.

❖ No matter how you preserve your eggs the after a couple of weeks the odd egg may become bad. At this time, **break each egg** into a separate container before adding it to the main dish so you don't ruin your entire meal.

❖ In **older eggs** the yolk becomes weak and runny so it's then hard to separate it from the white.

❖ Outside the U.S. eggs may be sold **without containers** so keep a reserve of egg cartons.

❖ **Styrofoam** egg cartons work well as they can reused for egg stowage after washing.

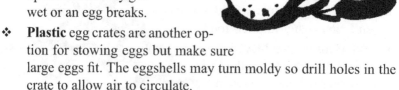

❖ **Cardboard** egg cartons may harbor insect eggs and don't hold up too well if they get wet or an egg breaks.

❖ **Plastic** egg crates are another option for stowing eggs but make sure large eggs fit. The eggshells may turn moldy so drill holes in the crate to allow air to circulate.

❖ Eggs are also available in **powdered** form in several countries. In the U.S. powdered eggs are available from Amazon.

Tips on Organizing the Fridge and Freezer

❖ **Motor yachts** often have a household-style front-loading refrigerator-freezer, while **sailing yachts** generally have top-opening refrigerators and freezers. On some yachts the space in top loading fridges and freezers is small and often an awkward shape. On *Mahina Tiare* I can't even reach the bottom of the fridge without doing a head-first dive, shoulders and all, into the compartment. It doesn't have a drain, so bailing it out is a little challenging.

❖ If your fridge has a **drain**, check where it drains to. If it drains into the bilge bad odors may occur. To prevent the cold air from escaping down the drain an option is to install a valve or plug on the drain.

❖ You need to be **organized** in the refrigeration department to avoid continually opening and closing the lid to acquire your desired items, rearrange the contents each time you create a meal or search for misplaced items.

❖ Some foods that we might otherwise cool at home – pickles, mustard and mayonnaise – **do not require refrigeration** if they're not contaminated with dirty utensils each time they're consumed.

❖ **Transfer bulk goods** that you might otherwise refrigerate at home, such as the above items, into smaller containers for weekly use so that they accommodate less space in your fridge.

Organizing the Fridge

❖ Lynn Kirwin on the yacht *Constance* had stacking clear **plexiglass containers** with fold-down handles made for her fridge. These worked well for organization and space utilization.

❖ To **maximize efficient use of the odd dimensions** of our fridge I use six 15 quart lidded plastic containers that stack; either Rubbermaid or Sterilite. The containers are labeled and the contents are organized according to meal plans and/or the items life expectancy. I can fit 2 stacks of three containers plus 4 more containers, of various sizes, that that stand up on end against the hull.

❖ Here's how I pack the 15-quart containers for a 3-week passage from New Zealand to Tahiti.

   Vegetables Week 1: avocados, bell peppers, carrots, cauliflower, celery, cucumbers, mushrooms, parsley, tomatoes, zucchini, limes and leeks.

Vegetables Week 2: avocados, bell peppers, carrots, cauliflower, celery, cucumbers, zucchini limes and leeks.

Vegetables Week 3: This tub will contain hardy and long-lasting vegetables such as carrots and green peppers along with citrus.

Dairy, Luncheon Meats and Condiments: cheese, yogurt, butter, salami, luncheon meats, smoked seafood, dips, hummus, pesto, and salsa. These items are keep in the three remaining 15-quart containers.

Lettuce: I've two containers for lettuce. Each container holds 3 iceberg lettuces and I place a damp paper towel in the bottom.

Tomatoes: I keep the tomatoes all together in their own container so that I can monitor them. I allow for the consupmtions of 1 medium tomato per day.

Fruit: I pack a container of long lasting apples, stone fruit and citrus which will be consumed in week three at sea. The remaining apples and citrus are stowed in containers kept in the bilge at the beginning of the passage. As space opens up in the fridge I'll then add these items to the fridge vegetable containers.

Open Condiments: I have two open bins that contain the daily condiments, cheese, milk, juice, luncheon meat, butter, jam, bread, herbs etc. The bins can be easily lifted out to obtain access to the containers stacked beneath them.

Cabbages are wrapped in newspaper and placed in a plastic bag. If space allows, I place them in the fridge, but if there is no space I store them in the bilge until room opens up in the fridge.

I purchase cheese, luncheon meats and butter in **large sized packs.** When I open a pack I transfer the item into smaller containers for daily/weekly consumption.

Organizing Your Freezer

❖ For the **efficiency of the freezer** it's vital to keep air spaces to a minimum.

❖ For optimum **utilization of freezer space** and to assist in meal planning I package all freezer meats, seafood and vegetables into quart Ziploc bags.

❖ I **alternatively layer** food items of meats, poultry, seafood and vegetables according to my passage menu plan. For a planned meal it's then **easy to choose the required pack** and defrost it. The meat and poultry are precut to size acording to the recipe.

❖ When space occurs in the freezer I'll either **pack it with blue ice packs**, loaves of bread or bottles of water.

❖ **Vacuum-packing** freezer items helps avoid freezer burn, tainting, and prolongs their freezer life.

Transporting Supplies to the Boat

❖ When shopping bring your own **sturdy nylon/canvas tote bags** preferably with a zip. L.L. Bean has a great selection. These bags make the packing of groceries and transporting of provisioning items much easier. If I'm doing a major shop and have access to transport I'll also take large duffel bags as these work well for loading light goods such as paper towels, toilet paper and bread.

❖ Consider having a **strong-wheeled cart** for transporting groceries, fuel and water.

At the Grocery Store or Market

❖ Plan on shopping **early** in the morning to avoid the lunchtime and evening rush.

❖ Try to **reduce all unnecessary packaging** while at the checkout counter.

❖ Pack all **related items** into designated bags (i.e., frozen, canned, dry and fresh goods). This makes for easier stowage once aboard.

❖ Many supermarkets don't have people to help pack your groceries, so you need to **take someone with you** to give you a hand. Otherwise, you hold up the customers behind you as it's nearly impossible to unload your cart, reduce the packaging and sort your groceries into their designated bag by yourself.

Pest Control

❖ Try to **avoid tying ashore,** as this provides easy access for pests to board your boat. When moored stern-to for the night lift your gangplank and if possible move your boat further away (6 feet or so) from the quay.

❖ Don't leave garbage bags on deck overnight.

❖ Install **mesh screens** over hatches and portholes to keep bugs out.

❖ **Baygon** insect spray (not available in the U.S.) is extremely effective.

❖ Treat all items that you bring aboard as **potential carriers** of bugs and eggs.

❖ **Ants** are best killed by spraying or with ant-bait traps.

❖ **Cockroaches** are hardy critters. They fly, have a three-week hatching cycle and are adept at changing their resistance to pesticides. They don't like light, hiding away anywhere dark and are very wary of poisons.

❖ Combat or Raid **roach baits** work very well killing roaches, as they arrest their three-week hatching cycle.

❖ **Boric acid** is often a recommended method for killing roaches. It can be either mixed with sugar, sprinkled around the boat or combined with water and sugar then painted on surfaces. I find this rather messy and prefer roach baits and spray.

❖ **Bug bombs** (insect foggers) are pest control products that are intended to fill a room with a pesticide solution. They're ideal for extensive and widespread infestations that have not responded to bug sprays and other methods of pest control. Because they're more powerful and widespread than some of their counterparts bug bombs and foggers should only be used after you have familiarized yourself with their pros and cons.

    Activating a bug bomb:

        Remove all open food, dishes and utensils.

        Block all dorades and vents.

        Open all lockers, storage areas and bilges spraying a handheld can into each space.

        Activate the bomb and leave the boat closed for 12 hours.

Air well and repeat bombing three weeks later, as a new batch of eggs might of hatched.

❖ To kill or repel **mosquitoes** use smoke coils in the cockpit, which are less noxious than spraying insecticide below decks. Never scratch a bite, as staph infection can easily occur in broken flesh.

❖ **Weevils** are rapacious little critters that live and reproduce in cake mix, cereal, flour, pasta, grain, nuts and rice, generally preferring wholesome foods. They're recognized by their small, dark bodies and threads that appear throughout the packaging.

People think that weevils come from the outside searching for food however most weevil infestations come from grocery items which during the process of harvesting and packaging the item becomes contaminated by weevils or by their eggs. Once weevil eggs are in your flour, for example, they'll lay dormant until the outside conditions are good for hatching such as stable temperatures. Upon hatching they'll start eating your flour, rice and other items in your food pantry. Weevils will eat through Ziploc bags.

Weevils don't bite, sting or contain any toxins which could be harmful to a person. They can be picked out of food but cooking is suggested of infested products to kill the weevil and bacteria which they contain. Often a few herbs will disguise them in rice or mixing brown rice with white rice. I remember my young brother and I arguing over who had the most weevils in their breakfast cereal.

Four ways of **avoiding weevils:**

Place a **bay leaf** or two in with the stored dry food.

Freeze packets of potential weevil food for 24 hours.

Microwave questionable foods for 30 seconds.

Vacuum-pack dry goods.

❖ **Rats:** Each year I encounter at least one cruising boat that has a rat aboard so I hope that you never have this misfortune. They're extremely difficult to exterminate and love chewing through anything in order to wear their teeth down. I visited a steel boat with a rat that was gnawing the paint off the inside of the hull.

Suggestions to help you **eliminate Mr. Ratty:**

Rat trap set with cheese or peanut butter. Don't set the trap for the first few days so that the rat gets used to the idea that there's food easily available.

A **rat trap tray** with the sticky goo and tasty poison in the middle so that when the rat steps onto the tray its feet get stuck.

Stowage

Insect fogger with an escape hatch for the rat. This may not smoke it out but it will cause it to become drowsy.

Poison will kill the rat but pray it doesn't go off to die in an inaccessible place.

Rats love to eat the **insulation on electrical wires** so check all wiring closely after a rat has been aboard.

❖ When **leaving your boat** for and extended period of time, it's a good idea to place ant, cockroach and possibly rodent traps around the boat and have someone periodically check the boat.

Chapter 4

PASSAGE
PREPARATION &
COOKING AT SEA

Provision Planning

Before Leaving Your Homeport

❖ For a week write down a basic **menu plan** of the foods you generally eat. Check that these items are easy to stow onboard and prepare at sea. If not, amend your plan accordingly.

❖ Dee on *Penguin* writes out her favorite recipes, either on **recipe cards** or in a notebook. She makes the steps logical and easy to read. This way, when at sea, she doesn't have to deal with a large cookbook and fine print that provides too much information on what otherwise should be an easy-to-follow recipe.

❖ Use your menu plan to help with your provisioning. It allows you to **calculate the amounts** required and ensures that you don't forget anything.

❖ At sea I generally plan a **two-week rotation** for my menus allowing for rough weather and the catching of a fresh fish if we're in suitable waters.

❖ Once your menu plan is established you can then **arrange your dry provisions**, refrigerator and freezer items accordingly.

❖ **Make a list of the items you use** and the quantity you use of them several months before you set out cruising. This will give you a basic guideline when buying provisions.

❖ **Collect and sample recipes** that will take advantage of your long-term on board provisions.

❖ Cabbage is reasonably priced and keeps well. I'm always on the lookout for **interesting recipes** that utilize cabbage so that at the end of a four-week passage it's not something the crew will be bored with.

❖ At a **cruiser's potluck** dinner in the Marquesas there were 10 pasta dishes, two rice dishes and luckily one fish dish from a fortunate yacht that had caught a tuna just before arrival that day. I should have written down the recipes as that would be 12 more for your collection!

❖ Make provisioning less daunting and save money on bargains by provisioning over **several months**.

❖ You may not be an avid rice, beans and pasta consumer when you set out cruising. It's rare that people **change their eating habits drastically** when starting their cruise but they do slowly alter them while they're cruising usually out of necessity.

The Cruising Diet

I was raised on an English diet of meat, potatoes and two vegetables. The only spaghetti I was familiar with came out of a can. Even racing in the Whitbread Race our boat was very British with our freeze-dried meals consisting of roast beef and beans, roast lamb and peas, smoked fish and carrots, lamb stew plus macaroni and cheese. It was not until I spent 18 months cruising the remote Chilean Patagonia region, with its infrequent and minimal provisioning stops, that I became interested in using herbs and spices.

The Chileans are big red meat and potato eaters and for spice they use cumin and red chili. I was starting to become bored with meals on board and after studying cookbooks my cooking style slowly started to change as I tried out new recipes and meal ideas.

A newly arrived crew member brought down a packet of dried taco seasoning mix. After reading through the ingredients with gusto I set out to recreate the mix so that I could create future taco meals using fish instead of ground beef. I realized that taco shells were unavailable so I researched how to make tortillas and after my first successful meal I was hooked!

My Dad is another example of how cruising can change ones diet. With English parents and 15 years in the Royal New Zealand Air Force Dad's eating habits were an ingrained English affair. Back in the 80's after our first week in Tahiti Dad slowly began to question how much of our cruising kitty Mum was spending on provisions. One day Mum threw down her wallet in frustration saying, "You go buy your pork chops, sirloin steaks and fresh asparagus." Two hours later, Dad returned and sheepishly unpacked his bags. While Mum sat in the saloon nonchalantly reading a book Dad stowed away canned tomatoes, pasta, rice and tuna fish. He'd no idea of the high cost of imported meat and vegetables and to this day Dad has never again complained of spaghetti for dinner.

Calculating How Much You Need

Calculate your **passage time** in days.

Next **add extra days** for unfavorable winds such light air or heavy weather and a few more for rigging or engine troubles.

Double this time amount.

This then amounts to the minimum number of days you'll need to provision for.

Tips on Provision Planning

❖ **Seasickness** may lay claim to appetites for the first few days of any ocean passage. Plan for simple bland meals when putting to sea to ensure you don't encourage your crew's stomachs to churn.

❖ **Heavy weather** makes cooking at sea difficult. Plan easy-to-prepare meals for at least 10% of your passage time. These may be any combination of the following:

Frozen precooked meals: chilis, curries, hearty soups, lasagnas, pies, quiches, pizzas and stews.

Canned meals come in a few options ranging from chili con carne, spaghetti, ravioli to soups, baked beans and stews.

Freeze-dried meals ranging from complete gourmet camping meals to instant two-minute noodles.

❖ **Research your first landfall port**. Many cruisers crossing the Pacific from Mexico and Panama to the Marquesas are often surprised at the high cost of food and fresh produce available from the few small stores and the lack of selection. There's often another month of cruising the isolated islands of the Marquesas and Tuamotus before reaching the major port of Tahiti with its super stores and thriving local market.

❖ Check if any **quarantine restrictions** apply to the food items you have before arriving in a foreign port.

❖ Maintaining a **well-stocked yacht** gives you the freedom to stay places longer and change your plans without the burden of endless trips to the store.

❖ Find out what items are **unavailable or expensive** in your planned cruising ground and purchase extra provisions accordingly.

❖ **Menu variety is important** so don't restrict yourself to large quantities of few items.

❖ **Special events** such as birthdays, anniversaries, equator crossings, halfway celebrations and holidays should not be forgotten. Think of interesting ways to cater for these occasions maybe a cake mix or special treat.

❖ If you're **unfamiliar with the products** you're choosing it may be best to purchase one of each brand and try it out. I've often done this with different brands of canned tuna as the size of meat flakes versus water quantity varies from brand to brand. One label of canned stew might just taste awful, another too fatty, while a different variety may have too much added sugar or salt for our taste. Quite often I'll mix different brand/products of ready-to-go meals and when I discover a favorite brand I'll stock up on extra cans.

Stretching the Limit

The finish line for the Auckland, N.Z.-to-Nouméa, New Caledonia yacht race had been changed the year I did the race. Previously, it had ended at the Amédée lighthouse on the barrier reef 20 miles from the town of Noumea but the local French sailors decided to finish the 1993 race off the yacht club headland inside the lagoon. The reason for the change was to offer the public a view of the finish line and to save the committee boat from bouncing around in the lagoon while they recorded the finishers.

We arrived at Amédée lighthouse after eight days of hard sailing from Auckland to discover that the wind dies at night inside the lagoon. We then spent the night drifting around the coral heads in the strong tidal currents and there went all our hopes of a good race result as we lost 12 hours being becalmed!

Our race was not the only one finishing as Australia also had its own race arriving from Gosport. So here we were, inside the reef like a sitting duck with an Aussie boat also heading for the finish. Well, these Aussies weren't happy that the finish line had been changed as they weren't notified of the switch until we told them on the radio.

To drown our sorrows we decided to have a party as we still had a supply of rum, a few munchies and we could get the local FM dance station on our stereo. These poor Australians were not in luck having eaten everything on board.

Every hour or so they'd contact the race committee trying to get a response. They were hoping the race committee would let them finish at the lighthouse and just add extra time to account for the lack of wind in the lagoon. This way they could finish and all would not be lost. What they didn't know was that the race committee, knowing that no one would finish in the dark due to the lack of wind, had gone home for the evening.

The Aussie's were pretty persistent, calling the race committee every hour. By 3 a.m. they were extremely agitated and were starting to sound quite angry while our crew were truly merry having demolished most of our rum. It was then that one of our crew members picked up the radio microphone and spoke in a very French accent: "Would you *pleeze* stop calling *zee* race committee. We are not going to talk to you, and are even prepared to deduct time off your race result if you continue to be so rude." There was a period of silence, and a very quiet voice came back saying they were sorry for being impolite.

The breeze picked up early in the morning and by dawn we'd drifted across the finish line with the Australians. They were very quiet and glum, though exceedingly polite to the officials.

No harm was done but it perhaps pays to carry a few extra provisions for the sake of crew moral.

Menu Planning

This is the menu plan I created for our 2,300 mile passage from Tahiti to Hawaii with a crew of eight. I was worried when Juha, one of our crew, informed me that he had a moderate intolerance to wheat products. I'd an established supply of canned and dried goods onboard and just required fresh and frozen food provisions in Tahiti for the passage.

At sea I used to take one day at a time when it came to meals but now on expeditions I write up a plan for the entire passage to ensure that I provide a balanced and varied diet.

Day	Lunch	Dinner with Wheat	Dinner Non-wheat
Mon.	Sandwiches		Garlic chicken with rice and salad
Tue.	Sandwiches		Quiche, baked potatoes and salad
Depart Port Wednesday at 10 am			
Wed.	Sandwiches	Chicken, black bean, corn, tortillas	
Thu.	Sandwiches	Pre-frozen lasagna and salad	
Fri.	Rice salad		Chicken lentil stew
Sat.	Sandwiches		Shrimp stir-fry, rice
Sun.	Tabouleh salad	Spaghetti and salad	
Mon.	Pasta		Fresh wahoo, rice salad
Tue.	Poisson cru		Chicken pumpkin curry
Wed.	Fish cakes	Tortellini and salad	
Thu.	Mac & cheese		Satay shrimp stir-fry
Fri.	Sandwiches		Tuna, potatoes and beans
Sat.	Poisson cru	Spaghetti carbonara and salad	
Sun.	Sushi		Fresh fish tacos
Mon.	Tuna salad		Mexican chili
Tue.	Left over chili	Seafood & couscous	
Wed.	Pasta salad		Mahi, potatoes & corn
Thu.	Chickpea salad		Greek tomato chicken
Fri.	Sandwiches		Curry and rice
Sat.	Tuna bean salad	Shrimp pesto pasta	
Sun.	Crackers		Fish tacos
Mon.	Soup		Salmon, farro salad

Breakfast

John cooks breakfast and although most breakfasts contain wheat Juha had the option of fruit and yogurt or eggs. French toast, yogurt, fruit (either canned or fresh), eggs, cereal, toast, fresh baked muffins, pancakes, egg muffins and porridge are all breakfast options.

Lunch

Lunches are usually toasted sandwiches and the previous night's leftovers and I always gave Juha the option of salad. French baguettes were cheap at 50 cents each but a small loaf of local bread was expensive at $5 and imported brown bread from the U.S. or New Zealand ran as high as $9. I provisioned with 15 baguettes that lasted four days and 4 loaves of brown bread, 2 of which I froze as soon as there was space in the freezer. I planned to bake a large loaf of bread at least two days of the trip and I always carry a large supply of crackers for lunch options.

Fresh Vegetable Quantities

When provisioning the fresh food, I count out my vegetable items per day. I allow 3 onions, 3 carrots, 1 tomato, 3 apples and 2 oranges per day. Apples and oranges are best kept in the refrigerator for an Equator crossing, as they stay fresh longer. At lunch I cut them into quarters and give each person a few slices. Such a small portion may seem stingy if you are a fruit fanatic but a fresh, cool, crispy apple slice is a big treat especially with a squeeze of lime or a slice of tasty cheese.

For this passage, I counted out four meals using potatoes, allowing two medium potatoes per person. I selected four medium cabbages, two that were red to give a dash of color in salads and stir-frys. Other fresh vegetables were imported and rather expensive so they needed to be kept in the fridge for maximum longevity. I included six green peppers, five zucchini, five cucumbers, fresh green beans, and mushrooms for two meals. Imported frozen peas, beans and corn were inexpensive and helped supplement stir-frys, salads and stews.

Local lemons were inexpensive and I purchased eight of medium size to use in salads, poisson cru and a garnish for fish. A bunch of imported parsley was $4 at the supermarket while locally-grown bunches of basil, parsley and cilantro were only $1 at the market. A big bag of dried imported Herbs de Provence was $3 at the supermarket. These herbs were absolutely incredible and I wish I'd bought several more.

Red Meat

Red meat imported from New Zealand was good quality and inexpensive but we generally don't eat much red meat on board. It would be very easy to substitute red meat for the fish, chicken or shrimp dinners in the previous menu chart.

Chicken

Local chicken was very expensive but 5-lb. boxes of frozen chicken breasts imported from the U.S. were only $8. One box easily fed our crew for a meal and before I stowed the boxes in the freezer, I slightly thawed them, removed the skin and cut the chicken into fist-sized pieces. This reduced the size of the package and cut preparation time while under way. Roasted chickens were $10. I bought two and deboned them, freezing the meat in quart Ziploc bags, enough for three meals: chicken tortillas, chicken lentil and chicken stir-fry or pasta.

Seafood

Shrimp were reasonably priced and I like them as a meal plan because they don't require defrosting until you're ready to use them. Shrimp are a good standby, along with pasta dishes if you don't catch that fish you were hoping for, if weather conditions deteriorate and you aren't able to bake the gourmet quiche dish you planned or you simply forgot to defrost the chicken.

On this trip I only set the fishing lines on three days because each time the lines were payed out we only had to wait a few hours before catching a fish. Each fish was a different variety so it kept the meals interesting. I generally cook the fish on the day we catch it.

Stowage

The menu plan greatly helped in my stowage organization as I was able to layer the refrigerator and freezer with each week's provisions according to when they'd be required.

Surprises

We baked bread twice and fresh bread is always a big hit. Unfortunately John accidentally cut the power supply to the bread machine on the second time around. He switched off the inverter to get a clearer radio signal and as the bread machine has no memory of its time sequence it has to start all over again. Luckily the loaf was on its second rise and I could punch it down, place it in two pans, wait for it to rise again before baking it in the oven. We'll now place tape over the inverter switch whenever the bread machine is on.

For our equator crossing ceremony I concocted an awful mixture of oats, Tabasco and coffee grounds, tinted with green food coloring. This was administered to the pollywogs as part of their initiation rite into the realm of shellbacks. A celebratory batch of walnut-peanut brownies was baked but the rest of the passage was a bit bouncy for further baking. For snacks we have a cracker box that stays in the cockpit. Each night after dinner we open a packet of cookies for dessert and use the remainder to stock the cracker box for night watches, along with crackers.

Planning Overview

I was amazed at how my daily concern of what to cook was eased by having created a menu plan and this then allowed me more time to concentrate on the meals of the day.

Catching fish was a bonus, providing more spare meals to add to the menu plan and the chance to eliminate some repetitive meals. Most meals had an accompanying salad made with both lettuce and cabbage to stretch the lettuce further. I try to keep the evening salad interesting: Greek with olives and herbs, orange and ginger, nutty with sesame and pumpkin seeds or mixing a tasty dressing if I feel inspired.

Many times the leftovers from previous evenings meal were easily expanded to provide a tasty lunch. Weather conditions were favorable though winds were either beam-on or just forward of the beam at around 18 knots which made for a bumpy ride. Some nights it was difficult to juggle the pasta pot and it was often easier to lock the stove than have it gimbal away. My next galley project is to modify the gimbal locking mechanism enabling the oven to be locked-off at different angles when the boat is on a steady tack.

The temperature was hot, hot, hot and I was grateful for the Hella turbo galley fan as we had spray over the decks so we couldn't open the hatches or ports. I did not use the oven and cooked with the pressure cooker whenever possible to reduce the heat below.

By the end of the passage my estimates had worked out extremely well. On our arrival in Hawaii, State Agriculture confiscated the fresh food which consisted of one tomato, two lemons, one orange and one grapefruit, a quarter of a cabbage, three carrots and two onions. The crew was very complimentary of the meals saying they were better than what they eat at home and not at all what they had expected.

Cooking While Underway

Tips on Cooking While Underway

* **Plain crackers** can be kept in a small sealed container, always at the ready for the seasick sailor.

* Have a container of **snacks** – cookies, dried fruit, health bars or crackers – handy for night watches or for quick inbetween meal pick-me-ups.

* Use **Scoot-Gard** on the counter tops to keep items from sliding.

* **Prep and cooking time** for a meal at sea takes twice as long as does at anchor. Have patience, be organized, replace items as you use them, clean up as you go and don't let it get you down.

* At sea, it's a lot easier to prepare the evening meal in **daylight**. Remember that in the tropics it gets dark at six in the evening.

* For some reason, the wind always seems to increase at **sunset**, interrupting cooking. Sail reduction is often required and conditions become more uncomfortable below in the galley. I've nicknamed this scenario the "sunset puff-up".

* If my evening meals require a lot of **vegetable preparation**, such as with a salad, stir-fry or stew, I'll sometime do the chopping in the early afternoon so that in the evening I don't have to spend as much time in the galley.

* Quite often at sea I find it's easier to prepare and chop vegetables sitting down **at the table** than standing at the counter top. I'll use Scoot-Gard on the table to keep articles from sliding around.

* I enjoy having **a daily cartoon calendar** on my galley wall. Being able to view a joke scenario from the New Yorker helps my sense of humor, especially when it's rough and I'm not enjoying the current situation.

Heavy Weather Menu Planning

❖ The **simplest menu** in heavy weather is one that doesn't require a lot of prep work or unnecessary time watching pots on the stove top.

❖ Cooking and washing dishes in rough conditions is challenging and difficult and you shouldn't expect just one person to do it all. You need to be able to **trade off** such duties.

❖ After you've been at sea for a few days you and your crew will have a hearty appetite although if heavy weather occurs rich food might be a little hard to stomach whereas tasty **one-pot meals** will be welcome.

❖ When it's **extremely rough** and we're sailing with the two of us we generally plan only two hearty meals a day. John will cook a large brunch around 10:00 consisting of either eggs, French toast, pancakes or hot cereal and at 16:00 I'll prepare a hot one-pot evening meal.

❖ Even the simple task of **boiling water** may becomes difficult when it's rough. For this reason consider a dedicated sealed kettle and hot thermos. These will give you a convenient source of hot water for drinks and instant soups.

❖ When heavy conditions occur I try not to attempt any dish that requires more than half a potful of water such as meals with **rice, pasta or boiled potatoes** as the water might slosh over the edge of the pot.

❖ **One-pot meals** such as chili, curries, hearty soups and stews can be prepared before a passage and frozen. When heavy weather occurs these meals can then be thawed and easily heated in a pot.

❖ **Frozen meals** like lasagna, pizza, quiche and pie require a hot oven or microwave to reheat them although you can use a fying pan with a lid on the stove top. These food items may be difficult to impossible to find ready made in less developed countries.

❖ Prepared frozen meals are generally the first choice in rough conditions but if you've consumed these you'll be resorting to **canned food** unless your budget has allowed you to provision with freeze-dried meals.

❖ **Canned meals**. Often I'll mix them with soup to stretch them out, and maybe add a meat, tuna, shrimp or vegetables for variety.

❖ The **pressure cooker** provides a safe method for cooking one-pot meals in all weather conditions. My one good standby in stormy weather is a pressure cooker pot filled with potatoes, carrots and onions sprinkled with Italian or French herbs. It may sound plain, but when its cold, wet and miserable out there's something comforting about the old spud and his pals. Toppings can vary from a knob of butter, to bacon bits, Parmesan cheese, grated cheddar cheese, salt and pepper, canned tuna or relish. Any leftovers can be diced and sautéed for lunch the next day see *"Bubble and Squeak."*

Navigating The Galley In Heavy Weather

❖ Know and **anticipate the movement of your stove**. If my stove is gimballing too erratically, I will simply lock it so that I'm not having to deal with its movement.

❖ Make sure that your stove is fitted with sturdy **adjustable locking arms** so that all your cookware can be secured in position on the stove top.

❖ In heavy weather, my mum also uses a **spring tie-down**, a setup of a stainless spring with a hook on each end. She simply hooks one hook to the side fiddle, stretches it across the pot, lid and all, then hooks the other end onto a fiddle on the other side. It saves the worry of a flying pot or its lid slipping off.

❖ Pack new sponges into **gaps in galley cupboards** to stop items from sliding and rattling around.

❖ Ensure that **drawers have a sturdy catch** to prevent them from jumping and sliding out of position. In heavy weather, I place a webbing strap with buckle across the front of the drawers.

❖ Ensure that your **drawers have a stop** to prevent them from sliding out all the way. I've seen the odd heavy drawer go flying across the cabin when someone has let it go after removing an item.

❖ If your **sink** is an outboard installation, make sure your shut off valve is easily accessible so you can prevent the regurgitation of water.

❖ Having a Hella Turbo **fan** installed in the galley ensures adequate ventilation for the cook. Remember that in heavy weather all ports and hatches will be closed.

❖ Invest in sturdy, deep, stable **non-skid bowls** for serving meals in storm conditions. Some people recommend paper plates but I find that you can't set them down and that food gets cold too quickly.

❖ Plastic or stainless **thermal mugs** with tight sealing lids are invaluable in heavy weather for serving hot drinks and meals. Their large handles makes them easy to hold and the insulation keeps food and liquids hot in cold weather.

Chapter 5
APPETIZERS &
LIGHT MEALS

Drinks

Sangria

Sangria always reminds me of summertime afternoon yacht club lawn functions in South England. Great for a large crowd where you don't want to go to the trouble of attending "the bar," sangria can be served in jugs, though I prefer a punch bowl with ladle as you can scoop up which fruit you wish to nibble on.

1 bottle	wine – white or red
1 bottle	soda – cold ginger ale, 7-Up or equivalent
	sliced fruit such as lemons, oranges, apples and berries
	mint leaves to garnish

❖ Combine wine and fruit in a punch bowl and let soak for at least 2 hours.

❖ Add soda, mint leaves and ice cubes.

Hot Buttered Rum

While wintering over in White Rock, Canada, my Dad and I would row out from the pier in the afternoons to check our three crab pots. Often the weather was miserable and upon arriving back to the boat we'd share a hot buttered rum before cooking up the crabs.

1/2 C	brown sugar
1/4 lb.	butter – salted
	*cinnamon, nutmeg and allspice

❖ Combine ingredients.

❖ Spoon 2 T of mixture into a mug, add desired measure of rum and fill with boiling water.

Nibbles

Spicy Fruit and Nuts

2 C	cashew – toasted
1 C	almonds – toasted
2/3 C	dried apricots
2/3 C	raisins

```
  2/3 C   dates – diced
      1   egg white
      2 T   olive oil
      2 T   lemon juice
  1 1/2 T   lemon zest
      1 T   ground cumin
      1 T   ground coriander
      1 t   hot paprika
    1/2 t   turmeric
```

❖ Heat oil, add spices, cook and stir until fragrant.

❖ Whisk egg white until it peaks, stir in spice mixture and remaining ingredients.

❖ Spread mixture onto a greased oven tray.

❖ Bake 25 minutes or until crisp and dry, stirring occasionally.

Makes 5 cups of mixture that keeps well in an airtight container.

Sugared Nuts

```
      1 C   almonds – whole
      1 C   pecans
      1   egg white
    1/3 C   sugar
    1/4 C   butter – melted
    1/2 t   cinnamon
```

❖ Bake nuts until slightly roasted.

❖ Beat egg white until it forms soft peaks, gradually beat in sugar and cinnamon.

❖ Mix in melted butter, add nuts, stir and spread onto a greased oven tray.

❖ Bake 25 minutes, stirring occasionally.

Deviled Nuts and Seeds

```
      1 C   walnuts
      1 C   pecans
      1 C   peanuts
      1 C   pinenuts or pumpkin seeds
    1/2 C   Brazil nuts
    1/4 C   butter
```

Appetizers and Light Meals

4 T   Worcestershire sauce or chili and soy sauce
salt

❖   Roast nuts in butter for 10 minutes, stirring often.

❖   Add sauce and seeds, cook 5 minutes.

❖   Sprinkle with salt and cool.

Keeps well in airtight container

Island Coconut Chips

❖   Extract coconut meat from a fresh coconut and cut into thin strips. A vegetable peeler works well for this.

❖   Spread chips on a cookie sheet and bake at 375° until chips begin to brown, about 10 minutes.

Sprinkle with Island Seasoning, *page 167.*

Coconut Slices

A simple and inexpensive nibble is chilled coconut meat cut into bite sized pieces. It provides a nice tropical touch with sunset drinks and can be ready at short notice with minimal fuss.

Dips and Spreads

Aïoli

Carol~Yacht Elyxir

This dip can be used with vegetables, cold potatoes and as an addition to fish soup.

2 C   olive oil
5   egg yolks
1   lemon – juiced
6   garlic cloves
1 t   salt
1/2 t   sugar
1/2 t   mustard
pepper

❖   Puree all ingredients in a blender while slowly adding olive oil.

Quick Aïoli

Carol~Yacht Elyxir

        1 C   mayonnaise
         5   garlic cloves – crushed
               lemon juice – to taste
               *red pepper – roasted
               *roasted garlic

❖ Blend all ingredients together.

Chutney and Cream Cheese Spread

Judi~Yacht Long Passages

    1 block   cream cheese
               chutney or sweet relish

❖ Place cream cheese in a dish and cover with chutney.

Serve with crackers.

Baba Ghanoush ~ Eggplant Dip

Anu~Yacht Kialoa II

This recipe, along with the other Turkish recipes, was given to me by Anu, a professional chef who works on both sailing and motor yachts around the world. Anu spent 6 years as a guide in Turkey and while learning to speak Turkish she collected many wonderful recipes. Having recently traded land life for the sea Anu says she now feels more at home in the galley cooking Turkish food than her national dishes from the Netherlands.

When Anu gave me her favorite dishes she also included the following paragraph, perhaps to enlighten you to be creative in the galley.

Because the Turks are very hospitable people, you will not be able to leave their homes before drinking the specially brewed çay tea or kahve coffee accompanied by home made tatli sweets and meze starters. If you're ever in Istanbul, you'll enjoy an interesting visit to the imperial kitchens of the Topkapi Palace.

Turkish cuisine, often rated amongst the top three in the world, emerged during the time of the Ottoman Empire conquests across the Mediterranean. Here in these kitchens lavish dishes were created for the sole pleasure of the Sultan and his court. Chefs were employed under

Appetizers and Light Meals

strict rules resulting in a basic Ottoman cuisine that spread across the Mediterranean incorporating Chinese, Mongolian, Persian, Arab and Greek cuisine.

4	eggplants
1/2 C	olive oil
3 T	white wine vinegar or 2 T of tahini
1	egg yolk or 3 oz yogurt
1	lemon – juiced
3	garlic cloves – minced
	pinch of sugar
	S&P

❖ Grill eggplants whole under a hot grill turning them at least once until their skins are split, blistered and soft. May take up to half and hour. An option is to roast them, see *Eggplants,* page 153, in Fruits and Vegetables,.

❖ Peel eggplants when they have cooled and blend in a food processor or mash.

❖ Add garlic, vinegar, lemon juice, sugar and egg yolk.

❖ Blend ingredients while slowly drizzling in olive oil, stop every now and then to check the consistency, it should be light and rather thin but you may choose to make it thicker.

❖ Adjust flavor with S&P.

Serve slightly rounded and smoothed on a serving platter decorated with tomato wedges, black olives and parsley sprigs. This dip goes well with Shepherd's Salad *and warm bread.*

Quick Baba Ghanoush

❖ Peel eggplant and dice into cubes, sprinkle with salt, mix and let drain for an hour.

❖ Squeeze eggplant and steam in the pressure cooker for 3 minutes, eggplant should be very soft.

❖ Saute garlic in olive oil until brown, this gives baba ghanoush the smoky roasted flavor traditionally achieved when grilling the eggplant.

❖ Continue to make baba ghanoush by following the traditional directions above, substituting the prepared eggplant and garlic.

Guacamole

2	avocados
3 T	lemon juice
1	garlic clove – crushed
several drops	chili sauce
	S&P

❖ Blend all ingredients together.

Hummus

Hummus is a Mediterranean dip or spread made from chickpeas. It can be flavored with pesto, roasted red peppers, sun-dried tomatoes, olives or cumin.

3 C	chickpeas – cooked or canned
1/2 C	water
1/2 C	olive oil
1/4 C	vinegar or lemon juice
1/4 C	sesame seeds – toasted
8	garlic cloves
1 t	salt
	*substitute *Tahini* for vinegar and sesame seeds

❖ Blend all ingredients together to the consistency of peanut butter and chill.

Traditionally served rounded and smoothed on a flat tray, together with a dribble of olive oil and a garnish of paprika crisscrossed over the mound, finished with a sprinkling of parsley.

Serve with warmed pita pockets or tortillas, as a vegetable dip or a spread on brown toast or crackers.

Olive Tapenade

25	olives
1/4 C	olive oil
1/4 C	cilantro
3	garlic cloves – diced
2	anchovy fillets or fish sauce
2 T	lemon juice
2 T	basil
2 T	capers

3 t   Dijon mustard
    salt

❖ Blend all ingredients together.

Sun~Dried Tomato Tapenade

1 C   sun-dried tomatoes
1/3 C   capers
3   garlic cloves – diced
3   anchovy fillets or fish sauce to taste
2 T   olive oil
2 T   cilantro
1 T   basil
2 t   vinegar
    ground pepper

❖ Blend all ingredients together.

Tahini Dip

1/2 C   tahini or sesame seeds – toasted
1/4 C   lemon juice
1/4 C   parsley
1   garlic clove
3 T   water
1/4 t   salt

❖ Blend ingredients together, adding enough water to achieve the consistency of whipped cream.

❖ Cover and refrigerate

Keeps up to one week.

Westri Dip

I first tasted this dip at a cruisers New Year's Eve party in Patagonia with great friends on the yacht *Westri*. It's more of a temperate climate dish, as baking it in the boat oven makes the boat too hot in the tropics, perhaps then use a microwave.

1 C   Parmesan cheese
1 C   mayonnaise

1 C   canned artichokes, asparagus or mushrooms

❖   Combine ingredients and bake one hour at 350°F or until golden
brown.

Serve dip warm with toasted pita bread, crackers or vegetables.

Railroad Dip

Fran~Yacht Aka

Fran says this dish is super easy, and people just go crazy over it.
They sit there smacking their lips saying,
"Hmmmm is it quiche?"
"Tastes like there's cream in it"
Very good hot or cold. You can add crab or shrimp but it definitely
stands on its own with no need to fluff it up.

2 C   cheese – grated
2 C   mayonnaise
1 1/2 C   minced onion

❖   Combine ingredients.

Serve with pita bread, crackers or vegetables.

Turkish Yogurt Dip

Anu~Yacht Kialoa II

This tangy yogurt dip goes well with Turkish food as both a dip
and a dressing. I've also had it served as a side dish to chili beans and
was surprised at the refreshing taste it added.

1 C   yogurt – preferably thick and creamy
1   garlic clove
3 T   water
1/4 t   salt
1/2 T   olive oil
*1 t   cilantro

❖   Combine all ingredients except olive oil and chill.

*Just before serving, swirl oil over the top, garnish crosswise with pa-
prika and fresh dill.*

Vietnamese Dipping Sauce

2/3 C	soy sauce
1/4 C	rice wine or dry sherry
2	garlic cloves – crushed
2 T	lime juice
1 t	chili paste or chili pepper flakes
	*grated carrot, cilantro or diced scallion

❖ Combine all ingredients.

Serve with sushi, fish cakes or seafood.

Salsas

Made from fresh ingredients, salsas are a simple, low calorie addition to any meal enhancing the flavors of fish, poultry, meat and vegetables. Salsas are also wonderful spread on crusty bread or served as a dip for crackers and vegetables.

Grapefruit Salsa

2	grapefruit – diced with membranes removed
1	orange – pieced
2	scallions – sliced
1	chili – minced
2 T	mint – diced

❖ Combine all ingredients.

Hawaiian Salsa

1 C	fresh pineapple – cubed
2	tomatoes – cubed
1/4 C	cilantro – diced
1/2	Maui (sweet) onion – diced
1	garlic clove – minced
1	chili pepper – minced
1 t	coriander seed – crushed
3/4 t	cumin
1/2	salt

❖ Combine all ingredients, chill and serve.

Italian Salsa

5	tomatoes – diced
1	onion – diced
2	garlic cloves – crushed
2 T	basil – diced
3 t	chili pepper flakes
1 t	lemon juice
	S&P

❖ Combine all ingredients.

Mexican Salsa Fresca

5	tomatoes – diced
2	jalapeño chilies – seeded and diced
1	red onion – diced
3 T	cilantro – diced
2	garlic cloves – crushed
2 t	lime juice
	S&P

❖ Combine all ingredients.

Orange Salsa

3	oranges – diced with membranes removed
1/2 C	olives
	lemon juice

❖ Combine all ingredients.

Roasted Garlic Salsa

Roast a whole garlic head in the oven then squeeze the garlic out of the peel like paste. A quicker method – though it that does not provide the same taste – is to peel and chop the garlic then toss it in a pan with olive oil until brown.

```
    5   tomaotes – diced
    2   onions – diced
1/4 C   cilantro – diced
1 head  roasted garlic
    1 T tomato paste
        fresh chili to taste
```

❖ Combine all ingredients.

Tropical Salsa

Fran~Yacht Aka

```
    1   papaya, 2 mangoes or 1/4 C pineapple –
        diced
1/4 C   lemon or lime juice
1/4 C   onion – grated
    1   garlic clove – minced
        chili powder or chilies to taste
        cilantro
        salt
```

❖ Combine all ingredients, chill and serve.

Equatorial Meltdown

Tahiti to Hawaii 1980

Cool bliss – the first time I've felt chilled all day. An electric blue surrounds me as I sink deeper, feet first into the ocean, watching the light rays extended beyond an unknown galaxy as the dark-green hull of our yacht glides by like the mother ship from *Star Wars*. I feel free in my own cool outer space wishing it would last forever.

Soon it's over and I'm back on deck to the hot blazing reality of crossing the Equator. I long for tomorrow when once again dad will slow the boat down just long enough for me to jump off the bow and catch the stern as *Swanhaven II* sails by. I never imagined that it could be this hot.

We've an invasion of fleas aboard. I'm covered in bites from head to toe. Heidi, our cat, is the culprit, but we have long since used up our only can of insect repellent. We'd no fleas in Tahiti but the Equator has

Appetizers and Light Meals

caused them to hatch and multiply. Dad has resorted to drastic measures to rid us of the fleas by submerging Heidi in a bucket of water to drown them. With each dunking, his arms emerge with more scratches from her sharp claws as she resists. I can't watch these wild moments, as Heidi's Siamese cries are very haunting. She's now avoiding him. I don't know who's winning out – the fleas or Heidi.

In this heat it's hard to get excited about food. We've no refrigeration and the provisions we purchased in Tahiti were not all that fresh. In the Chinese supermarket mum noticed my brother David and I gazing wistfully at expensive American brands of breakfast cereal lining the shelves so she let us each choose a box. David chose Fruit Loops and I chose Alphabets; a big treat as we'd never had American cereal before.

On an appointed day we eagerly opened our cereal in celebration. My Alphabets looked great as I quickly tipped them out into a bowl and covered them in milk but when I raised my spoon to my mouth I didn't like the taste. I asked our American crew girl if she liked Alphabets and Kini replied, "Sure," but on tasting them she promptly announced they were stale. I was devastated.

Our cheese is fitted into square plastic containers and surrounded by cooking oil to stop it from molding. I have to pull hard at the large slimy block to release it from the oil. It's like pulling your gumboot out of a mud hole. I place the slippery cheese on the chopping board and watch it smartly slide off and slowly skate around the countertop to its own private tune. All I want is a small slice of cheese to eat with my cracker not a moving performance.

On night watch when I reach my hand into the jar of sweets it closes around a sticky jumbo lump. The wine gums have all melted together and in the morning their individual colors have merged, resembling the murky chunk I created one Christmas when I melted down my new packet of crayons with candles. Even the can of Coke I share with David holds no magic. The warm liquid tastes flat and sickly sweet while it lingers in my mouth.

When we sight a ship we all dream of ice cream, imagining big freezers loaded with wonderful flavors. Maybe the ship is a "Mr Whippy" ice-cream truck of the high seas and will soon come steaming by playing its jingle, a loudspeaker hailing that chocolate flakes are free today with a double cone. No such luck. But we catch a fish and David writes a log entry. He draws a picture of a shop with a neon sign flashing "Fish and Ships."

Twenty days after leaving Tahiti, we arrive in Honolulu. We pull alongside the Texaco fuel dock in the Ala Wai Yacht Harbor with our boat looking smart, our Kiwi and yellow quarantine flags snapping in the tradewind breeze.

"Aloha, Where you folks sail from?" asks the attendant.

"Tahiti," we reply.

"Well, you just go on inside and help yourselves to a cold drink from the cooler," he offers. With the first slug of the cold fizzy tropical punch meltdown images are wiped away and 20 days blend themselves into one to be stored away on a small meteor floating in a dark cool space inside my head.

Finger Foods

Falafels

Falafels are a Mediterranean patty that can be served with *Turkish Yogurt Dip* or in a warm pita pocket with tomatoes, bean sprouts, diced lettuce and yogurt or *Tahini Dressing.*

2 C	chickpeas – cooked
1/3 C	water
1/4 C	whole wheat bread crumbs
1/4 C	parsley or cilantro – chopped
1	onion – diced fine
5	garlic cloves – crushed
1/4 T	chili pepper – minced

```
1 t    basil – chopped
1/2 t  cumin
1/2 t  ground turmeric
       S&P
       flour for coating
       oil for frying
```

❖ Blend chickpeas until smooth, add remaining ingredients and mix well.

❖ Form mixture into 2" patties.

❖ Fry patties in hot oil until they are brown and crispy, drain on a paper towel.

Serve falafels warm from the oven.

Tortilla Wrap

Mary~Yacht Kismet

This may seem a basic appetizer but on a hot steamy night in Samoa at a memorable cruisers dinner party hosted by Diane aboard *Impossible* it proved to be a delightful treat. This recipe also reminds me that entertaining doesn't have to be too fancy.

```
tortillas
cream cheese
ham
green chilies – minced
cilantro
```

❖ Spread tortilla with cream cheese, ham, chilies and cilantro.

❖ Wrap tightly, cut into rounds and arrange on a plate.

Pita Chips

```
6     pita pockets – cut into chip triangles
1/2 C butter
2 T   parsley – diced
2 T   chives – diced
4     garlic cloves – crushed
1 t   lemon juice
```

❖ Blend above ingredients and spread onto pita chips.

❖ Bake at 350°F for 5 minutes until crispy or toast in a frying pan.

Turkish Zucchini Patties

Anu~Yacht Kialoa II

1/2 C	flour
1/3 C	parsley – chopped
2	zucchini – grated
1	onion – grated
1	egg
1	garlic clove – crushed
	chili pepper – any kind
	S&P
*1 C	feta cheese – mashed

❖ Mix ingredients together.

❖ Heat enough olive oil (or 1/2 olive and 1/2 vegetable oil) in a deep skillet to float patties.

❖ Note: before frying the entire batch, first fry one tester, if patty doesn't hold together add more flour and possibly another egg, taste check the seasoning.

❖ Drop a fork full of batter into the oil and flatten with the fork, fit in as many patties as you can.

❖ Cook patties until golden on the bottom, about 3 minutes, turn and brown the other side.

❖ Remove when done and drain on paper towels, add new patties.

To serve, arrange patties on a large platter with Turkish Yogurt Dip *in the middle.*

Tomato Basil Bruschetta

3 C	tomatoes – diced
1	green onion – diced
1/4	red onion – finely diced
2	cloves garlic – minced
3/4 C	basil – chopped
2 T	Parmesan cheese – grated
1/8 t	salt
	fresh ground pepper
	olive oil
1	baguette – sliced
1	garlic clove

❖ Combine tomatoes, onions, garlic, basil, olive oil, parmesan cheese, salt and pepper.

- ❖ Let sit 1 hour for flavors to combine.
- ❖ Brush baguette slices with olive oil and toast in oven 5 minutes.
- ❖ Rub garlic clove into one side of toast then top with tomato mixture.

Marinated Salmon ~ Gravlax

1	salmon fillet – skin on, scales removed
4	lemons – juiced
5 T	olive oil
4 T	coarse salt – not fine table salt
3 T	sugar
	ground pepper
	parsley

- ❖ Place fish skin down on a shallow dish, sprinkle with lemon juice, salt, pepper and sugar.
- ❖ Cover with plastic wrap and marinate 12 hours in the fridge.
- ❖ Scrape off salt and pat with a paper towel.
- ❖ Cut diagonally into thin slices, dress with olive oil, lemon juice and chopped parsley.

Serve with bread.

Sushi

Sushi is the Japanese name given to seafood served with cooked, room temperature rice.

- ❖ The two most **common sushi** are *Maki* and *Nigiri.*
- ❖ Sushi is **served with** sliced preserved ginger and a dipping sauce of wasabi and soy sauce or try Vietnamese hot sauce.
- ❖ As you can use leftover rice with a small amount of fresh seafood, sushi is a **versatile and economical** appetizer or meal.

Sushi Rice

- ❖ For **2 C of rice** use 1/4 C rice wine vinegar.
- ❖ If **rice wine vinegar is unavailable** heat 1/4 C vinegar and dissolve 2 T sugar, add to rice.

❖ To use **leftover rice** from the day before, heat vinegar and stir in the rice until it is soft and moist.

❖ **Store rice** in a cool dark place covered but not in the fridge as it will dry out.

Maki Sushi

Maki sushi is seafood, vegetables and rice rolled in nori seaweed and sliced.

❖ Maki sushi contains a **three color** combination achieved by combining 3 fillings.

Ideas for fillings

thin omelet
cream cheese
sesame seeds – toasted
spam – Allie Boys' favorite
smoked chicken
teriyaki chicken

vegetables

avocado
asparagus
julienne carrots
cucumber with skin on
spinach
dried mushrooms – soaked
scallions
spinach
sprouts
daikon radish

seafood

raw tuna or other firm raw fish
smoked salmon
smoked fish
canned tuna
crab
lobster
caviar
salmon eggs
shrimp
scallop

Nigiri Sushi

Nigiri sushi is seafood placed on an elongated rice ball spread with wasabi and sometimes belted with a strip of nori.
It's less fussy to make than *Maki* sushi but doesn't look as impressive. I like to make both for a contrast in presentation.

Chapter 6

SOUPS

Cold Soups

Gazpacho

2 C	stewed tomatoes – pureéd
1 1/2 C	tomato sauce
3/4 C	celery – diced
3/4 C	cucumber – diced
1/2 C	onion – diced
1/2 C	water
1/4 C	green pepper – diced
1/4 C	red wine vinegar
2 T	parsley – chopped
2 T	olive oil
1 t	Worcestershire sauce
1/4 t	pepper
	garlic crushed
	*assorted seafood poached in white wine

❖ Combine ingredients and chill several hours.

Serve with a dollop of yogurt.

Bean and Grain Soups

Spanish Chickpea and Spinach Soup

2 C	spinach – shredded or frozen
1 C	chickpeas – soaked
1 C	ham – diced
1	potato – diced
1	slice bread
2	garlic cloves
2 T	olive oil
	salt
	saffron

❖ Drain chickpeas and cover with water, pressure cook 15 minutes or simmer 1 hour.

❖ Add potatoes, ham, salt and pressure cook 5 minutes, or simmer 20 minutes, add saffron.

❖ Fry bread and garlic in oil, mash into a paste and add to chickpeas, this thickens and flavors the soup.

❖ In same pan sauté spinach in garlic and oil until soft, add to soup and simmer 3 minutes.

Serve hot with a sprig of basil.

Italian Black Bean Soup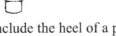

In Italy, it's customary to include the heel of a piece of Parmesan cheese to soups and stews, this adds a distinctive cheesy flavor that compliments the dish.

Although this classic soup is usually made with pasta and either rice or beans, I generally eliminate two of these ingredients as I find yet another step inconvenient. I will however add any leftover rice, pasta or beans from a previous meal.

If I'm lazy or it's rough I sometimes use a can of red beans or chickpeas instead of cooking black beans and add rice or shell pasta with a cup of water.

Extra liquid can be soaked up with couscous to make a thicker soup.

6 C	water
2 C	black beans – cooked
2 C	cabbage – shredded
3	tomatoes
2	red peppers – diced
2	zucchini – diced
2	potatoes – diced
1	onion – diced
1	celery stalk – diced
1	carrot – diced
3 T	olive oil
2 T	red wine
2	bay leaves
1 t	sugar
1	garlic clove – chopped
	S&P
	*cooked chicken can be added at the end of cooking, allow it to heat through

❖ Heat olive oil and sauté onion until brown.

❖ Add remaining ingredients and pressure cook 10 minutes, or simmer 20 minutes until vegetables are tender, season to taste.

Garnish with grated Parmesan cheese and parsley.

Caribbean Lentil Soup

4 C	boiling water
1 C	lentils
1/2 C	parsley – chopped
3	potatoes – diced
2	celery stalks – diced
2	carrots – diced
1	onion – diced
2	scallions – diced
2	bay leaves
2	garlic cloves – crushed
1	chili pepper – whole
2 T	olive oil
2 t	cider vinegar
	salt

❖ Combine all ingredients, except vinegar and parsley, pressure cook 10 minutes or simmer 1 hour until lentils are soft.

❖ Mix in vinegar and parsley, remove bay leaves and chili pepper.

Serve hot garnished with a swirl of yogurt.

Jamaican Split Pea Soup

4 C	boiling water
1 C	split peas
2	scallions – diced
1	onion – diced
2	garlic cloves – 1 whole and 1 crushed
1	chili pepper – whole
3 T	oil
4	allspice grains
2	bay leaves
1 t	ground cumin
1 t	curry powder
1/2 t	chili pepper – seeded and chopped
1/2 t	ginger – grated
1/4 t	thyme

❖ In pressure cooker or saucepan place split peas, whole garlic clove, ginger, bay leaves, allspice, whole chili, scallions and curry powder, cover with water.

❖ Pressure cook 15 minutes, or simmer 1 hour until split peas are tender, add thyme at end of cooking.

- ❖ Pour off excess liquid, discard chili and bay leaves, mash peas.
- ❖ Sauté onion, chopped chili and garlic until soft, mix in cumin.
- ❖ Add onion to split peas.

Serve hot with Yogurt Dressing.

Black Bean Chipotle Soup

6 C	vegetable broth
3 cans	black beans
1 can	diced tomatoes
1 C	corn
1	onion – diced
1	carrot – diced
2 T	olive oil
1 1/2 t	ground cumin
1/2 t	cayenne pepper
3	garlic cloves
1	chipotle pepper in adobe sauce – chopped
1 T	lime juice
1 pinch	of salt
1 pinch	of sugar

- ❖ Sauté onions 3 minutes.
- ❖ Add remaining ingredients and simmer 15 minutes.

Serve topped with grated cheese, sour cream, diced avocado and chopped cilantro.

Portuguese Sausage and Bean Soup

Patty~Hawaii

I met Patty in Hilo, Hawaii and on a visit to the boat she offered me this family recipe given to her by her mother. The Portuguese came to Hawaii as cowboys and sugarcane workers and along with the ukulele they also introduced many new recipes. This one became a favorite among the locals. Portuguese sausages are large and spicy, and many butchers in Hawaii create their own specialty blend.

1 1/2 C	kidney beans – soaked overnight
1	ham hock

```
        1    Portuguese sausage – 12oz.
        2    carrots – diced
        2    potatoes – diced
      1/2    cabbage – sliced
        1    celery stalk – sliced
        1    onion – diced
    1 can    tomato sauce
             S&P
```

❖ Cover ham hock with water and pressure cook 10 minutes or simmer 20 minutes.

❖ Sauté sausage and onion and add to ham hock along with beans, carrots, potatoes and tomato sauce.

❖ Pressure cook 15 minutes or simmer 2 hours.

❖ Add cabbage and simmer until cooked, season to taste.

Serve with chopped basil.

White Bean and Farro Tuscan Soup

Tessa~Yacht Kiwi Lass

```
      3 C    chopped kale, chard or spinach
      3 C    vegetable broth
    1 can    cannellini beans
        2    carrots – diced
        2    celery stalks – diced
        1    onion – diced
      1/2 C  farro
      1/4 C  diced bacon
        1 T  olive oil
        2    cloves garlic – minced
        2 t  Italian seasonings
        2 t  tomato paste
    pinch    red pepper flakes
             S&P
```

❖ Sauté bacon 2 minutes. Add farro and cook 2 minutes.

❖ Add onion, carrots, celery, garlic and cook 2 minutes.

❖ Add remaining ingredients except kale and beans.

❖ Pressure cook 10 minutes or simmer 30 minutes.

❖ Add kale and beans and cook until kale is wilted.

Garnish with grated Parmesan cheese and fresh chopped herbs.

Soups

White Bean and Pesto Soup

Emma~Svalbard

The tablespoon of pesto added when serving this versatile Mediterranean soup provides an elegant addition.

6 C	water
1 1/2 C	fresh white haricot beans or cooked white beans such as navy or even chickpeas
1 C	green beans – diced
3	tomatoes – diced
2	potatoes – cubed
2	carrots – diced
1	onion – diced
1	celery stalk – diced
2 T	olive oil
	S&P
	pesto

❖ Sauté onion until soft and add remaining ingredients except pesto.

❖ Pressure cook 10 minutes or simmer 1 hour.

❖ Season to taste.

Serve each bowl with a tablespoon of petso and grated Parmesan cheese.

Chicken and Combo Grain Soup

Vicky Witch~Cape Horn

8 C	water or chicken broth
2 C	brown rice, barley and split peas – combined
2	chicken breasts – cut into strips
2	onions – diced
2 C	assorted vegetables – diced
4	garlic cloves – crushed
	parsley, sage, thyme,
	S&P

❖ Pressure cook combo grains in water 15 minutes, or simmer 1 hour until barley is tender.

❖ Add remaining ingredients and simmer until chicken is cooked.

Garnish with a drizzle of Yogurt Lime Dressing *to add a pleasant refreshing taste.*

Miso Soup

Carol~Yacht Lorraine

This simple soup is wonderful as a quick warm-me-up and tasty low calorie treat.

I was first served this recipe in Port Townsend during a fly-by visit with my sailmaker friend Carol. She threw it together in no time at all, leaving us plenty of time to catch up on news. I was impressed! A hearty salad tossed with *Tahini Dressing* followed before I sadly bid my farewell and made a dash for the ferry.

Later in New Zealand I purchased plastic tubs of red miso and used it across the Pacific and for our extensive expeditions in Alaska. The crew never tired of *Miso Soup* served at lunch and although the soup alone is not fulling enough for a hungry crew it certainly helps take the chill off an icy day.

        4 C   water
        1 lb. tofu – cubed
        4 T   miso paste
        4 T   brewers yeast
        2 T   dried seaweed
          4   scallions – sliced
              *sliced mushrooms

❖   Simmer ingredients for 5 minutes and serve.

The Queen's English

We'd rounded Cape Horn in the early morning, the tall headland an impressive sight in the gray light. Although it was the middle of summer, 30-knot winds and hailstorms were blasting around the Cape as we tied to the mooring buoy beneath the steep hill that provides access ashore to the lighthouse, chapel and several monuments. Due to the precarious location I offered to stay aboard and keep watch while our expedition crew visited ashore.

The three Chilean lighthouse keepers hadn't received any visitors for three weeks and were eager for their mail and packages which we were delivering from Puerto Williams. While the moorage was calm I decided to make *Chicken and Combo Grain Soup* for lunch and also bake the lighthouse keepers a *Hawaiian Carrot Cake*. I was busy with the cake mix when a British voice came over the radio.

"Cape Horn lighthouse, Cape Horn lighthouse, Cape Horn lighthouse, this is the HMS *Endurance* calling."

No reply.

"Cape Horn lighthouse, Cape Horn lighthouse, Cape Horn lighthouse, this is the HMS *Endurance* calling."

No reply.

Thinking that the lighthouse keepers were being aloof to such a British voice I left my cooking and radioed the HMS *Endurance* suggesting that they try calling the lighthouse in Spanish.

"Farro Carbo de Hornos, Farro Carbo de Hornos, Farro Carbo de Hornos, HMS *Endurance* se llama."

Still no reply.

It then occurred to me that I'd been mistaken - the lighthouse keepers weren't ignoring HMS *Endurance* they were greeting our crew and receiving their mail. In the middle of placing the cake in the oven, I radioed back HMS *Endurance* and apologized for my mistake advising them that the lighthouse keepers were engaged with our landing party.

"Thank you very much madam and what vessel are you?" came a British voice.

"We're the yacht *Mahina Tiare* and our position is the mooring buoy stationed beneath the lighthouse," I answered.

Suddenly an extremely loud rumbling noise occurred and I instantly thought Oh No!!, we're adrift near the rocks.

Then a calm voice came over the radio and stated "Ah yes madam, quite right you are. We're the helicopter from the *Endurance*, on her way to Antarctica, and we can see quite clearly that you're in the bay and that your crew are ashore. Good day to you."

Vegetable Soups

Curried Carrot Soup

10	carrots – diced
4 C	water
1/2 C	rice
1/4 C	milk powder or cream
1	onion – diced
1	celery stalk – diced
3	garlic cloves
2 T	butter

      1 T   ginger grated
      1 t   curry paste
            S&P

❖ Sauté onion, curry, garlic and ginger, add remaining ingredients.

❖ Pressure cook 12 minutes or simmer until carrots are soft.

❖ Blend together and season to taste.

Serve garnished with dollop of chutney and fresh cilantro.

Irish Carrot Soup

Carol~Yacht Elyxir

      10   carrots – sliced
      4 C   vegetable or chicken broth
      1   onion – chopped
      6   garlic cloves – crushed
      1 T   lemon juice
      5   whole cloves
            honey

❖ Sauté carrots, onions, garlic and cloves until onions are transparent.

❖ Add broth and pressure cook 8 minutes, or simmer 15 minutes, remove cloves and mash.

❖ Add lemon juice and honey.

Garnish with a drizzle of yogurt and a sprinkle of parsley.

Mushroom Soup

Jenn~Yacht Ocean Light II

      2 C   mushrooms – sliced
      1 1/2 C   milk
      1 C   chicken stock – hot
      1/3 C   parsley
      2 T   onion – chopped
      2 T   flour
      1 T   butter
      1 t   tarragon
            S&P

❖ Sauté onion for 2 minutes, add mushrooms and cook 3 minutes.

❖ Sprinkle in flour and stir in chicken broth.

- ❖ Bring to a boil, stir in milk and herbs, simmer 5 minutes.
- ❖ Season to taste, *blend with hand blender.

Serve garnished with sliced mushroom caps.

Leek and Broccoli Soup

3	leeks – sliced
6 C	broccoli florets
1	potato – diced
2 T	olive oil
4	garlic cloves – minced
	salt

- ❖ Sauté leeks and garlic 3 minutes.
- ❖ Add remaining ingredients and pressure cook 8 minutes or simmer 15 minutes.
- ❖ Puree using a hand blender.

Serve garnished grated cheese.

Pumpkin Lentil Soup

2 1/2 C	vegetable stock
2 C	pumpkin
1 C	lentils – soaked
2	onions – diced
2	potatoes – grated
1 T	oil
4	garlic cloves – crushed
1 t	ginger – grated
1/2 t	each – cumin, coriander and basil
	parsley
	S&P

- ❖ Sauté onion and pumpkin until tender, approximately 5 minutes.
- ❖ Add spices, potatoes, lentils and stock, pressure cook 13 minutes or simmer 90 minutes until lentils are tender.

Garnish with parsley and serve with freshly baked bread or crackers.

Soups

Pumpkin Orange Soup 🍲

Ben~Yacht Katherine

1	pumpkin – cubed and skin removed
4 C	vegetable or chicken broth
1 C	orange juice
2	onions
6	garlic cloves – crushed
1 t	cinnamon
1/2 t	thyme
	* honey or sugar
	* cooked barley, rice, ham, bacon, ginger or curry

❖ Sauté pumpkin, garlic and onions.

❖ Add broth, cinnamon and thyme.

❖ Pressure cook 10 minutes, or simmer 20 minutes until pumpkin is soft, mash.

❖ Add honey and S&P to taste.

Garnish with a drizzle of yogurt and a sprinkle of parsley.

Curried Potato Soup 🍲

Carol~Yacht Elyxir

4 C	chicken broth
1 C	orange juice
5	potatoes – diced
4	carrots – diced
2	onions – diced
2	garlic cloves – crushed
1 T	ginger – grated
1 t	curry powder
	S&P

❖ Sauté carrots, potatoes, onions, garlic, ginger and cumin.

❖ Stir in chicken broth and pressure cook 5 minutes, or simmer 15 minutes, mash.

❖ Add orange juice and heat through, season to taste.

Garnish with cilantro and a spoon of Mango Chutney.

Spinach and Parmesan Soup

4 C	spinach – chopped
2 C	milk
1 C	chicken broth
1/4 C	Parmesan cheese – grated
1/4 t	nutmeg

❖ Heat broth and cook spinach, add milk and nutmeg simmer 10 minutes.

❖ Add Parmesan and simmer 2 minutes, season to taste.

Garnish with grated Parmesan.

Miscellaneous Soups

Clam Chowder

2 C	clams – chopped and sautéed in their own nectar
2 C	water
1 can	evaporated milk
5	potatoes – cubed
4	bacon rashers – diced
1	onion – diced
1	celery stalk – diced
1	carrot – sliced
2	garlic cloves – crushed
1 t	Worcestershire sauce
	lemon juice
	chili pepper of some form
	S&P

❖ Sauté bacon, onion, potatoes, celery, carrot and garlic.

❖ Add water, chili, Worcestershire sauce and S&P.

❖ Simmer until potatoes are tender.

❖ Add clams, lemon juice and milk, stir well and heat.

Soups

New England Fish Chowder

2 C	milk
2 C	water
1 lb.	white fish
1/2 C	white wine
1/4 C	flour
1/4 C	water
2	bacon rashers – diced
1	onion – diced
1	bay leaf
2	whole allspice
1	garlic clove – crushed
	nutmeg

❖ Sauté onion, garlic and bacon, add 2 C water, wine, bay leaf and allspice, bring to boil.

❖ Add fish, cover and simmer until fish flakes, about 10 minutes.

❖ Remove fish with slotted spoon and flake.

❖ Mix flour and 1/4 C water until smooth, gradually stir into soup, simmer until soup thickens.

❖ Stir in milk, return fish and stir over medium heat until heated through.

❖ Add nutmeg, season to taste, remove bay leaf and allspice before serving.

Queen Charlotte Salmon Chowder

Jenn~Yacht Ocean Light II

1 1/2 C	salmon or 1 can, including juice
1 can	evaporated milk or 2% milk
1 can	creamed corn
1 C	water
1 C	chicken stock
1/2 C	parsley – chopped
4	potatoes – diced
3	carrots – diced
1	onion – diced
1	celery stalk – diced
1	zucchini – diced
1	green pepper – diced
3	garlic cloves – crushed
2 t	butter

    1/2 t   ground pepper
    1/2 t   dill seed

- ❖ Sauté onion, green pepper, celery and garlic 3 minutes.
- ❖ Add potatoes, carrots, stock, water, pepper and dill.
- ❖ Pressure cook 7 minutes or simmer 20 minutes.
- ❖ Add zucchini and simmer 5 minutes, add salmon, milk and corn, heat through and stir in parsley just before serving.

Serve hot with crusty bread.

Chicken Tortilla Soup

Juan~Acapulco Yacht Club

    8 C   chicken stock
    3 C   cooked shredded chicken
    2   stalks celery – diced
    2   tomatoes – diced
    1   onion – diced
    1   bell pepper – diced
    1   carrot – diced
    2   jalapeños – diced
    3   garlic cloves – minced
    1 T   olive oil
    1 t   ground coriander
    2 t   ground cumin
        S&P

- ❖ Sauté onions 3 minutes.
- ❖ Add remaining ingredients and simmer 15 minutes.

Serve with diced corn tortillas, diced avocado, chopped cilantro and lime wedges.

Thai Chicken Soup

Roland~Iceland

    4   chicken breast – sliced
    1 1/2 C   milk
    1 C   chicken broth
    1 can   coconut milk
    1 can   bamboo shoots

1/2 C	sugar peas
1	onion – sliced
3	scallions – sliced
3	ginger slices
3 T	fish sauce
1/2 t	lemon zest
	chili of some form
	cilantro

❖ Combine broth and coconut milk, add chicken, onions and ginger.

❖ Cook gently for 15 minutes, add lemon zest, chili, cilantro, scallions and vegetables, heat through.

❖ Add milk and simmer 10 minutes, stir in fish sauce.

Garnish with thin slice of lemon and sprig of cilantro.

Thai Fish Soup

Cow Bay Café~Prince Rupert, Canada

Adrienne uses fresh halibut for this soup but any firm white fish is suitable.

4	fish fillets
4 C	fish stock
1 C	coconut milk
1 C	clam nectar
1	onion - chopped
1 T	vegetable oil

Curry

2	curry leaves
1 t	paprika
1 t	dried dill
1/2 t	cayenne pepper
1/2 t	cumin
1/2 t	mustard
1/4 t	turmeric
	grated ginger

❖ Toast curry seasoning in dry frying pan to release flavor, add olive oil, onion and ginger, sauté.

❖ Add stock and nectar, bring to a boil, add pieced fish and simmer until nearly cooked.

❖ Stir in coconut milk and simmer 5 minutes, season to taste.

Garnish with sliced lemon and serve with crusty bread.

Thai Salmon Soup

3	salmon fillets – cubed
3 C	chicken stock
1 C	pineapple – cubed
1/2 C	white wine
1/4 C	red pepper – diced
2	scallions – sliced
4	garlic cloves – crushed
3"	lemon grass – crushed
2	lime leaves – sliced
1 T	cilantro – chopped
1 T	vegetable oil
1/2 t	salt
	*1 chili

❖ Sauté garlic and chili in hot oil for 30 seconds to release flavors.

❖ Add red pepper, lemon grass, scallions and lime leaves, sauté 30 seconds.

❖ Pour in stock and wine, bring to a boil.

❖ Add salmon and simmer 2 minutes.

❖ Reduce heat, add pineapple and simmer 5 minutes.

Serve hot, garnished with cilantro.

Chapter 7

SALADS AND
SALAD
DRESSINGS

Salads with Fruit

Apple, Nut and Chicken Salad

2 C   cooked or canned chicken – pieced
2   apples
1/2 C   Chinese cabbage – shredded
1/2 C   peanuts – toasted
1/2 C   bean sprouts
2 T   lemon juice

❖   Dice apples and sprinkle with lemon juice to prevent discoloring.

❖   Combine remaining ingredients.

❖   Chill and dress with *Coconut Peanut Dressing*.

Green Papaya and Carrot Salad

2 C   green papaya – grated
1 C   carrots – grated
1/2 C   rice vinegar
1/4 C   scallions – sliced
2 t   honey
ginger – grated
Asian fish sauce or salt

❖   Combine vinegar, honey and ginger.

❖   Stir in papaya, carrots and scallions.

❖   Add fish sauce to personal taste.

Green Papaya Salad

This salad can be made with the addition of any raw vegetables such as carrots, bell peppers, diakon radish etc.

5 C   shredded green papaya
2   tomatoes – diced
1 C   Chinese long beans – diced
1/2 C   bean sprouts
1/4 C   peanuts – roasted and unsalted
2   garlic cloves – peeled
2   bird's eye chilies
1 T   crumbled palm sugar
2 t   fish sauce

2 limes – juiced
fresh cilantro

❖ In a mortar and pestle pound garlic and chilies until finely ground.

❖ Add sugar and pound until it starts to dissolve.

❖ Add peanuts and pound until broken into small pieces.

❖ Add beans and pound a couple times, add fish sauce and lime juice.

❖ In a large bowl combine tomatoes and papaya.

❖ Mix in dressing just before serving.

Waldorf Salad

2 apples – diced
2 C celery stalks – diced
1 C grapes – sliced in half
1 C walnuts – toasted
1 T yogurt
2 t lemon juice

❖ Combine all ingredients.

Vegetable Salads

Antipasto Salad

1 C cauliflower florets
1 can black olives
3 small onions – diced
1 carrot – diced
1 celery stalk – diced
1 red pepper – diced
1/2 C green beans
1/2 C water
1/2 C wine vinegar
1/4 C vegetable oil
1 garlic clove – crushed
1 T olive oil
1 T sugar
1 t oregano
S&P
*vegetables may be varied

- ❖ Combine all ingredients, cover and simmer 5 minutes.
- ❖ Cool and refrigerate, allowing a day or more to marinate before serving.

Seeded Beet Salad

1 1/2 lb.	cooked beets or 2 large cans – sliced
2	green apples – sliced
1/2 C	scallions – diced
2 T	red wine vinegar
1 T	salad oil
1/2 t	mustard seeds
1/2 t	cumin seeds
	S&P

- ❖ Toast seeds in a dry frying pan until they become fragrant.
- ❖ Combine seeds with remaining ingredients, adding apple just before serving to maintain color contrast.

Thai Broccoli Salad

Carol~Yacht Elyxir

5 C	broccoli florets
3 T	red pepper – diced
3 T	red onion – diced
3 T	rice vinegar or unflavored white vinegar
1 T	sesame oil
2 t	brown sugar
1 t	chili pepper flakes
	salt to taste

- ❖ Steam or parboil broccoli until al denté, rinse in cold water to halt cooking.
- ❖ Combine remaining ingredients.
- ❖ Toss with broccoli just before serving.

Garnish with toasted peanuts and/or raisins.

Moroccan Carrot Salad

         4   carrots – grated
     1/2 C   dates – chopped
     1/2 C   dried apricots – chopped
     1/4 C   parsley – chopped
         1   lemon juiced
       1 T   olive oil
       1 t   Moroccan spice

❖   Combine all ingredients.

Carrot Salad

         3 C   carrots – grated
       1/2 C   raisins
         2 T   olive oil
         1 T   honey
               lemon juice
               mint
               S&P
               *grated apple
               *chopped nuts
               *yogurt

❖   Combine all ingredients, chill and serve.

Pickled Cucumbers

Affectionately known as bread and butter pickles, this is a simple way of preserving cucumbers, especially when they start to turn bad. They keep well, are appealing in salads and serve as a tasty snack with crackers and cheese.

         1 C   vinegar – any kind
       1/2 C   white sugar
           3   cumbers – sliced
           2   onions – sliced
         1 T   salt
         1 t   celery seeds

❖   Combine all ingredients, chill and serve.

Cauliflower and Broccoli Salad

2 C cauliflower florets
2 C broccoli florets
1 C sharp cheddar cheese – cubed
      mayonnaise

❖ Mix all ingredients together.

Chill and serve.

Cucumber and Yogurt Salad

3 cucumbers – sliced

❖ If you are preparing this salad in advance, arrange the cucumber slices in a colander and sprinkle with salt to allow the juices to drain.

❖ Mix cucumber slices with *Yogurt Garlic Dressing.*

Eggplant and Tomato Salad

3   eggplants – cubed
2   onions – sliced
2   red peppers – diced
1 can whole tomatoes
5   garlic cloves – crushed
3 T   olive oil
2 T   lemon juice
3/4 t ground turmeric
      salt
      pinch of sugar
      cilantro – chopped

❖ Sauté eggplant in half the olive oil until golden, drain on paper towel.

❖ In remaining oil sauté onions, garlic, peppers, tomatoes and turmeric.

❖ Simmer mixture until it thickens slightly.

❖ Add eggplant and sugar, reduce heat and simmer 6 minutes.

❖ Stir in lemon juice and salt, cool.

Garnish with cilantro just before serving with Yogurt Lime Dressing.

Kale Salad

1 large bunch	kale – shredded
1/3 C	sliced almonds – toasted
2	hard-boiled eggs – diced
1/4 cup	grated Parmesan cheese
3 T	olive oil
1 T	sherry vinegar
1/2 t	smoked paprika
	S&P

❖ Combine oil, vinegar, paprika and S&P, work dressing into kale.

❖ Add remaining ingredients.

French Potoato Salad

Mary-Ann~Yacht Southern Star

4	potatoes – cubed and cooked
1 C	celery – diced
1/2 C	olive oil
1/4 C	cider vinegar
1/4 C	parsley
2	carrots – grated
2	scallions – diced
1	onion – diced
1	green pepper – sliced
1	garlic clove – crushed
2 T	Dijon mustard
1/2 t	oregano
	chili of some form
	S&P

❖ Blend oil, vinegar, salt, oregano, mustard and garlic until smooth, pour over hot potatoes and marinate until potatoes are cool.

❖ Add remaining ingredients, mix well and season to taste.

Serve chilled on shredded lettuce.

Turkish Potato Salad

4	potatoes – cubed
3	eggs – hard boiled, peeled and quartered
1/2 C	red cabbage – shredded

1/3 C fresh parsley – chopped
1/3 C Greek black olives
1/4 C olive oil
  1 T mayonnaise
  1 T ground cumin
       lemon juice
       S&P

❖ Boil potatoes in salted water, or chicken broth for more flavor, until tender, rinse under cold water to stop further cooking, cool.

❖ When potatoes are cool, mix in cabbage, eggs, parsley, olives and cumin, chill.

❖ Before serving add olive oil, lemon juice, mayonnaise and S&P.

Mediterranean Potato Salad

10 new potatoes – cooked
1 C green beans – sliced and cooked
1 can tuna – drained

Dressing

1/2 C olive oil
1 can anchovies
    3 shallots – diced
  2 T lemon juice
  1 T capers
  1 T parsley

❖ Heat oil and sauté shallots for 2 minutes, add remaining dressing ingredients and continue sautéing for 3 minutes.

❖ Combine potatoes, beans and tuna. Mix in dressing.

Shepherds Salad

Anu~Yacht Kialoa II

100 g feta cheese – cubed
   12 Greek olives
    2 tomatoes – diced
    1 red onion – finely diced
    1 cucumber – diced
    1 green pepper – diced
1/4 C fresh parsley – chopped
       lemon juice or white wine vinegar

olive oil
S&P

❖ Combine feta, tomatoes, cucumber, green pepper, onion, olives and parsley

❖ Chill and toss salad with lemon juice, olive oil and S&P just before serving.

Garnish with lemon wedges.

Tomato and Citrus Salad

6	tomatoes – sliced into wedges
1/2 C	celery, kale or radish leaves – diced
1	onion – sliced

Dressing

1 T	cider vinegar
1 T	oil
1 T	brown sugar
1 T	citrus zest

❖ Combine tomatoes, greens and onion.

❖ Blend dressing ingredients together and mix with salad.

Coleslaws

Asian Coleslaw

2 C	cabbage – shredded
2	oranges – segmented with membranes removed
1	cucumber – sliced
1	avocado – sliced
2 T	sesame seeds – toasted

Dressing

3 T	rice wine vinegar
3 T	soy sauce
1 T	sesame oil
1 t	sugar
	ground pepper

❖ Blend dressing ingredients together.

❖ Combine remaining ingredients and mix in dressing.

Apricot and Broccoli Coleslaw

2 C   broccoli florets
3 C   cabbage – shredded
5   dried apricots – sliced
1 t   caraway seeds

Dressing

1   onion – diced
1   garlic clove – crushed
2 T   sugar
2 T   vinegar
2 T   oil
   S&P

❖ Blend dressing ingredients together.

❖ Combine remaining ingredients and mix in dressing.

Pineapple Coleslaw

Lisa~Yacht Westri

3 C   red cabbage – shredded
1/2 C   pineapple – crushed
1/2 C   raisins or chopped prunes
3   celery stalks – sliced
2 T   parsley

Dressing

2 T   cider vinegar
1 T   oil
1/2 T   honey

❖ Blend dressing ingredients together.

❖ Combine remaining ingredients and mix in dressing.

Jamaican Coleslaw

3 C   cabbage – shredded

Dressing

1 C   honey roasted peanuts – chopped, in a pinch you can use peanut butter

1/4 C rice wine vinegar
2 limes – juice and zest
  chili of some form
  cilantro – chopped
  ginger – grated
  *coconut flakes

❖ Blend dressing ingredients together.

❖ Combine remaining ingredients and mix in dressing.

Quick Cabbage Kimchi

1 cabbage – sliced
1/2 C julienned carrot
1/4 C unseasoned rice vinegar
2 T coarse sea salt
2 T Korean red pepper
1 T honey
1 T grated ginger
1 T soy sauce
1 bunch scallions – sliced

❖ Combine cabbage with salt. Set aside for 1 hour.

❖ Rinse cabbage and add remaining ingredients.

Grain and Pasta Salads

Couscous Salad

3 C couscous – cooked
1/2 C corn – frozen or canned
1/2 C peas – frozen or canned
1/2 C raisins
2 scallions – diced
1 carrot – grated
  parsley

❖ Combine all ingredients.

Serve chilled with your favorite salad dressing.

Chickpea Salad

Simple and casual, this salad originates in North Africa though the addition of chili easily modifies it to Asian cuisine.

2 C	chickpeas – cooked
3/4 C	scallions or red onion – diced
2	tomatoes – diced
	cilantro – chopped
	*some form of chili for an Asian flavor

❖   Toss all ingredients together.

Serve chilled with Toasted Cumin Vinaigrette.

Egyptian Lentil Salad

1 C	lentils
4	scallions – sliced
	lemon juice
1 t	cumin
	parsley or mint – chopped
	S&P

❖   Cook lentils until tender, drain.

❖   Mix hot lentils with remaining ingredients, this allows the lentils to absorb the dressing.

Serve chilled.

Minted Lentil Salad

1 1/2 C	bean sprouts
1 C	lentils
1/2 C	mint leaves – chopped
1/4 C	red onion – minced
1/4 C	orange juice
2 T	olive oil
1 T	balsamic vinegar
1 t	orange zest
1 t	salt
	ground pepper

❖   Cook lentils until tender, drain.

❖   Combine lentils with remaining ingredients and toss well.

Serve chilled.

Chinese Chicken Noodle Salad

Carol~Yacht Elyxir

500g	2-minute noodles or linguine
2	chicken breasts – grilled and sliced, or 1 can
a selection	salad vegetables of your choice:

cabbage	green beans
carrots	snow peas
red peppers	broccoli
green onions	cilantro

❖ Cook noodles, rinse in cold water and drain.

❖ Thinly slice vegetables and slightly blanch those you don't want crunchy such as carrots, green beans and broccoli.

❖ Mix noodles and vegetables together, scatter chicken on top.

Sprinkle with toasted sesame seeds and drizzle with Peanut Dressing.

Crunchy Chicken Noodle Salad

Elliot~Magellan Straits

3 C	cabbage – shredded
1	chicken breast – cooked and sliced
1 pkg.	2-minute noodles – broken and raw
2	scallions – sliced
2 T	sesame seeds – toasted
2 T	sliced almonds – toasted
	S&P

❖ Mix all ingredients together.

❖ Dress with your favorite dressing, or mix sugar, vinegar, and oil with the noodle spice packet.

Indonesian Rice Salad

Leila~Yacht Reveille

This salad feeds many and is always a hit at potlucks. It's the perfect use for leftover rice and a versatile way to stretch salad greens. We generally make it aboard once a week and depending on what salad ingredients we

have at hand it's often varied. I never alter the dressing and generally use a mix of wild and brown rice to make it healthier.

```
            2 C    rice – cooked
any combination    diced vegetables:
                     bell peppers
                     bok choy
                     kale
                     cabbage
                     celery
                     carrots
                     bean sprouts
                     parsley
                     scallions
   a selection    long lasting foods:
                     nuts – toasted
                     coconut – grated
                     corn – canned or frozen
                     dates – chopped
                     pineapple – crushed
                     peas
                     seeds – pumpkin, sunflower or sesame
                     raisins and or dried fruit
                     water chestnut slices
```

❖   Mix all items together with rice and chill.

Just before serving dress with Indonesian Dressing.

Tabbouleh Wheat Salad

Middle Eastern

I've found that fresh parsley keeps well (see herbs), so I often enjoy this salad at sea. It can be made with dried herbs equally well. Cracked wheat is not common worldwide so I generally stock up with it when I can. I was delighted to find it in southern Chile. Although it was slightly unprocessed with husks throughout it still made a wholesome, healthy salad. As parsley was unavailable I used cilantro and for added flavor, crunch and color I added radishes.

```
  1 C    bulgar (cracked wheat)
  1 C    water
  1 C    tomatoes – diced
  1 C    parsley – chopped
1/4 C    olive oil
1/4 C    lemon juice
    4    scallions – sliced
```

1 t fresh mint – chopped
1 garlic clove – crushed
S&P
*chili pepper of some form

❖ Place wheat in a bowl and cover with boiling water, let stand 30 minutes.

❖ Drain if necessary, add remaining ingredients and mix well.

Chill and serve.

Autumn Tabbouleh Salad

Cow Bay Café~Prince Rupert

1 C bulgar
1 C water
1/2 C wild rice – cooked
1/2 C raisins
1/2 C red pepper – diced
1/2 C corn
1/2 C cucumber – diced
1/4 C parsley – chopped
1 lemon – juiced

❖ Place wheat in bowl and cover with boiling water, let stand 30 minutes.

❖ Drain if necessary, add remaining ingredients and mix well.

Chill and serve.

Bean Salad

1 can black beans
1 can kidney beans
1 can cannellini beans
1 red onion – finely diced
1 C corn
1/2 C cilantro – chopped
1 bell pepper – diced
2 limes – juiced
1 clove garlic – crushed
1 T ground cumin
1/2 t cayenne pepper
1/2 t salt

❖ Drain and rinse canned beans.

❖ Mix all ingredients together.

Tuscan Bean and Tuna Salad

2 C	white beans – cooked
1 can	tuna – drained and flaked
1/3 C	black olives – diced
1/4 C	parsley – chopped
5	sun-dried tomatoes – sliced
3 T	vinegar – balsamic
2 T	olive oil
1 T	pesto
	ground pepper
	*marinated artichoke hearts

❖ Combine beans, tuna, tomatoes, olives and parsley.

❖ Blend pesto, vinegar and olive oil, pour over salad.

Season with pepper and serve chilled.

Seafood Salads

Hawaiian Poke

1 lb.	fresh tuna – cubed
1/4 C	red onion – minced
2	tomatoes – diced
2	scallions – sliced
1	garlic clove – crushed
2 T	soy sauce
1 T	sesame seeds – toasted
2 t	coarse salt
1 t	dried chili pepper
1 t	grated ginger

❖ Combine salt, ginger, garlic and chili, add tuna and coat well.

❖ Stir in remaining ingredients, cover and refrigerate 2 hours.

Serve on a small bed of salad greens.

Poission Cru ~ Tahitian Marinated Fish

2 lb.	fresh white fish
1 C	coconut milk
	limes or lemons
	Tabasco or chili peppers – chopped
	ginger – grated
	garlic – crushed
	tomatoes – diced
	carrots – grated
	onions – diced
	scallions – sliced
	*any vegetables you think go well
	S&P

❖ Cut fish into strips or small bite size pieces.

❖ Squeeze enough juice to cover fish and marinate for an hour until the fish turns white.

❖ Drain juice and combine fish with remaining ingredients.

Serve chilled on a bed of shredded lettuce.

Seared Peppered Tuna Salad

3	tuna fillets – 1" thick
3 T	olive oil
1 T	green peppercorns
1 T	black peppercorns
1 T	red peppercorns

❖ Grind peppercorns and oil together to form a paste.

❖ Spread paste over tuna and chill 3 hours.

❖ Barbecue or sear tuna in a hot dry skillet, about 1 minute each side.

❖ Wrap tuna in plastic and chill 2 hours, slice thin.

Serve tuna on top of greens and drizzle with Chinese Dressing.

Dressings

Salad Vinaigrette

This classic recipe can be changed endlessly, it is always refreshing and keeps well in the cupboard. I usually make it the day before leaving on a passage so that I can use fresh parsley and then not have to worry about messing with it at sea. The longer it sits the better the flavors develop. I make it in a quart-size squeeze bottle that I shake before serving to combine the flavors.

1 C	olive oil
1/3 C	red wine vinegar
1/4 C	parsley – chopped
2 T	balsamic vinegar
1 T	capers
3	garlic cloves – crushed
2 t	Dijon mustard
1 t	honey
	S&P

❖ Combine all ingredients in a bottle and shake well, adjust ingredients to taste.

❖ Variations: * use white wine or cider vinegar instead of red

* add tarragon, basil, oregano, or rosemary

* use lemon juice instead of vinegar

* use half-and-half instead of vinegar

Blue Cheese Dressing

1 C	blue cheese
1/4 C	milk
1 T	sour cream or yogurt

❖ Blend all ingredients together and let sit 1 hour to thicken.

Caesar Dressing

1/2 C	olive oil
1/3 C	Parmesan cheese – grated
3 T	sour cream or yogurt
2 T	lemon juice
1 T	Worcestershire sauce
1	Dijon mustard
1	garlic clove – crushed
	pepper

❖ Blend all ingredients together.

Chutney Dressing

1/3 C	olive oil
1/4 C	red wine vinegar
2	garlic cloves – crushed
3 T	mango chutney
1 T	honey
2 t	mustard
	*chili sauce

❖ Blend all ingredients together.

Cumin Vinaigrette

2	garlic cloves – crushed
3 T	olive oil
3 T	lemon juice
1 t	cumin seeds
	S&P

❖ Toast cumin seeds in small pan until fragrant, about 30 seconds.

❖ Blend all ingredients together.

Peanut Dressing

1/4 C	peanut oil, peanut butter or chopped nuts
3 T	sesame oil
2 T	cider or rice wine vinegar
2 T	soy sauce
2 T	basil or cilantro – chopped
2 T	honey or brown sugar
1 T	lemon juice
1 t	chili sauce
	garlic and ginger – crushed
	S&P

❖ Blend ingredients together until smooth.

Chinese Dressing
❖ Make *Peanut Dressing* using olive oil and add:
2 t   mustard

Indonesian Dressing
❖ Make *Peanut Dressing* and add:
1/2 C   orange juice

Thai Dressing
❖ Make *Peanut Dressing* and add:
1/4 C   coconut milk

Kiwi Vinaigrette
1/2 C   salad oil
2   kiwifruit – peeled and diced
1   garlic clove – minced
3 T   white wine vinegar
2 t   Dijon mustard
1 t   ginger – grated
chili to taste
S&P

❖ Blend all ingredients together.

Serve on grilled chicken salad.

Lemon Tahini Dressing
1/4 C   water
1/4 C   tahini
1/4 C   olive oil
2 T   lemon juice
2 T   soy sauce
*celery and onion – diced

❖ Blend all ingredients together.

Serve on salad greens or vegetables.

Miso Dressing

1/4 C	olive oil
1/4 C	vegetable oil
1/8 C	balsamic or rice vinegar
2 T	sherry
1 T	miso
3	garlic cloves – minced
	S&P

❖ Blend all ingredients together and store in a bottle.

Serve on salad greens or vegetables.

Papaya Seed Dressing

The seeds of the papaya have an elaborate peppery taste that enhance this dressing and give an added zip to any salad.

1/4 C	balsamic vinegar
1 T	honey
1 T	papaya seeds
1 T	poppy seeds
1 T	lemon juice
2	garlic cloves – crushed
1/2 t	cumin
	S&P

❖ Blend all ingredients together and serve with salad.

Sesame Dressing

1/2 C	salad oil
1/4 C	lemon juice
1/8 C	sesame oil
2	garlic cloves – crushed
2	scallions – diced
3 T	sesame seeds – toasted
1 T	honey
1/2 t	salt

❖ Blend all ingredients together, saving 1 T of sesame seeds to toss on the salad when serving.

Tofu Dressing

Leila~Yacht Reveille

1 box	tofu or feta cheese
1/4 C	olive oil
1/4 C	vinegar
1 T	honey
1 T	tarragon
1	garlic clove – crushed
	pepper

❖ Blend all ingredients together.

Wasabi Salad Dressing

1/2 C	salad oil
3 T	rice wine vinegar
2 t	wasabi

❖ Mix all ingredients together.

Wasabi Seafood Dressing

This dressing is exquisite with cold fish or seafood.

1/2 C	mayonnaise
1 T	wasabi paste
2 t	rice wine vinegar or lemon/lime juice
1 t	grated ginger

```
1/2 t   garlic – crushed
*1/2 t  sesame oil or sesame chili oil
```
❖ Mix all ingredients together and serve chilled.

Yogurt Garlic Dressing

This refreshing dressing is often mixed with diced cucumbers and served as an accompaniment to Mediterranean dishes.

```
1 C   yogurt
 2    garlic cloves – crushed
2 T   olive oil
1 T   diced mint
```
❖ Blend ingredients together.

Yogurt Lime Dressing

```
1 C   yogurt
 2    limes – juiced
1 t   coriander
1/2 t salt
      *mint – chopped
      *onion – diced
```
❖ Blend ingredients together.

Chapter 8

FRUITS AND
VEGETABLES

Beets

Cooking Tips for Beets

❖ **Don't peel beets** until after they're cooked or they'll lose some of their color.

❖ To cook beets until tender, simmer 45 minutes on **stove top** or

❖ **Pressure cooker beets:** Place beets in steamer basket. Fill pressure cooker with 2-inches water. Pressure cook 15 minutes.

Beet and Potato Salad with Lemon

From Ethiopia, this salad is a delightful marriage of colors and flavors.

1 lb.	red skinned potatoes – cooked and diced
1 lb.	beets – cooked and diced
1/4 C	lemon juice
1/2	onion – diced
3 T	vegetable oil
1	jalapeño chili – seeded and minced
	S&P

❖ Combine all ingredients.

Serve warm or at room temperature.

Morroccan Beets

3 C	beets – diced
1/2 C	parsley – chopped
2 T	olive oil
2 T	lemon juice
2	garlic cloves – minced
1 t	cumin
	S&P
	*orange juice and zest
	*mint

❖ Mix all ingredients together.

Serve chilled.

White Beets

2 C	beets – diced
1/2 C	yogurt
2 T	mayonnaise
2 t	horseradish
1/2 t	Dijon mustard
	chives – chopped

❖ Mix all ingredients together.

Serve either warm or cold.

Cabbage

Bubble and Squeak

When I was growing up this old English standby for stretching leftovers was always a favorite when we went sailing. My earliest memories of this dish go back to when I was five, I loved it so much that I named my two pet mice Bubble and Squeak.

	cabbage – shredded
	potatoes – cooked and diced
	S&P

❖ Sauté cabbage in pan and when al denté add potatoes and heat through.

*an egg can be added to hold it together

Serve with ketchup or chili sauce.

Fran's Bubble and Squeak Patties

Fran from the yacht *Aka* makes another variation of *Bubble and Squeak*

❖ Make mounds of mashed potato and throw everything into it; peas, cabbage, carrots, onion, pea shoots, brussel sprouts, ground beef, chopped ham etc.

❖ Sauté patties in a large frying pan.

These are is great on a passage as once it's on your plate it doesn't move.

Fruits and Vegetables

Coconut Cabbage

4 C	cabbage – shredded
1/2 C	coconut – grated
1	onions – diced
2	green chilies – chopped
2 T	oil
1 T	Dijon mustard
1	garlic clove – crushed
1/4 t	cumin
1/4 t	turmeric

❖ Sauté onion, add remaining ingredients, cover and cook until done.

Cabbage Pancakes

Carol~Yacht Elyxir

4 C	cabbage – shredded
1	onion – diced
1	green pepper – diced
3	eggs
2 T	flour
1 T	milk
	parsley – diced
	salt to taste

❖ Sauté onion and green peppers.

❖ Combine eggs, flour and milk, add remaining ingredients and mix well.

❖ Spoon mixture into frying pan, like a pancake and cook until done.

Cabbage Peking

4 C	cabbage – shredded
1	onion – sliced
1/4 C	rice vinegar
1 T	honey
1 T	salad oil
1 T	ginger – grated
	soy sauce

- ❖ Sauté onion, ginger and cabbage 2 minutes.
- ❖ Stir in vinegar, honey and soy sauce.
- ❖ Sprinkle with sesame seeds.

Serve hot or cold.

Spiced Red Cabbage

6 C	red cabbage – shredded
3/4 C	red wine
1	onion – diced
1	apple – diced
2 T	brown sugar
1 T	butter
1 T	cooking oil
2 t	balsamic vinegar
3	cloves garlic
1	star ansie
1/4 t	cinnamon
1/4 t	nutmeg – freshly grated
	salt

- ❖ Sauté onion in oil until translucent.
- ❖ Add butter and cabbage, cook 5 minutes.
- ❖ Add remaining ingredients, cover with lid and simmer 30 minutes.

Sweet and Sour Red Cabbage

1/2	red cabbage – shredded
1/4 C	raisins
1	onion – diced
2	garlic clove – crushed
2 T	vegetable oil
2 T	apple cider vinegar
2 T	honey

- ❖ Sauté onion and garlic, add cabbage and toss quickly to coat.
- ❖ Splash cabbage with vinegar, add honey and raisins, toss and cover.
- ❖ Steam until al denté.

Serve hot.

Versatile Cabbage

1/2	cabbage – shredded
1	onion – diced
1 t	vegetable oil
	salt

* ❖ Sauté onion in the oil, add cabbage and cover.
* ❖ Steam over low heat until al denté.
* ❖ Variations: * use butter instead of oil
  *   * add a dash of nutmeg
  *   * sprinkle with grated cheese
  *   * mix with cooked pasta and 1 T caraway seeds

Cauliflower

Mustard Cauliflower

Carol~Yacht Elyxir

4 C	cauliflower florets
2 T	vegetable oil
2 t	mustard seeds
2 t	ginger – grated
2 t	lemon juice
1/2 t	turmeric
	cilantro
	salt

* ❖ Toast mustard seeds in a dry pan until they begin to pop.
* ❖ Add ginger and turmeric, sauté for 30 seconds.
* ❖ Add cauliflower, stir to coat, splash with 1/2 C water, cover and steam until al denté.
* ❖ Stir in lemon juice and season with S&P.

Garnish with cilantro.

Carrots

Moroccan Carrots

4	carrots – sliced
2	garlic cloves – crushed

2 T   whole cloves
2 T   whole cumin seeds
2 T   olive oil
2 T   lemon juice
parsley – chopped
salt

❖   In enough water to cover carrots, add garlic, cloves and cumin, bring to a boil.

❖   Add carrots and cook until al denté.

❖   Drain carrots and toss with oil, lemon juice, salt and parsley.

Serve hot or cold.

Eggplant

Purging Eggplant

Eggplant is often purged to remove some of the bitterness and make it less absorbent.

❖   Slice or cube eggplant and place in a colander.

❖   Sprinkle with salt and let drain 30 minutes.

Roasted Eggplant

The roasted pulp of the eggplant is used in dips and spreads, *see Baba Gonash.*

❖   Place whole, oil coated, eggplant in roasting pan, pierce the skin in a few places.

❖   Roast or grill until skin is blacken and wrinkled. Peel off skin.

Braised Eggplant

3   eggplants
4 T   olive oil
2 T   lemon juice
garlic – crushed
orgeano
salt

- ❖ Slice eggplants crosswise and sprinkle both sides with salt, when "sweaty" wipe off liquid.
- ❖ In a very hot skillet, braise eggplant until golden and tender, drain on a paper towel and salt.
- ❖ Dress with lemon juice, garlic, oregano and chill.

Eggplant and Tomato Casserole

Carol~Yacht Lorraine

2	eggplants – sliced
1 C	cheese – grated
1 C	red wine
1	onion – diced
1 can	tomato pureé
1/2 C	bread or cracker crumbs
1/2 C	mushrooms – sliced
1/4 C	celery – diced
2	egg yolks – beaten
	olive oil

- ❖ Dip eggplant slices in eggs and bread crumbs, brown in olive oil.
- ❖ Layer baking dish with tomato pureé, eggplant and vegetables.
- ❖ Cover with cheese and bake 15 minutes.

Greek Vegetable Stew

2	Italian eggplants – diced
2	zucchini – diced
1/2	butternut squash or 2 potatoes – diced
2	tomatoes – diced
1	onion – diced
1 bunch	scallions – sliced
4	garlic cloves – crush

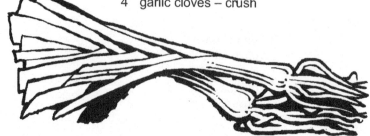

1/2 C olive oil
1/2 C red wine
1 t salt

❖ Cook vegetables over medium heat until liquid bubbles.

❖ Add olive oil, wine and salt, simmer 15 minutes until vegetables soften.

Serve garnished with fresh parsley and hearty bread.

Ratatouille

2 eggplants – cubed and purged
3 zucchini – diced
2 green peppers – diced
2 tomatoes – diced
1 onion – diced
2 garlic cloves – crushed
2 T parsley – chopped
2 T basil – chopped
1 T tomato paste
1 t thyme
1/2 t sugar
  S&P
*1 C coconut milk may be added for a tropical flavor

❖ Sauté eggplant with peppers and zucchini until brown, drain on a paper towel.

❖ Sauté onion, add tomatoes and seasoning, simmer 15 minutes.

❖ Add eggplant, heat through and serve.

Sicilian Caponata

2 eggplants – cubed and purged
3 tomatoes – diced
2 celery stalks – diced
1 onion – diced
10 green olives
3 T wine vinegar
2 T cocoa powder
2 T capers
1 T sugar

Fruits and Vegetables

2   bay leaves
1   dried chili
    olive oil
    thyme
    S&P

❖   Sauté eggplant in hot olive oil until soft.

❖   Add remaining ingredients and simmer 15 minutes.

Serve warm garnished with parsley and toasted almonds.

Leeks

Curried Leeks

3 C   leeks – sliced
1/2 T   butter
1 t   cumin seeds
1 t   turmeric
1 t   ginger – grated
1/2 t   *Garam Masala*

❖   Sauté cumin seeds in butter.

❖   Add leeks, tumeric and ginger, cover and cook until tender.

❖   Stir in *Garam Masala* and serve.

Papaya

Green Papaya Curry

2   green papaya – peeled and diced
1/2 C   coconut milk
1   onion – diced
2 T   butter
2   garlic cloves – crushed
2   green chilies – minced
2 t   ginger – grated
1 t   curry powder
    S&P

❖   Sauté onion, garlic and ginger in butter.

❖   Add chilies, curry powder and S&P, cook paste until golden, about

5 minutes.

❖ Stir in the coconut milk and add papaya.

❖ Cook 30 minutes stirring occasionally, add more coconut milk if curry dries out.

Peppers: green, red and yellow

Roasted Peppers

Many Mediterranean dishes include roasted peppers. To achieve this distinct flavor follow these directions:

❖ Roast, grill or turn whole pepper over a flame until skin is blacken and blistered.

❖ Place roasted pepper in a paper bag to cool for 10 minutes.

❖ Peel the skin off, slice the pepper open and scrape out the seeds and ribs.

Potatoes

Curried Potatoes

3 C	potatoes – diced
2 C	peas or beans
1/2 C	water
3	tomatoes – diced
1	onion – diced
2	garlic cloves – crushed
2 T	vegetable oil
1 T	ginger – grated
1 t	cumin
1/4 t	chilies

❖ Sauté garlic, ginger and onion in oil, stir in spices and tomatoes.

❖ Add peas, potatoes and water, cover and simmer until potatoes are cooked.

Garnish with fresh cilantro.

Fruits and Vegetables

Hash Browns

1 potato – per person

❖ Grate potatoes and rinse in a sieve with salt water.

❖ Sauté in oil.

Irish Potato Pancakes~Fadge

Commodore Alex

It was a sunny day in B.C., Canada, and we were tied up at the Prince Rupert Yacht and Rowing Club after our arrival from Hawaii. John and I were busy scrutinizing our varnish work, wondering if the August weather would let us place a touch-up coat on the toerails. Alex was next door working away on his boat and overhearing our conversation he offered a magnifying glass for our inspection.

"Sure thanks, as this is the only thing in life I have to worry about." I replied.

Alex laughed, and I explained that I was officially handing over the job of varnishing to John as I had to continue writing a book. I'd caught his interest.

"What's your book about?" Alex asked.

"If you'll give me your favorite recipe you'll know." I replied.

"It's Irish fadge and it's great for brunch when you're out cruising," came the reply.

6 potatoes – boiled and mashed
1/2 C flour
2 scallions – diced
S&P

❖ Combine all ingredients and shape mixture into pancakes.

❖ Sauté pancakes until golden brown.

Serve hot with Canadian bacon, scrambled eggs and fresh fruit.

Mexican Potatoes

6 potatoes – sliced
2 C cheese – grated
1/2 C olives – sliced
2 tomatoes – diced
1 onion – diced

     3 T olive oil
          chili of some form
          S&P

❖ Layer a baking dish with potatoes, onion, chili and tomato, sprinkle with olive oil.

❖ Cover with another layer of potatoes, drizzle with olive oil and top with cheese.

❖ Bake 45 minutes at 425° until potatoes are cooked.

Garnish with cilantro and serve with salsa, sour cream or guacamole.

Potato and Zucchini BBQ

Barbara~Tahiti 98

     5 potatoes – sliced
     5 zucchini – sliced
     4 onions – sliced
        Italian herbs – basil, rosemary and oregano
        butter or olive oil

❖ Place all ingredients on a large sheet of aluminum foil, sprinkle with Italian herbs and S&P, dot with knobs of butter.

❖ Wrap foil into a tight package and place on a corner of the barbecue, cook vegetables until tender, about 20 minutes.

Spanish Potatoes

Dr Michel~Southern Ocean

This is delicious way to dress up leftover potatoes.

     4 C potatoes – cooked and cubed
    1/4 C olive oil
       5 garlic cloves – crushed
     2 T paprika
     2 T wine vinegar
          salt

❖ Sauté potatoes in half the oil.

❖ In a small pan sauté garlic in remaining oil, stir in paprika and vinegar, pour dressing over warm potatoes.

Fruits and Vegetables

Taro Leaf

Taro Leaf

Grown in the Caribbean and Pacific, the cooked leaves of the taro plant can easily be substituted for spinach. The desired leaf should be young and tender, take caution in choosing the plant variety as some contain calcium oxalate resulting in an itchy mouth and throat. When cooked, the leaves can be frozen in plastic bags for later use in quiches, pastas or green curry.

1 1/2 lb. young taro leaves – no bigger than 16"

❖ Wash leaves. Cut out the middle stalk, pinch off the tip of the leaf and coarsely shred the leaf.

❖ Simmer leaves in water for 20 minutes.

❖ Drain and mash.

Coconut Creamed Taro Leaf

South Pacific

Baking powder is used in this recipe to remove the "sting" from the taro leaf and to preserve the green color.

1 1/2 lb	young taro leaves
1/2 C	coconut milk
1	onion – diced
3 T	butter
pinch	baking powder
	S&P

❖ Cook taro leaves following the directions above, squeeze out excess liquid.

❖ Sauté onion in butter, add coconut milk, taro leaves and baking powder, heat through.

❖ Season to taste.

Zucchini

Zucchini Provçencal

6 zucchini – sliced

```
4    tomatoes – diced
1    onion – sliced
1 T  olive oil
2    garlic cloves – crushed
     basil – chopped
     S&P
```

❖ Sauté onion and garlic, add zucchini and cook 3 minutes.

❖ Add tomatoes and simmer 10 minutes.

Serve with basil and S&P.

Lemon-Garlic Zucchini Ribbons

```
4     zucchini – cut into ribbons or rounds
4     garlic cloves – minced
2 T   olive oil
1     lemon – juice of
1/2 C feta cheese
1/4 C pine nuts – toasted
      S&P
```

❖ Sauté garlic in oil until sizzling.

❖ Add zucchini ribbons and S&P, cook 5 minutes.

Serve with lemon juice, feta and pine nuts.

Vegetables

Fijian Vegetable Curry

```
2 C  coconut milk
1 C  vegetable stock
1 C  Curry Paste
1 C  pumpkin – cubed and par boiled
1 C  green beans – sliced
1 C  cauliflower florets
2    carrots – sliced
2    onions – diced
2    potatoes – cubed and par boiled
1    eggplant – diced
1    green pepper – diced
```

2 T   butter
1 T   mustard seeds
2 t   chili pepper – chopped

❖ Toast mustard seeds in a dry frying pan until they pop, add butter and onions, cook until soft.

❖ Add green pepper, curry and chili, cook 3 minutes.

❖ Add remaining vegetables, stir in stock and coconut milk, cook vegetables until al denté.

Serve on rice, garnish with chopped basil or cilantro.

Chapter 9
SEASONINGS
MARINADES
AND SAUCES

Herb Mixes

Italian Herb Mix

I make up an Italian herb mix in a 2-cup sized container and use it in most of my dishes that require herbs. At sea it's a lot easier to shake one seasoning into a dish than find, open, close and stow each indivdual herb. At first I thought that by consolidating my herbs food might get a little boring as every dish would result in the same flavor but with the addition of fresh herbs and or a pesto a dish can easily take on a different flair.

I renew my dried herbs at every major provisioning stop adding to the Italian herb mix to keep it fresh and interesting. French and Italian dried herbs seem superior to American brands so I always stock up on them when I'm cruising in French territories.

These herbs mixed together make a great mix blend that is quick to use.

1/4 C	basil
1/4 C	oregano
1/8 C	rosemary
1/8 C	savory
1/8 C	sage
1/8 C	thyme

❖ Combine all ingredients and store in a cool place.

Spice Mixes

Cajun Spice

1 T	paprika
2 t	garlic powder
1 t	cayenne pepper
1 t	ground pepper
1/2 t	salt
1/2 t	oregano
1/2 t	thyme

❖ Combine all ingredients and store in a cool place.

Curry Powder

2 T	ground coriander
1 T	turmeric
1 T	mustard seeds
1 T	ground cumin
2 t	cinnamon
1 t	ground cardamom
1 t	fenugreek
1 t	chili powder
1 t	ground black pepper
1 t	ginger

❖ Mix all ingredients together with a hand blender for 4 minutes.

Curry Paste

1 C	stewed tomatoes
1/4 C	coconut milk
1	onion – chopped
2	lemons – juice and zest
2 T	*Garam Masala*
2 T	curry powder
1 T	soy sauce
6	garlic cloves – crushed
2 t	turmeric
1 t	ginger – grated
1 t	chili peppers – chopped
1 t	mustard seeds

❖ Blend all ingredients together until chunky.

Keeps refrigerated for a week, or frozen for several months.

Moroccan Spice

5 T	cumin
2 T	allspice
2 T	cinnamon
1 T	cayenne
1 T	turmeric
1 T	coriander
1 t	ginger

❖ Combine spices, keep in a glass jar and use as needed.

Seasonongs, Marinades and Sauces

Thai Green Curry Paste

Green curry is wonderful with fish, vegetables and chicken, *see Thai Fish Green Curry.*

1 t	coriander seeds – toasted
1/2 t	cumin seeds – toasted
1/2 t	white peppercorns – toasted
1 stalk	lemongrass – chopped
1/2 inch piece	galangal root – chopped
1/2 inch piece	turmeric – chopped
3	shallots – chopped
4	cloves garlic – chopped
10	green bird's eye chilies – chopped
10	green/serrano chilies – chopped
3 T	chopped coriander
1	kaffir lime peel
3	kaffir lime leaves
1 t	shrimp paste
1 t	sea salt

❖ In a mortar and pestle grind coriander seeds, cumin seeds and peppercorns.

❖ Add remaining ingredients grinding each ingredient into a coarse paste before adding another.

Makes 1 1/4 cups of curry paste.

Thai Red Curry Paste

4	chilies – chopped
3	garlic cloves – crushed
5	young lime or lemon leaves
1	lime – juice and zest
2	scallions – chopped
1 bunch	cilantro – chopped
1 T	ginger – grated
2 t	paprika
2 t	peanut oil
1 t	fish sauce
1 t	cumin seeds – toasted and ground
1 t	nutmeg
	S&P

❖ Blend all ingredients together until smooth.

Garam Masala

1/4 C	ground coriander
2 T	cumin
1/2 t	ground black pepper
1/2 t	cardamom seeds
1/2 t	cinnamon
1/4 t	black pepper
1/4 t	ground cloves
1/4 t	nutmeg

❖ Combine all ingredients together and store in an airtight container.

Island Seasoning

This Seasoning is excellent on grilled bananas, grilled chicken, fish, curries and veggies.

1 T each	allspice, nutmeg and cloves
1/2 T each	cinnamon and mace
1 t each	thyme and pepper

❖ Combine all ingredients and store in a cool place.

Mustard

2/3 C	wine vinegar
1/2 C	yellow mustard seeds
3 T	honey or brown sugar
1 t	salt
1/4 t	cinnamon

❖ Soak mustard seeds in vinegar for 36 hours.

❖ Blend all ingredients together until smooth, add extra vinegar if it's too thick.

Mustard will keep for a year in sterile sealed jars.

Taco Seasoning

1 T	oregano
1 T	cilantro
1 T	paprika
1 T	cumin

1 garlic clove
2 t lime juice
2 t chili pepper flakes
sugar
S&P

❖ Combine all ingredients together.

Fish Marinades

Wasabi Fish Marinade

1/2 C rice wine vinegar
1/4 C Dijon mustard
2 T ginger – minced
2 T soy sauce
2 T brown sugar
2 shallots – minced
3 garlic cloves – minced
2 t wasabi paste

❖ Combine all ingredients and marinate fish 4 hours.
❖ Barbecue, grill or sear fish in hot dry frying pan.

Serve with brown rice and salad.

Fish in Mustard Marinade

1/4 C Dijon mustard
1/4 C olive oil
1/4 C lime juice
1/4 C orange juice
2 scallions – chopped
3 garlic gloves – minced

❖ Marinate fish 15 minutes then poach in marinade.

Jamaican Fish Marinade

1/3 C brown sugar
1/4 C dark rum
2 T olive oil
2 T orange juice

1 T	lime juice
1 T	ginger – grated
1 T	garlic – crushed
1 t	diced fresh or dried chilies
1/4 t	allspice

❖ Blend all ingredients together.

❖ Marinate fish 2 hours then poach in marinade.

Thai Fish Marinade

1 T	brandy
2 t	oyster sauce
2 t	soy sauce
3	cilantro sprigs
2	garlic gloves – crushed
2	whole black peppers – ground

❖ Grind ingredients together to form a paste.

❖ Spread paste onto fish then barbecue, broil or poach until done.

Meat Marinades

Citrus and Ginger Chicken Marinade

1/2 C	orange juice
1/4 C	lemon juice
2 T	sugar
2 T	mint – chopped
2 T	ginger – grated
2 T	oil
	S&P

❖ Combine all ingredients and marinate chicken overnight.

❖ Grill, poach or barbecue chicken until done.

Teriyaki Marinade

1/2 C	soy sauce
1/2 C	water

```
1/4 C   sherry
1/4 C   sugar
    2   garlic cloves – crushed
    1   scallion – diced
  1 T   ginger – grated
```

❖ Combine all ingredients and marinate meat for 2 hours.

❖ Grill, poach or barbecue meat until done.

Sauces

Apple Sauce

```
    3   apples – peeled and diced
  1 T   water
  1 T   butter
    2   cloves
        lemon juice
        sugar
```

❖ Simmer all ingredients until apples are cooked.

❖ Beat with a fork until smooth.

❖ Add sugar to taste.

Black Bean Sauce

Jenn~Yacht Ocean Light II

```
  1 C   water
    1   onion – diced
    5   garlic cloves – crushed
  2 T   honey
  2 T   sherry
  2 T   fermented black beans – chopped
  1 T   soy sauce
  1 T   peanut oil
  2 t   cornstarch – mixed with 1 T cold water
  1 t   fish sauce
 *1 t   ginger
        *chili pepper flakes
```

❖ Sauté onion, garlic, and back beans in hot oil for 1 minute.

❖ Add water, soy sauce, fish sauce, and sherry, bring to a simmer.

❖ Add honey and simmer 2 minutes.

❖ Drizzle in corn starch mixture and stir over a low heat until sauce thickens, about 1 minute.

Thai Sweet and Sour Sauce

2/3 C water
2/3 C sugar
1/2 C rice wine vinegar
3 T chili paste
2 garlic cloves – crushed
cilantro

❖ Combine all ingredients to form sauce.

Add to stir-fried meat and or vegetables.

Barbecue Sauce

1 C ketchup
2 T Dijon mustard
2 T vinegar or sherry
2 T maple syrup
1 T Worcestershire sauce
1 garlic clove – crushed
chili of some form

❖ Blend all ingredients together.

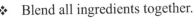

Mango Barbecue Sauce

2 mangoes – pureéd
1/4 C sherry
3 cloves garlic – crushed
2 T tomato paste
1 T Worcestershire sauce
1 T oil
1 T lime juice
2 t ginger – grated
2 t brown sugar

Seasonongs, Marinades and Sauces

2 t vinegar
2 t Dijon mustard
1 t chili paste
S&P

❖ Sauté garlic and ginger in oil for 30 seconds, add sherry and simmer 2 minutes.

❖ Add remaining ingredients and simmer 10 minutes.

❖ Marinate ribs, chicken or shrimp in sauce.

❖ Bake or barbecue, brushing with sauce until done.

Peanut Sauce

1/2 C water
1/2 C peanut butter
3 T soy sauce or teriyaki sauce
1 T lemon juice
1 T oil (not olive)
1 garlic clove – minced
2 t sesame oil
2 t brown sugar
1 t chili pepper flakes

❖ Brown garlic and chili pepper in oil 1 minute.

❖ Add remaining ingredients and simmer until smooth.

Tarragon Mustard Sauce

2 T butter – melted
2 T Dijon mustard
1 T honey
1 T lemon juice
1 T tarragon – chopped
2 scallions – chopped
ground pepper

❖ Blend all ingredients together until smooth.

Serve with fish baked in wine.

Tartar Sauce

1/2 C mayonnaise
2 T dill pickles – diced
2 T capers
2 T chives or scallions – chopped
1 t lime or lemon juice

❖ Combine all ingredients, chill and serve.

Vegetable Sauce

Honey Glaze

This sweet glaze is delightful on a variety of roastable vegetables such as sweet potato, carrots, parsnip, yam, pumpkin and potatoes.

4 C vegetables – chunked
2 T honey
1 T vinegar
1 T butter
pepper

❖ Combine all ingredients in a baking dish and bake 25 minutes.

Mustard Cheese Sauce

This wonderful tangy cheese sauce adds a zip to steamed cauliflower, carrots, broccoli, spinach or cabbage.

1 C milk
1/4 C cheese – grated
2 T butter
2 T flour
2 T Dijon mustard
ground pepper

❖ Melt butter, stir in flour and cook until frothy.

❖ Slowly stir in milk until mixture boils and thickens.

❖ Remove from heat, add cheese, mustard and S&P.

Seasonongs, Marinades and Sauces

Vegetable Dressings

Grilled Vegetable Dressing

1/2 C	olive oil
3 T	salt
3 T	brown sugar
2 T	paprika
1 1/2 T	ground black pepper
1	garlic clove – crushed
1 1/2 t	cayenne pepper
	basil

❖ Mix spices together and moisten with oil until you reach the consistency of paint.

❖ Brush seasoning onto sliced vegetables and grill both sides, about 8 minutes.

Lemon Vegetable Dressing

3 T	olive oil
2 T	bell pepper – diced
1 T	lemon juice
1 T	lemon zest
1/2	salt

❖ Mix all ingredients together and serve over steamed vegetables.

Chapter 10

BEANS AND GRAINS

Beans

Readily found worldwide, in many varieties, long lasting and cheap, beans are an excellent source of protein. Beans combine well with tomatoes, onions, cheese and garlic making them a simple nutritious addition to any galley especially in bouncy conditions when nourishing one-pot meals are needed most.

Cooking Time for Beans

Beans - 1 Cup	Soak Time	Stove-top Time	Pressure Cooker Time
Black beans	8 hrs	45 min	10 min
Black-eyed peas	8 hrs	1 hr	10 min
Chickpeas	8 hrs	1 hr	13 min
Kidney beans	8 hrs	1 hr	10 min
Lima beans	8 hrs	1 hr	10 min
Navy beans	8 hrs	45 min	7 min
Northern beans	8 hrs	45 min	8 min
Pinto beans	8 hrs	90 min	10 min
Soy beans	8 hrs	3 hrs	35 min
Split peas	none	2 hrs	10 min
White beans	8 hrs	3 hrs	15 min

Tips on Cooking Beans

❖ **Soak beans,** in water for 8 hours, generally overnight.

❖ **Discard** any beans that float as they're bad.

❖ **A quicker option** to soaking beans is to blanch them for 3 minutes then let them rest 1 hour tightly covered.

❖ Use **3 cups** of fresh water to cook 1 cup of beans.

❖ The above times are for 1 cup of beans. Cooking time will need to be **increased** if more beans are cooked.

❖ **1 cup of beans** will increase to 2 1/4 cups during cooking.

- **Cooking time for beans varies** as the older they are the longer they take to cook.
- **Don't salt beans** until they're cooked as the skin becomes tough.
- To **test if beans are cooked** place a few on a spoon and gently blow on them. If the skin peels back they're done.

Eco Burgers

Nicholas~Tahiti 98

Nicholas created these burgers with leftover refried beans from our previous nights dinner.

3 C	couscous
2 C	refried beans
1 C	salted peanuts – chopped
1	onion – diced
1	carrots – grated
1	egg
2	garlic cloves – crushed
1 T	sesame seeds
	S&P

- Combine all ingredients and shape into patties.
- Fry in olive oil until golden.

Serve with tossed garden salad.

Baked Beans

4 C	water
1 can	tomatoes
1 C	bacon – sliced
1/2 C	navy beans
1/4 C	tomato sauce
1/4 C	brown sugar
1	onion – diced
1	green pepper – diced
1	celery stalk – diced
3 T	Dijon mustard
	salt

- Place beans in 2 C water and pressure cook 5 minutes, or simmer 15 minutes, drain.

- ❖ Mix all ingredients together and pressure cook 10 minutes or bake covered 1 hour.
- ❖ Simmer uncovered 5 minutes to thicken.

Serve with toast.

Chili Beans

2 C	black, red or kidney beans – cooked
1 can	whole peeled tomatoes
1 can	tomato paste
1	onion – diced
1	green pepper – diced
1	celery stalk – diced
4	garlic cloves – chopped
2 T	Dijon mustard
1 T	chili pepper – chopped
2 t	cumin
1 t	lemon juice
	fresh basil and oregano
	S&P
*1/4 C	bulgar wheat
*3 T	barbecue sauce
*1 small can	Mexican salsa or enchilada sauce may replace chili
*1	apple – diced
*5	bacon rashers – diced

- ❖ Combine all ingredients and pressure cook 10 minutes or simmer 25 minutes.
- ❖ Simmer 10 minutes to allow flavors to develop.

Serve garnished with cilantro, grated cheese, sour cream and or Pink Onion Relish.

Portuguese Sausage and Beans

2 C	red kidney beans – cooked
2 C	spicy sausage or salami – sliced

1 can	stewed tomatoes
1	onion – diced
1	green pepper – diced
2	celery stalks – sliced
3	garlic cloves – crushed
2 T	basil – chopped
	chili of some form
	S&P

❖ Sauté sausage until browned, add onion, pepper and celery, cook 3 minutes.

❖ Add beans, tomatoes and seasoning.

❖ Pressure cook 10 minutes or simmer 20 minutes.

Serve over rice.

Pumpkin and Bean Stew

2 C	pumpkim – cooked
2 C	white beans – cooked
1 C	water
1/2 C	scallions – diced
2	carrots – diced
2	apples – diced
8	mushrooms
	ginger – grated
	soy sauce

❖ Combine all ingredients and pressure cook 10 minutes or simmer 20 minutes.

Who's Coming to Dinner?

It was my turn to be cook and I was mentally going through our lockers contemplating what to prepare for dinner. We were sailing north on a cold afternoon through the labyrinth of Patagonia's archipelago and it had been three days since our last contact with civilization; a radio call giving the required identification information while passing a remote lighthouse.

Sunlight rays were streaming from the sky turning the steel water blue and basting the distant hillside in a mellow light. Briefly a white triangle shape appeared inside a beam of light and I wondered if an angel had decended from heaven. All thoughts of food vanished as I realized it was a sailboat. Excitement broke out onboard as John gave call on the radio announcing our position. A reply came stating that they were the yacht *Chiloe* on their way south. In his elation at sighting another vessel John asked them to consider stopping for the day to join us for dinner. "Yes," was the reply and I was quickly down to two dinner options rice and beans or spaghetti.

As their white sail grew larger I began to question how big *Chiloe* was and more importantly how many were onboard so I placed a radio call asking how many to expect for dinner.

"There's thirteen of us and a dog," came the reply.

Yikes!!!! Not only did I have our crew of six to feed but thirteen more, too. It amazing how quickly the enchantment of the prospect of company became daunting even though our crew kept reassuring me that beans and rice would be fine for dinner - again.

Five minutes later a providential crackle came across on the radio.

"This is the 32' yacht *Chiloe* and Charlie and I will be happy to join you for dinner, we'll bring the beers!"

Yeah, party time! Shrimp stir-fry and jasmine rice was my new dinner plan with apple cobbler to follow.

Polenta with Mushrooms and Gorgonzola

4 C	water	
2 1/2 C	mushrooms – diced	
3/4 C	instant polenta	
1/2 C	gorgonzola – crumbled	
1/2 C	parsley – torn	.
2	garlic cloves – crushed	
1 T	olive oil	
1 t	fresh minced rosemary	
	S&P	

❖ Bring water to a boil and whisk in polenta, whisking until creamy, 10 minutes.

❖ Meanwhile sauté mushrooms, garlic and rosemary, 6 minutes.

❖ Season to taste.

Serve mushrooms over polenta with gorgonzola and parsley.

Couscous

Originally from North Africa, couscous is fine milled wheat that only requires hot water and 5 minutes until ready to serve. It's a perfect onboard staple especially in heavy weather as it's safer to prepare than rice or pasta. I boil hot water in an enclosed kettle and fill the galley mounted thermos so that I'm at the ready to prepare the couscous, thus eliminating a pot on the stove-top that requires attention.

I often add couscous at the end of cooking stews and soups to absorb the juices and thicken the dish thus making it easier to serve to crew.

Traditionally couscous was served at the end of the week to use up all the vegetables before market day on Saturday. Served in a large round dish, the grain is piled into a mound with a depression at the top. Chicken or meat is placed in the hollow with the vegetables on top or around the side.

Inexpensive and available worldwide couscous keeps well in an airtight, waterproof container.

Tips on Cooking Couscous

❖ Add 2 cups of boiling water to 2 cups of couscous and let stand 5 minutes. Makes 4 cups.

❖ Couscous can be dressed with with a variety of ingredients including almonds, pine nuts, raisins, dates, apricots, cranberries, herbs, feta or sun-dried tomatoes.

Almond Couscous

1 1/2 C	couscous
1 1/2 C	vegetable broth
1/4 C	raisins
2	zucchini – diced
1	onion – diced
3 T	slivered almonds – toasted
1 T	butter
1 T	cilantro
1 T	mint
1/4 t	cumin
	S&P

❖ Sauté onion and zucchini, heat broth and butter, add couscous and let stand 5 minutes.

❖ Toss in remaining ingredients and sesaon to taste.

Serve with lamb or fish.

Vegetable and Date Couscous

1 1/2 C	vegetable broth
1 1/2 C	couscous
1	onion – diced
1	red pepper – diced
1	zucchini – diced
1/2 C	dates – chopped
1/4 C	coriander – chopped
4 T	olive oil
1/2 T	paprika
1 t	cumin
	salt
	coriander
	*chicken – cooked and diced

❖ Sauté onion, add zucchini and red pepper, cook 2 minutes.

❖ Bring broth to a boil, add all ingredients.

❖ Remove from heat, cover and let stand 5 minutes.

❖ Add coriander and fluff with a fork.

Serve with crumbled feta and a wedge of lemon.

Lentils

Inexpensive, long-lasting, nutritious, nourishing and simple, lentils are a staple provision and I enjoy using them at least a couple of times throughout a passage. They obtain a sophisticated taste when seasoned with spices and herbs while enhancing vegetables, poultry, seafood and meats.

Tips on Cooking Lentils

❖ **One cup** of lentils equals 2 1/2 cups cooked.

❖ **Red lentils** disinterate when cooked.

Beans and Grains

Cooking Time for Lentils

Lentil	Soak Time *optional	Stove-top Time	Pressure Cooker Time
Large green/ brown	1 hr	40 min	10 min
Red	25 min	25 min	8 min

Jamaican Curried Lentils

```
    3 C   water
1 1/2 C   lentils
  1 can   pineapple – diced
      1   onion – diced
      2   garlic cloves – crushed
    2 T   oil
    2 T   curry powder
          S&P
```

❖ Sauté onion and garlic, add curry, lentils, pineapple and water.

❖ Pressure cook 10 minutes or simmer 25 minutes until lentils are soft.

Serve with salad.

Lentil Loaf

Lynne~Yacht Kirwin

```
    1 C   lentils
    1 C   rice
    1 C   bread crumbs
  1/2 C   vegetable broth
      1   onion – diced
      1   green pepper – diced
      2   eggs – beaten
    2 t   soy sauce
    2 t   vinegar
      3   garlic cloves – crushed
```

1/2 t   sage and thyme
         sesame seeds
         S&P

❖ Cook lentils and rice together.

❖ Combine all ingredients except sesame seeds, add more bread-crumbs if mixture is too moist.

❖ Place mixture in an oiled bread pan and sprinkle with sesame seeds.

❖ Bake 30 minutes at 350°F covered with foil then uncovered for 10 minutes.

❖ Let sit 15 minutes before slicing.

Serve with salad.

Mditerranean Lentil Stew

Dr Michel~Southern Ocean

    4 C   water
1 1/2 C   lentils
      3   tomatoes – diced
      2   onions – diced
      2   carrots – diced
      2   celery stalks – sliced
      4   garlic cloves – peeled but left whole
    2 T   butter
    2 T   brown sugar
    1 T   vinegar or lemon juice
      2   bay leaves
          French Herbs de Provençe – rosemary,
            oregano and basil
          S&P
          *pre cooked roasted chicken or canned
            chicken
          *cooked shell pasta

❖ Sauté vegetables, add water and heat.

❖ Add lentils, S&P and bay leaves.

❖ Pressure cook 10 minutes or simmer 1 1/2 hours.

❖ Add sugar, vinegar, spices and herbs.

Serve with grated Parmesan, diced cilantro and a twist of lemon.

Fijian Lentil Stew

1/2 lb.	chicken, beef or lamb – cubed
1 1/2 C	lentils
3 C	water
1 C	spinach, peas or green beans
1/2 C	raisins
2	carrots – diced
1	onion – diced
3	garlic cloves – chopped
2 t	ginger – grated
1 t	cumin seeds
1/2 t	cinnamon
1/4 t	allspice
	S&P
*1 C	coconut milk

❖ Sauté onions, add spices, lentils, meat, carrots, water and raisins.

❖ Pressure cook 10 minutes or simmer 30 minutes.

❖ Add vegetable greens and simmer 5 minutes.

Walu's Lentils

LeeAnne~ Yacht Juliet

4 C	water
2 C	lentils
1 can	coconut milk
1 can	chopped tomatoes
1 lb	spinach – chopped
1	onion – diced
2 T	butter
2 t	*Gram Masala*
1 1/4 t	cumin
1 1/4 t	mustard seed
1 t	salt
1 t	turmeric
1/2 t	cayenne pepper
*3 C	shredded cooked chicken, pork or beef

❖ Sauté onions in butter with spices until fragrant.

❖ Add lentils, water and tomatoes, pressure cook 10 minutes or simmer 30 minutes.

❖ Add spinach and simmer until tender.

❖ Add coconut milk and heat through.

Middle Eastern Lentil Stew

Dyan~Yacht Ascension

3 C	water
1/2 C	barley
1/2 C	lentils
1/2 C	brown rice
1/2 C	raisins or currants
1/2 C	mint – diced
2	onions – chopped
2	garlic cloves – chopped
2 T	olive oil
1 T	vinegar
1 t	cumin
2 t	sugar
1/2 t	cardamom
	S&P

❖ Sauté onions and garlic, add remaining ingredients except raisins, mint and S&P.

❖ Pressure cook 15 minutes or simmer 40 minutes.

❖ Add raisins and mint, season to taste.

Rice

Jambalaya, risotto, pilaf, nasi goreng, sushi and biriyani are names of distinguished rice dishes from across the Northern Hemisphere. Originating in India, rice traveled throughout the trade routes and became integrated into local dishes. As varied as the dishes themselves, so are the cooking methods

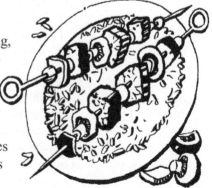

of each particular variety of rice. From short grain to long grain, arborio, basmati, black, brown, carolina, jasmine, patana, sticky and wild, the choices are endless.

As an all-round favorite rice I use basmati and stock up in large quantities when available. Basmati rice stores well in plastic sealed containers and doesn't require rinsing.

Tips on Cooking Rice

❖ Allow **2 cups of water** for every **cup of rice.**

❖ One cup of uncooked rice yields **3 cups of cooked** rice.

❖ For **four people** I cook 1 1/2 cups of rice in 3 cups of water.

❖ Bring **water to a boil**, add the rice and cover with a lid.

❖ Cook on low heat **15 minutes** until tender.

Let rice stand 5 minutes before serving.

Cooking Time for Rice

Rice Variety	Stovetop Cooking	Pressure Cooker
White Rice	20 minutes	7 minutes
Brown Rice	45 minutes	15 minutes

Cardamom Rice

Carol~Yacht Elyxir

3 C	vegetable or chicken broth
1 1/2 C	rice
1/2 C	raisins
1 T	butter
1	bay leaf
1 t	curry powder
1 t	cardamom
1/4 t	cumin

❖ Sauté rice in butter, add remaining ingredients except broth and cook 1 minute.

❖ Add broth and cook until rice is done.

Beans and Grains

Coconut Rice

From Burma, this dish is a pleasant accompaniment to a main course.

3 C	water
1 1/2 C	rice
3/4 C	coconut milk
1	onion – sliced

❖ Place all ingredients in a saucepan and cook until rice is done.

Indian Curry Pilaf

3 C	chicken broth
1 1/2 C	rice
1/2 C	raisins
3 T	vegetable oil
1 1/2 T	soy sauce
1/2 t	turmeric
1/2 t	curry powder

❖ Sauté curry and turmeric in oil for 30 seconds.

❖ Add rice and cook 5 minutes.

❖ Stir in broth, soy sauce and raisins, heat until boiling, cover and cook until rice is done.

Jambalaya

2 C	water
2 C	shrimp
1 C	spicy sausage – sliced
1 C	baked ham – diced
3/4 C	rice
1 can	stewed tomatoes
2	celery stalks – diced
1	onion – quartered
3	garlic cloves – crushed
2 T	oil
1	bay leaf
1 t	each – oregano and thyme

❖ Sauté sausage and ham for 2 minutes, remove meat from pan.

❖ Add garlic, onions and celery to pan, sauté 3 minutes.

❖ Combine all ingredients, except shrimp and bring to a boil, stirring occasionally.

❖ Cover and pressure cook 10 minutes or simmer 30 minutes.

❖ Stir in shrimp, cover, let sit 5 minutes to allow rice to absorb the liquid.

John's Seafood Paella

At Christmas we invite all our friends to join us for a kayak adventure from Roche Harbor to tiny Posey Island; a 1-acre state park islet with two campsites and a lovely beach. The only request we ask is that they bring something to add to a paella. We organize the firewood and the first order is to get a roaring camp fire underway in the fire ring.

John has done the paella prep work at home, so we enjoy chatting while we wait for the flames to reduce to hot coals before placing the paella pan on the grate. Once the rice gains some heat John artistically arranges the seafood on top according to its heating or cooking times before adding the peas and replacing the lid. It's always a success.

We've dinned on wonderful local treats like manila clams, Dungeness crab, Chinook salmon, and prawns all mixed in with spicy chorizo. Here's a toast to the holiday season and absent friends.

4 C	chicken, fish or vegetable stock
3 C	clams, mussels and or shrimp
1	chorizo sausage – sliced
1 1/4 C	short-grained rice
1	onion – diced
1 bell	pepper – diced
1 can	diced tomatoes
1/2 C	salmon – diced
1/2 C	crab
1/2 C	peas
1/2 C	olive oil
4	cloves garlic – minced

❖ Heat stock with saffron.

❖ Sauté rice in olive oil 2 minutes, add onion and cook 5 minutes.

❖ Add peppers and cook 3 minutes.

❖ Add tomatoes and garlic, simmer 5 minutes.

❖ Stir in broth and chorizo, simmer 10 minutes.

❖ Add seafood and peas, cover and cook 6 minutes.

Serve garnished with lemon wedges.

Spanish Tomato Pilaf

      3 C   vegetable broth
  1 1/2 C   rice
        2   tomatoes – diced
      4 T   butter
      1 t   tomato paste
            S&P

- ❖ Stir tomatoes, butter and S&P over moderate heat for 5 minutes, mash tomatoes with spoon.
- ❖ Add stock and tomato paste, cook 5 minutes.
- ❖ Stir in rice, cover and cook until rice is done.

Mexican Rice

      4   chicken breasts
    3 C   water
 1 1/2 C rice
    1 C   peas
      1   onion – diced
      1   carrot – diced
      1   red pepper – diced
    2 T   olive oil
    2 T   lemon juice
      2   mint sprigs
          S&P

- ❖ Cook chicken in water 10 minutes, cover and let stand 10 minutes, remove chicken and shred into bite size pieces, reserve stock.
- ❖ Sauté onion, add carrots and rice, cook 3 minutes.
- ❖ Stir in chicken stock and lemon juice, bring to a boil then turn heat to medium-low.
- ❖ Add chicken, mint, and red pepper, cover and cook 15 minutes.
- ❖ Add peas near end of cooking, remove mint.

Garnish with fresh mint leaves and serve with salsa.

Porcini Mushroom Risotto

       6 C   water
  2 1/4 C   arborio rice

```
     2 C   fresh porcini mushrooms – sliced
   1/4 C   olive oil
   1/2     onion – diced
     5     dried porcini mushrooms – soaked in warm
             water for 30 minutes
     3     garlic cloves – crushed
  bunch    parsley – chopped
           pecorino cheese – grated
           S&P
```

❖ Simmer water, onion, dried mushrooms and garlic 15 minutes.

❖ Add parsley, rice and fresh mushrooms, simmer 25 minutes until rice is done. Stir occasionally.

❖ Add cheese, season to taste and drizzle with olive oil.

Nasi Goreng

Carol~Yacht Elyxir

An Indonesian "national dish," nasi goreng is an ornately garnished fried rice studded with vegetables and meat, dressed with a flavorful sweet soy sauce.

```
     4 C   cooked rice
     1 C   shrimp or chicken – cooked
   1/2 C   cabbage – shredded
     1     green pepper – diced
     1     celery stalk – diced
     2     scallions – diced
     1     carrot – grated
     1     onion – finely diced
   1/4 C   coconut milk, yogurt or sour cream
     3     garlic cloves – crushed
     2 T   oil
     2 T   lemon juice
     2 T   sweet soy sauce
   1/2 t   each – cardamom, turmeric and chili
             pepper flakes
           ginger – grated
           S&P
```

❖ Sauté onion, garlic and spices.

❖ Add shrimp, lemon juice, soy sauce and vegetables, sauté 3 minutes.

❖ Stir in rice and coconut milk, heat through.

Ganish with diced tomatoes or omelet strips.

OATS

John's Porridge

There's no better way to start the day than with a steaming bowl of porridge, covered with berries, nuts and yogurt. John finds that using only oats to make porridge gets boring, so he searches for multi-grain cereals and makes his own mix. Knowing it's unlikely he'll find wholesome grains in isolated places, John stocks up our supplies at the start of the expedition season. In Scotland, he purchased 10 lbs of oats then added a mix of wheat, barley, rye and flax.

Adding a grated apple, sliced banana, dried blueberries, cranberries and or grated coconut into the water before bringing it to a boil creates interesting porridge. A sprinkle of nuts and dollop of yogurt on each serving has many an expedition member claim, "I don't care for oatmeal, but whatever you call this, it tastes fantastic!"

         4 C   water
         2 C   grains: oats, wheat, barley, buckwheat etc.
       1/2 C   dried fruit: blueberries, cranberries, raisins,
                  apricots etc.
           1   banana – sliced
       1/2   apple – grated
      *1/4 t   salt

❖ Bring water, apple, banana and dried fruit to a boil.

❖ Add grains, stir, cover and cook over on low heat for 5 minutes, stirring occasionally.

Serve topped with nuts, flax meal, diced fruit and yogurt.

Muesli

People of British extraction thoroughly enjoy this simple untoasted version of granola.

         4 C   rolled oats
         2 C   dried fruit: raisins, apricots, cranberries
         1 C   chopped nuts
       1/2 C   wheat germ, flax meal or bran flakes
       1/2 C   coconut

❖ Mix all ingredients thoroughly and store in an airtight container.

Bircher Muesli

We first enjoyed this muesli on a road trip in New Zealand's South Island when we stayed at a delightful B&B owned by a Swiss couple.

- 2 C rolled oats
- 1 C milk
- 1 C yogurt
- 1 apple – grated
- 2 T orange or apple juice
- 1/4 C raisins, cranberries or blueberries
- 1/4 C chopped nuts and or seed

❖ Combine oats, milk, yogurt and juice.

❖ Chill at least 3 hours.

❖ Mix in remaining ingredients.

Serve with fresh fruit, berries, yogurt and honey.

Granola

- 3 C rolled oats
- 1 C dried fruit
- 1/2 C chopped nuts
- 1/2 C seeds – sesame, pumpkin, sunflower, etc.
- 1/2 C coconut
- 1/2 C wheat germ, flax meal or bran flakes
- 1/4 C oil
- 1/4 C honey
- 1 t salt

❖ Combine all ingredients.

❖ Cover baking sheet with parchment paper and spread mixture over sheet in a thin layer.

❖ Bake 12 minutes at 300°F.

Oaty Banana Pancakes or Waffles

This is one of John's favorite breakfast dishes to cook at sea.

- 1 1/2 C milk
- 3/4 C flour or pancake mix
- 1/2 C whole wheat flour
- 1/2 C chopped walnuts or pecans
- 1/4 C buckwheat flour

```
1/4 C   oats
1/4 C   flax meal or wheat germ
1/4 C   coconut flakes
1/4 C   cooking oil
    2   bananas – mashed (pancakes only)
    1   egg
  1 T   baking powder
  1 t   vanilla
1/4 t   salt
```

❖ In sperate bowls, combine liquid ingredients and dry ingredients.

❖ Stir liquid ingredients into dry ingredients. If consistency is too thick, add water.

❖ Using a soup ladle pour batter into lightly oiled pan, sprinkle with chopped nuts and coconut.

❖ Flip pancake when edges turn dry and cook until done.

Oatmeal Pear Breakfast Bake

```
    3   pears – diced
  2 C   rolled oats
  2 C   milk
1/2 C   walnuts
1/2 C   hazel nuts
1/3 C   maple syrup
    1   egg
  3 T   unsalted butter – melted
  2 t   vanilla extract
1 1/2 t cinnamon
  1 t   baking powder
1/2 t   salt
```

❖ Combine oats, nuts, baking powder, cinnamon and salt.

❖ In another bowl, whisk together milk, maple syrup, egg, half the butter and vanilla.

❖ In a buttered 9-inch pie dish spread out pears in a layer.

❖ Scatter oats mix over pears. Drizzle with milk and egg mix.

❖ Bake 35 minutes 350°F, until oats are set.

❖ Serve drizzled with remaining melted butter and yogurt on the side.

Beans and Grains

Oatmeal Energy Balls

1/2 C	rolled oats
2 T	quick-cooking oats
1/4 C	ground flax seeds
1/4 C	smooth natural peanut butter
2 T	honey
1/2 t	vanilla
1/4 t	salt (if using unsalted peanut butter)
*2 T	dark chocolate chip
*2 T	crushed banana chip
*2 T	finely chopped dried apple slices and 1/8 t ground cinnamon
*2 T	unsweetened coconut

❖ Combine first 7 ingredients.

❖ Divide mixture into 4 and add the * ingredients or make as one mix adjusting the * ingredients.

❖ Refrigerate mixture 10 minutes.

❖ Press and roll mixture into 1-inch balls.

Makes 24 balls.

Chapter 11

PASTA

Tips on Cooking Pasta

❖ I generally allow **3 oz of pasta per person** for a hungry crew.

❖ When it's **rough at sea** it's safer to cook pasta in the pressure cooker with the lid on but no weight.

❖ Add a dash of **cooking oil** to the pasta water to stop the pasta from sticking together.

❖ To stop cooked **pasta from sticking** after it's cooked run it under cold water or don't totally drain the pasta.

Italian Cheeses that go well with Pasta

❖ **Mozzarella:** is a mild stringy cheese used on pizza. You may substitute 1/2 cheddar and 1/2 Parmesan.

❖ **Parmesan:** is a hard, long lasting cheese often available grated, though it's best served freshly shaved or grated from a block. The rind from a block of Parmesan is called the heel and it goes well in soups and stews.

❖ **Ricotta:** is a mild soft cheese that can be made from milk and vinegar, *see Cheese.*

Chicken Enchilada Pasta

2 C	fusilli pasta
2 C	chicken stock or water
2 C	corn
1 1/2 C	chicken – cooked and shredded
1 C	bell peppers – diced
1 can	diced tomatoes and green chilies
1 can	red enchilada sauce
1 can	black beans
3/4 C	cheddar cheese – grated
3 T	taco seasoning
	*toppings: tomatoes, green onions, cilantro fresh lime, sour cream, guacamole, tortilla chips

❖ Combine tomatoes, sauce, pasta, and stock, bring to a simmer.

❖ Add beans, corn, bell peppers and taco seasoning, simmer 15 minutes.

❖ Add chicken and cheese.

Serve with toppings.

Pasta

Garlic Pasta

1 lb.	pasta – cooked
1/4 C	olive oil
4	garlic cloves – crushed
1	chili – minced
	S&P
	mint and parsley

❖ Sauté garlic, chili and a generous grinding of black pepper in half the olive oil until it begins to turn golden.

❖ Stir garlic into hot drained pasta, add remaining oil, mint and parsley, season to taste.

Pea Pasta

1 lb.	pasta shells – cooked
3 C	peas
1 C	white wine
1	onion – diced
3	garlic cloves – crushed
2 T	olive oil
	basil
	S&P
	*bacon

❖ Sauté onion and garlic until soft, add peas and white wine, heat through.

❖ Mix with pasta.

Serve hot with grated Parmesan cheese.

Kitty's Seafood Pasta

1 lb.	fettuccine – cooked
1 lb.	seafood mix or shrimp
4	tomatoes – diced
1 C	feta – crumbled
1/4 C	torn basil or pesto to taste
1/2 C	sun-dried tomatoes – sliced
1/4 C	white wine
3	cloves garlic – crushed
	crushed red pepper to taste

- ❖ Sauté garlic and fresh tomatoes 3 minutes.
- ❖ Add remaining ingredients and heat through.

Serve over hot fettuccine.

Red Wine Pasta

1 lb.	spaghetti
2 C	water
1 C	walnuts or 1/4 C pine nuts
1/2 C	Parmesan cheese – grated
1/4 C	olive oil
1/4 C	parsley – chopped
3	cloves garlic – crushed
1/2 t	red pepper flakes
	salt

- ❖ In a skillet bring wine, water, and salt to a boil.
- ❖ Add spaghetti and cook, stirring, until al dente. Remove pasta.
- ❖ In same skillet, heat 2 T oil, add garlic and red pepper, cook 1 minute.
- ❖ Stir in pasta, parsley, nuts, Parmesan and remaining oil.
- ❖ Season to taste.

Serve hot with tossed salad.

Shellfish and Spinach Pasta

1 lb.	pasta
1 lb.	clams
1/2 lb.	mussels
2 C	mushrooms – halved
2 C	spinach
1 C	white wine
1/4 C	stock
6	garlic cloves – sliced
3	scallions – diced
3 T	parsley – diced
2 T	olive oil
2 T	butter
1 T	chili pepper flakes
1/2 t	salt

- ❖ Sauté garlic, chili and scallions in oil and butter for 30 seconds.
- ❖ Add mussels and clams, cook 2 minutes.
- ❖ Add wine, stock, spinach and mushrooms, cook until shellfish open, about 5 minutes.
- ❖ Toss shellfish, parsley and hot pasta together.

Tomato Basil Pasta

6	tomatoes – diced
1/2 C	basil leaves – diced
2	garlic cloves – crushed
1/8 t	fresh ground black pepper
	red pepper flakes – optional
8 oz	brie – diced

- ❖ Combine tomatoes, basil, garlic and red pepper flakes. Let sit 1 hour for flavors to combine.

Serve over hot fettuccine and garnish with brie.

Vegetable Lasagna ~ Speedy

1 lb.	pasta
2 C	spinach or cabbage – shredded
1 C	broccoli or cauliflower florets
1 C	beans or zucchini
1 C	cheese – grated
3	potatoes – cubed
1	onion – cubed
4	garlic cloves – crushed
2 t	butter

- ❖ Sauté onion and garlic until soft.
- ❖ Boil enough water to hold all remaining ingredients, add potatoes and cook 10 minutes.
- ❖ Add broccoli, beans, spinach and pasta, cook 8 minutes.
- ❖ Layer drained pasta and vegetables and in a baking dish with onion and cheese.
- ❖ Bake in hot oven until cheese melts, about 10 minutes.

Pasta

Basil Chicken and Olive Pasta

1 lb.	pasta – cooked
4	chicken breasts – diced
2	tomatoes – diced
1	onion – diced
1/2 C	green pepper – roasted
1/2 C	mushrooms – sliced
1/4 C	white wine
1/4 C	black olives
6 T	olive oil
2 T	butter
2 T	herbs to taste – basil (pesto), oregano and thyme
1 T	capers
2	garlic cloves – crushed
	S&P

❖ Sauté chicken in butter 3 minutes, add garlic and onion, cook 2 minutes.

❖ Add tomatoes, green pepper and mushrooms, stir until vegetables cook.

❖ Add wine, olives, herbs and capers, heat through.

Serve over hot pasta.

Sesame Pasta

1 lb.	pasta – cooked
4	scallions – diced
1	red pepper – diced
4 T	sesame seeds
2 T	sesame oil
	hot sauce to taste
	fresh ginger to taste

❖ Toss all ingredients together.

Serve either hot or cold.

Walnut Pasta

1 lb.	pasta – cooked
1 1/2 C	walnuts – chopped

Pasta

2/3 C   Parmesan cheese – grated
1/2 C   olive oil
1/4 C   basil – chopped
    5   garlic cloves – crushed
  3 T   olive oil
        S&P

❖   Sauté garlic and walnuts until lightly toasted, about 5 minutes.

❖   Toss all ingredients together.

Zucchini and Mozzarella Pasta

1 lb.   pasta – cooked
  4 C   zucchini – sliced and sautéed
  1 C   mozzarella cheese – cubed
1/2 C   olive oil
1/2 C   Parmesan cheese – grated
    2   eggs – beaten
        S&P

❖   Stir mozzarella into hot pasta, add remaining ingredients, stirring
    to set eggs.

Serve with Parmesan and ground pepper.

Pancakes, Popcorn and Pasta

February 18 1990
Yacht *Maiden* – 1998-90 Whitbread Around the World Race
Latitude: 58° 39' S
Longitude: 118° 03' E

I now know it would be possible to for me to write my journal even if
I take up caving. I'm currently squashed into my bunk writing while
lying on my stomach with my head touching the bunk above me where
"Detroit" Dawn (Riley) sleeps. I dare not wiggle too much for fear I'll
wake her. As our generator has died we've no electrical power so I'm
writing by flashlight.

I hear water sloshing about the cabin sole like an underground river
and the side of the hull is dripping to such an extent that I wouldn't
be surprised to see stalagmites and stalactites forming as the dripping

water is slowly breaking down the insulating foam turning it into an alternative substance. Outside the raging continues.

This day has been one holding both amusement and fear. The wretched weather is still here, it's now our fourth day and apparently the entire fleet is experiencing our current low. The winds haven't dropped below 40 knots and *Maiden* is rocketing along averaging 15 knots in reduced visibility. With spray for miles we take turns standing 15-minute bow watches on the look out for icebergs. Rumor has it that behind us La Poste is experiencing a little let up in the conditions – phew, hopefully there'll soon be some moderation of this stuff for us.

Lying here I tend to forget the bone-chilling situation on deck – how the cold tends to bite into me after the second hour. After three hours I become weary of the smallest of movements; the lifting a hand that sends the chilly water inside my gloves running down my palm and up the length of my arm. As I switch with Angela to trim the spinnaker I brace against the incessant lashings of icy spray with hunched shoulders and clenched teeth, tired of the cold.

Michèle lies on the bunk be- low me, she's been out of action since this morning when we were struck by a rogue wave. It swept Tanja and I down the deck from our midship windward position and we ended up piled on top of each other like driftwood, along with the dorade. Michèle who was steering, was no where to be seen, she'd been compressed into the steering cockpit well, a bent and broken wheel testimony to the wave's force and Michèle's strength as she held on to the wheel when the wave hit her in the chest. We feared she'd broken her back but thankfully it is only muscle damage.

Food is one of our highlights. Yesterday was half way on this 6,000 mile leg from New Zealand to Uruguay, around Cape Horn. I produced the fruitcake nana had baked for us.... well, only half of it, as the whole cake was too heavy to bring aboard. It was fantastic and we ate the lot. Nana cried when she gave it to me, it was the first time I'd seen tears in her eyes. I miss her.

Today's breakfast was pancakes. It's hard work for Jo to cook pancakes for the 12 of us but she knows we love them so – they're such a welcoming comfort food. Popcorn was the main highlight dish at lunch, a total overdose, following carrots and New Zealand tasty cheddar cheese on crackers. Jo's evening menu plan was freeze-dried smoked fish but as I'm the only one who likes it she just heated up a small pouch and then made a large pot of our back up pasta. Pasta certainly gets the majority vote as everyone can then smother it according to their individual taste. Parmesan cheese, mayonnaise, salt and pepper, ketchup, hot sauce and butter all find homes on the pasta plates of the crew. I passed on the pasta and enjoyed my smoked fish followed by a chocolate bar.

I wonder what's for breakfast?

Pasta Sauces

Greek Artichoke Sauce

2 C	artichoke hearts
3/4 C	feta cheese – cubed
1/4 C	Greek black olives
4	tomatoes – diced
1 T	olive oil

❖ Sauté artichokes, olives and tomatoes.

❖ Add feta cheese and heat.

Serve over cooked pasta.

Carbonara

1 C	sour cream
1 C	sliced mushrooms
8	bacon rashers
1	onion – diced
1	egg yolk
2	garlic cloves – crushed
2 T	olive oil
	parsley
	pepper
	*1/4 t chili pepper flakes
	*tomato – diced
	*smoked salmon

❖ Sauté bacon, garlic and onion, add mushrooms and cook 3 minutes.

❖ Beat sour cream and egg yolk together, add to mushrooms and stir until sauce thickens.

Pour over cooked pasta and garnish with parsley.

Pasta

Caponata ~ Eggplant Sauce

1	eggplant – cubed and purged
2	yellow peppers – roasted and sliced
1 can	diced tomatoes
1/2 C	black olives
1/2 C	pine nuts – toasted
1/4 C	red wine
1	onion – diced
4	anchovy fillets – chopped
3	garlic cloves – crushed
2 T	olive oil
2 T	capers
	basil
	S&P
	Parmesan cheese

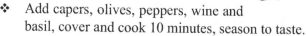

❖ Sauté garlic, eggplant, onion, tomatoes and anchovies 10 minutes.

❖ Add capers, olives, peppers, wine and basil, cover and cook 10 minutes, season to taste.

❖ Serve with pasta or as a pizza topping.

Garnish with basil, pine nuts and grated Parmesan.

Olive and Caper Sauce

1 can	stewed tomatoes
1 C	black olives – chopped if large
4 T	capers
2 T	olive oil
6	anchovy fillets – chopped
3	garlic cloves – crushed
	parsley
	basil

❖ Sauté garlic and anchovies until they're nearly melted.

❖ Stir in tomatoes, olives and capers, cook 5 minutes.

Serve mixed with hot pasta and garnish with parsley and basil.

Smoked Chicken Sauce

| 1 1/4 C | cream |
| 1 | smoked chicken breast – sliced |

```
1   onion
3 T butter
1 T lemon juice
1   egg yoke
2   garlic cloves – crushed
    parsley
    S&P
    *can replace chicken with smoked salmon
```

❖ Saute onion and garlic in butter.

❖ Add combined cream and egg yolk, heat until thick.

❖ Stir in lemon juice, add chicken, and heat through.

Serve on pasta and garnish with parsley.

Spaghetti Sauce

```
1 can  stewed tomatoes
1 can  tomato paste
  2 C  mushrooms – halved
1/2 C  red wine
1/4 C  olives
    2  carrots – grated
    1  onion – diced
    1  zucchini – diced
    1  green pepper – diced
    3  garlic cloves – crushed
  2 T  olive oil
  2 T  capers
  2 T  oregano – chopped
  2 T  basil – chopped
  2 t  thyme – chopped
       S&P
```

❖ Sauté onion and garlic.

❖ Add remaining ingredients and simmer 15 minutes.

Nicole's Pasta

```
    2  chicken breasts – sliced and sautéed
    4  garlic cloves – minced
  2 T  olive oil
1/2 C  Kalamata olives
```

Pasta

```
1/2 C  sun-dried tomatoes in oil – chopped
  2 T  caper juice, white wine or lemon juice
  2 T  capers
    3  garlic cloves – crushed
       S&P
       *pine nuts
```

❖ Combine all ingredients in a saucepan and heat through.

Serve mixed with hot pasta tossed with olive oil and garnish with parsley.

Tomato and Caper Sauce

```
1 can  stewed tomatoes
1 can  tomato paste
  1 C  red wine
    1  carrot – grated
    1  celery stalk – sliced
    1  onion – diced
    1  red pepper – diced
    1  zucchini – sliced
    3  garlic cloves – crushed
  3 T  capers
  2 T  olive oil
       basil, oregano, thyme and parsley
       S&P
       *Italian sausage
```

❖ Sauté garlic, carrot, celery, onion, red pepper and zucchini.

❖ Add wine, tomatoes and tomato paste, simmer 15 minutes.

❖ Stir in capers and herbs, season to taste.

Serve over hot pasta with grated Parmesan.

Tuna and Tomato Sauce

```
1 can  stewed tomatoes – drained
  2 C  tuna – cooked and flaked, or canned
  1 C  mushrooms – sliced
    1  onion – diced
  2 T  capers
  1 T  olive oil
    3  garlic cloves – crushed
       S&P
       *chili pepper of some form
```

❖ Sauté garlic, onion, chili and mushrooms.

❖ Add tomatoes and simmer 10 minutes.

❖ Add tuna and capers; simmer another 10 minutes.

Serve on hot pasta and garnish with diced parsley.

Niçoise Tuna Sauce

2 C	Tuna
1/3 C	Niçoise olives – pitted and diced
1/4 C	olive oil
2	scallions – chopped
2	garlic cloves – chopped
2 T	parsley – chopped
3 t	capers
	lemon juice
	S&P

❖ Sauté garlic, scallions and capers.

❖ Add remaining ingredients and serve over hot pasta.

Walnut Sauce

1 1/2 C	walnuts – chopped and toasted
1/2 C	Parmesan cheese – grated
1/2 C	ricotta or cream
1/4 C	olive oil
4 T	butter
1	garlic clove – crushed
	salt
	parsley

❖ Combine olive oil, butter and nuts.

❖ Add cheese and cream then salt to taste.

Serve mixed with stuffed pasta and garnish with parsley.

Pesto

Pesto is a thick, uncooked, blended sauce made with Parmesan cheese, olive oil and white nuts, such as almonds, pine nuts,

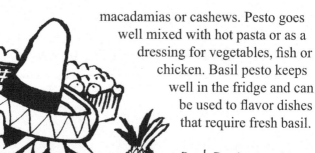

macadamias or cashews. Pesto goes well mixed with hot pasta or as a dressing for vegetables, fish or chicken. Basil pesto keeps well in the fridge and can be used to flavor dishes that require fresh basil.

Bail Pesto

Brian~Raivavae 98

Upon arriving in Raivavae, French Polynesia from New Zealand I noticed a huge basil bush on the end of the wharf. After picking a few basil sprigs I encouraged Brian to prepare pesto fettuccine for our dinner party with guests that night. I had no pine nuts, so substituted sesame seeds. I also rather underestimated the quantity of basil we required and throughout the preparation of this dish we had to send crew sprinting down the wharf in relays for more leaves.

2 C	basil leaves – chopped
1/2 C	olive oil
1/2 C	Parmesan cheese – grated
3	garlic gloves – crushed
1/3 C	pine nuts – toasted
	S&P

❖ Blend all ingredients together.

Serve mixed with hot pasta.

Black Olive Pesto

Susan~Yacht Moonshine

1 1/2 C	black olives – pitted
1/2 C	olive oil
4	garlic cloves – crushed
4	anchovy fillets
	lemon zest

❖ Blend all ingredients together.

Pasta

Roasted Red Pepper Pesto

2	red peppers – roasted and peeled or sautéed in oil
1/2 C	pine nuts – toasted
1/2 C	tomatoes – diced
1/2 C	Parmesan cheese – grated
1/2 C	olive oil
4	garlic cloves – crushed
	S&P
	lemon juice
	basil or parsley
	*chili of some form

❖ Blend all ingredients together.

If serving on pasta leave out the Parmesan and serve it on the side.

Spinach Pesto

2 C	spinach leaves – chopped
1 C	basil leaves – chopped
1 C	Parmesan cheese – grated
1/2 C	olive oil
2	garlic cloves – minced
	black pepper

❖ Mix spinach, basil and garlic together, slowly add olive oil.

❖ Stir in cheese and season to taste.

Sun-Dried Tomato Pesto

1 C	sun-dried tomatoes – chopped
1/2 C	basil – chopped
1/2 C	black olives – chopped
1/2 C	olive oil
3 T	lemon zest
3	garlic cloves
	ground pepper

❖ Blend all ingredients together.

Serve mixed with hot pasta.

Tuna and Walnut Pesto

2 C	tuna – cooked and flaked, or canned
3/4 C	olive oil
1/2 C	walnuts
2 T	lemon zest
1 t	Worchestershire sauce
	parsley
	basil
	S&P

❖ Blend all ingredients together while gradually adding olive oil.

Instant Ramen Noodles

Noodle Omelets

Fran~Yacht Aka

1 pkg.	instant ramen noodles
5	eggs – beaten
	vegetables of your choice – diced
	seasonings of your choice

❖ Cook noodles with enclosed packet, while noodles are cooking you may add vegetables to soften them.

❖ Mix all ingredients together and cook like omelets, you can make either one large one or smaller ones.

Serve hot or cold.

Thai Vegetable Noodles

Carol~Yacht Elyxir

2 pkg.	instant ramen noodles – cooked
3/4 C	water
3/4 C	coconut milk
2	carrots – julienne
2	zucchini – julienne
3	scallions – sliced
4	garlic gloves – crushed
2 T	*Thai Red Curry Paste*
1 T	soy sauce
1 T	olive oil

3 t ginger – grated
1 t sesame oil

❖ Sauté ginger and garlic until just sizzling.

❖ Add vegetables and stir-fry until al denté, remove to bowl.

❖ Add water, coconut milk, soy sauce and curry, reduce sauce for 5 minutes while stirring.

❖ Combine noodles, curry sauce and vegetables.

Garnish with chopped roasted peanuts and mint, basil or cilantro.

Chapter 12

EGGS AND

POULTRY

Eggs

Tips on Cooking Eggs

❖ Use **water** instead of milk to mix omelets, as milk will make them tough.

❖ Don't **salt** eggs until cooked.

Frittata

5	eggs
3 C	vegetables – grated carrots, zucchini, potatoes and mushrooms
1/4 C	Parmesan cheese – grated
1/4 C	butter
2	onions – diced
2 T	water
	S&P
	*spicy sausage

❖ Sauté onions, add vegetables and cook until tender.

❖ Beat eggs, water and cheese together, pour over vegetables and cook until set.

❖ Sprinkle with Parmesan and grill until golden.

Cut into wedges and serve hot.

Marmit's Egg Bake

7	eggs
1 1/2 C	cheese – grated
1 C	mushrooms – sliced
1 C	sausage or bacon – diced
1 C	potato – grated
1 C	cottage cheese
2	scallions – diced
	parsley
	chili to taste
	S&P

❖ Sauté bacon or sausage, add mushrooms and potato, cook until tender.

❖ Spread vegetables into greased baking dish.

- ❖ Beat eggs, chili, S&P, scallions and cheese together, mix in with vegetables.
- ❖ Sprinkle with parsley and grated cheese.
- ❖ Bake 35 minutes at 350°F.

John's Smoked Salmon Chipotle Scramble

8	eggs – beaten
1 C	kale, spinach or bok choy – chopped
1/2 C	smoked salmon – diced
2 T	chipotle in adobo sauce – chopped
1/4 C	olive oil
1/2 C	sliced mushrooms
1	onion – diced
1/4 C	Parmesan cheese – grated
	*diced beets, zucchini, broccoli and/or sweet potato

- ❖ Sauté vegetables until soft, about 4 minutes.
- ❖ Add salmon and chipotle, then eggs, cook until eggs are done.

Garnish with Parmesan.

Mediterranean Omelet

Kim~Yacht Misty

1 C	feta or ricotta cheese – crumbled
1/4 C	parsley – chopped
8	eggs
5	scallions – sliced
3 T	olive oil
	mint
	S&P

- ❖ Beat all ingredients together except oil.
- ❖ Heat 2 T oil in frying pan, pour in egg and cook on low for 10 minutes.
- ❖ Drizzle with remaining oil and grill until golden.

Cut into wedges and serve hot or cold.

Eggs and Poultry

Popeye's Scramble

Melissa~Yacht Sula

8	eggs
2 C	spinach – chopped
2 C	mozzarella cheese
1/2 C	bacon – cooked
	S&P

❖ Beat eggs together, stir in spinach and bacon, season to taste.

❖ Pour egg into pan to form either one large omelet or 4 individual ones.

❖ Add cheese when egg is half way through being cooked.

Quiche

Base

1 1/2 C	flour
1/4 C	butter
3 T	oil
3 T	water
1 t	sugar

❖ Rub butter, oil and sugar into flour with finger tips until mixture reaches an even consistency.

❖ Add water and mix to make a dough.

❖ Press mixture into a baking dish.

Filling

4	eggs
1 C	cubed cheese – try Brie or feta
3/4 C	milk
1	onion – sautéed
1	tomato – sliced
	Italian or French herbs – basil, parsley, oregano and thyme
	S&P

any combination: your choice of – asparagus, mushrooms, spinach, green pepper, peas, corn, olives, ham, cooked crab, smoked salmon, sautéed bacon, sun-dried tomatoes and or pesto.

❖ Beat eggs and milk together, add herbs, season to taste.

❖ Arrange remaining ingredients in base, pour in egg mixture and lay tomato slices on top.

❖   Bake 40 minutes until egg has set.
Serve with tossed green salad.

Tex~Mex Huevos Rancheros
Mac~who is boatless

6	eggs
2 C	refried beans
1/2 C	sour cream
1/4 C	salsa
1	green pepper – sliced
	chili sauce
	scallions

❖   Simmer beans, sour cream, salsa and pepper together in large skillet.

❖   Break eggs on top, cover and cook until eggs set.

Serve with grated cheese and hot sauce.

Chicken

Pressure Cooker Times for Chicken

Weight	Chicken Size	Cooking Time	Liquid
3 lb.	chicken - whole	20 minutes	1 C
2 lb.	chicken - pieces	10 minutes	3/4 C

Babootie
Amy~San Francisco

    At home on the water or hosting a dinner party, Amy is a dear friend. She's also a long treasured mentor and during my early sailing career she fueled my thoughts with her wild stories of Sydney-Hobart yacht races and sailing around Cape Horn. While I was sailing in Patagoina I recieved a letter from Amy that included this recipe as she'd recently served it at a dinner party and it had been a great success. This tried and true recipe has since travelled the test of time, like an old friend.

```
  2 lb.  chicken – diced
  1 can  tomatoes – diced
   1 C   dried apricots – diced
  1/2 C  slivered almonds
    2    onions – diced
    2    bananas – sliced
    1    apple – diced
    2    garlic cloves – crushed
   2 T   curry powder
         tomato juice as needed to thin
```

❖ Brown onion, garlic, curry and chicken.

❖ Add remaining ingredients and simmer until cooked.

Serve with rice, chutney and beer!

Caribbean Banana Chicken

```
    4    chicken breasts
  1/2 C  white wine
```

Banana Sauce

```
   1 C   coconut milk
    2    bananas – chunked
    1    onion – diced
    1    lime – juice and zest
    2    garlic cloves – crushed
   1 T   butter
   1 t   ginger – grated
  1/2 t  chili
         S&P
```

❖ Sauté onion, garlic, ginger and chili 3 minutes.

❖ Add bananas and cook 3 minutes.

❖ Stir in coconut milk and lemon juice, simmer 10 minutes, season with S&P.

❖ Sauté chicken breasts 5 minutes, add wine and cook until chicken is nearly done.

❖ Add banana sauce and cook until chicken is done.

Garnish with parsley and serve with rice and vegetables.

Cape Horn Chicken

Vicki Witch

4	chicken breasts
2 C	cooked grain or beans – rice, lima beans, or chickpeas
1 can	stewed tomatoes
1 C	corn
3	potatoes – diced
1	carrot – diced
1	onion – diced
1	celery stalk – diced
2	bay leaves
3	garlic cloves – chopped
2 T	Worcestershire sauce
1/2 t	thyme
	chili of some form
	parsley
	S&P

❖ Sauté chicken, add onions and garlic, stir in remaining ingredients except beans, corn and parsley.

❖ Pressure cook 10 minutes or simmer 20 minutes.

❖ Stir in beans, corn and parsley.

Citrus and Garlic Chicken

4	chicken breasts – cut into large pieces
1 C	white wine
1/3 C	juice – lemon, lime, orange or mixed
10	garlic cloves – peeled
3 T	olive oil
1 T	whole peppercorns
	basil
	S&P

❖ Combine all ingredients.

❖ Pressure cook 10 minutes or simmer covered 45 minutes.

❖ Remove lid and place pot on high heat for 10 minutes to reduce liquid by half.

Garnish with a slice of lemon and serve with potatoes and salad.

Eggs and Poultry

Chicken Cacciatore

4	chicken breasts
2/3 C	white wine
1 can	stewed tomatoes
6	mushrooms – sliced
1	onion – diced
1	green pepper – diced
1	celery stalk – diced
4	garlic cloves – crushed
4 T	olive oil
2	bay leaves
1 t	oregano
1/2 t	thyme
	citrus zest
	chili of some form
	S&P
	parsley

❖ Sauté onion and garlic, add chicken and brown, add remaining ingredients.

❖ Pressure cook 5 minutes or simmer 15 minutes.

Serve on pasta, rice or couscous.

Greek Black Olive Chicken

4	chicken breasts – diced
1 can	stewed tomatoes
1 can	tomato paste
2 C	Greek black olives
2 C	red wine
5	mushrooms – sliced
1	carrot – grated
1	onion – diced
1	zucchini – sliced
3	garlic cloves – crushed
2 T	capers
2 T	Italian herbs

❖ Marinate chicken in red wine.

❖ Sauté chicken, add garlic and onions, cook 3 minutes.

❖ Add remaining ingredients including red wine marinade and pressure cook 7 minutes or simmer 15 minutes.

Serve on rice, pasta or couscous and garnish with Parmesan.

Italian Green Olive Chicken

4 chicken breasts – diced
1/2 C green olives
1/4 C white wine
3 tomatoes
2 garlic cloves – crushed
2 T butter
2 T Italian herbs

❖ Sauté chicken in skillet until brown.

❖ Add butter, garlic and tomatoes, cook 3 minutes.

❖ Mix in wine, olives, and herbs, cook 5 minutes.

Serve on pasta or rice with garden salad.

Jamaican Chicken

4 chicken breasts
1/2 C white wine

Jamaican Sauce

3 oranges – peeled and segmented with membrane removed
1 onion – sliced
3 garlic cloves – crushed
4 T raisins
3 T ginger – sliced
6 allspice berries
2 t oil

❖ Sauté ginger in oil for 3 seconds, add onions, raisins, oranges, garlic and spice, simmer 10 minutes.

❖ Sauté chicken for 5 minutes, add wine and cook until chicken is nearly done.

❖ Purée Jamaican sauce, add to chicken and cook until done.

Serve with wild rice and tossed salad.

Lemon Yogurt Chicken

4 chicken breasts
1 C yogurt
1/4 C onion – diced
1/4 C mayonnaise

4 T	Parmesan cheese
2 T	Dijon mustard
2 T	flour
2 T	lemon juice
	dried oregano
	paprika
	Worcestershire sauce
	Tabasco sauce
	parsley

❖ Place chicken in baking dish, drizzle with lemon juice and sprinkle with Tabasco.

❖ Combine yogurt and flour, add mayonnaise, mustard, Worcestershire sauce, oregano and onions.

❖ Spread yogurt over chicken, sprinkle with Parmesan and paprika.

❖ Bake 30 minutes until cooked.

Garnish with parsley and serve with rice and salad.

Chicken Marabella

Jenny~Yacht Raven

6	bone-in skinless chicken thighs
1 C	chicken broth
1 C	green olives
1 C	prunes
1/4 C	white wine
1/4 C	red wine vinegar
1	onion – diced
4	garlic cloves – minced
2 T	brown sugar
2 T	capers
2 T	dried oregano
2 T	olive oil
1 T	lemon juice

❖ Sauté chicken 2 minutes per side.

❖ Add remaining ingredients and pressure cook 10 minutes or simmer 20 minutes.

Serve on couscous and garnish with parsley.

Mediterranean Chicken

4	chicken breasts

Sauce

1/2 C	sun-dried tomatoes
10	Greek olives
2 T	basil
2 T	parsley
3	garlic cloves
1 T	Dijon mustard
1 T	balsamic vinegar
2 t	capers
2 t	olive oil
	S&P

❖ Purée sauce ingredients together to form a paste, reserve 2 T of paste.

❖ Coat chicken with paste and chill 4 hours.

❖ Mix reserved paste with yogurt or sour cream to serve with chicken.

❖ Grill, bake or sauté chicken.

Serve with wild rice and tossed salad.

Mexican Chicken Chili

1 lb.	chicken – cubed
2 cans	mixed beans
1 can	diced tomatoes
1 C	corn
1 C	coriander leaves – chopped
1/2 C	chicken stock
2	onions – diced
1	red capsicum – diced
1	green capsicum – diced
1	long red chili or 2 chipotle chilies in adobo sauce – chopped
3	cloves garlic – crushed
2 t	ground cumin
2 t	smoked paprika
1 t	sugar
	sour cream
	S&P

❖   Sauté onion, chicken, capsicum, chili and garlic 5 minutes.

❖   Add cumin, paprika and sugar, cook 2 minutes.

❖   Add tomatoes, stock, S&P, simmer 10 minutes.

❖   Add corn and simmer 5 minutes.

Serve garnished with coriander and sour cream along with tortilla chips.

Moroccan Chicken

2	chicken breasts – cubed
1 C	chicken broth
1 can	diced tomatoes
1 can	chickpeas
1/2 C	dried apricots – sliced
1	onion – diced
1/4 C	slivered almonds
1 1/2 T	*Moroccan Spice*
1 T	olive oil
2	garlic cloves – crushed
1 t	fresh minced ginger
	S&P

❖   Sauté chicken, add onion, garlic and ginger, cook 3 minutes.

❖   Add broth, tomatoes, chickpeas, apricots, and *Moroccan Spice.* Pressure cook 7 minutes or simmer 15 minutes.

❖   Add almonds and season to taste.

Serve over couscous and garnish with cilantro.

Tahitian Fruit Chicken

6	chicken pieces
1 C	coconut milk

Marinade

1/2 C	coconut milk
1/2 C	white wine
1	onion – diced
1	lime – juice and zest
2	garlic cloves – crushed
2 t	soy sauce
2 t	honey
1	chili – diced

Tropical Fruit

4	pineapple slices
4	papaya slices
4	mango slices
2	bananas – sliced lengthwise
1 T	butter
1 T	lemon juice
2 t	brown sugar
1 t	cinnamon

❖ Combine marinade ingredients and marinate chicken for at least 2 hours.

❖ Remove chicken from marinade and roast 15 minutes.

❖ Cover chicken with fruit and marinade, bake 15 minutes.

❖ Remove fruit and chicken to serving dish, keep warm.

❖ Pour pan juices into a saucepan and bring to a boil.

❖ Add coconut milk and heat through, serve with chicken and fruit.

Garnish with basil and toasted coconut, serve with rice and salad.

Tandoori Chicken

Roger~Yacht Bella Luna

6	chicken pieces – skin removed
1/2 C	lemon juice
1	onion – diced
3	garlic cloves – crushed
2 T	paprika
1 T	ginger – grated
1 T	curry powder
1 T	*Garam Masala*
1 t	brown sugar
	chili of some form
	S&P

❖ Slice chicken with small cuts to allow spices to penetrate.

❖ Combine remaining ingredients and rub into chicken, marinate overnight.

❖ Roast chicken with marinade in butter, turning to coat with juices, until done, about 20 minutes.

Serve with rice and vegetables.

Coq au Vin Rosé

4 lbs	bone-in, skin-on chicken parts or 8 thighs
2 C	chicken stock
2 C	dry rosé wine
3/4 C	pancetta – cubed
1/4 C	brandy
4	medium potatoes – diced
2	carrots cut into 2-inch pieces
8	pearl onions
8	button mushrooms quartered
4	garlic cloves – crushed
3	spring fresh parsley
2	sprigs fresh thyme
	S&P

❖ Saute pancetta 5 minutes and remove.

❖ In batches brown chicken 5 minutes and remove.

❖ Add onions and garlic, cook 3 minutes.

❖ Add remaining ingredients.

❖ Pressure cook 9 minutes or simmer covered 30 minutes.

Serve garnished with fresh chopped herbs.

Chapter 13

FISH AND
SEAFOOD

Fish

Fish with Mango Sauce

4	fish fillets
1 C	orange juice
1/4 C	coconut cream
1/4 C	coconut – grated
2	mangoes – diced
1	lime – juiced
2 T	honey
2 T	butter
1 T	chutney
1 t	cinnamon
	S&P

* Layer fish in a buttered baking dish, dot with butter and sprinkle with S&P.
* Combine all remaining ingredients except coconut cream and coconut, spread over fish.
* Pour coconut cream over the mango and sprinkle with coconut.
* Bake fish until done.

Serve with rice and salad.

Fish Cakes

My mum Lesley~Yacht Taitoa

cooked fish
mashed potatoes
S&P
*sliced onions, parsley or garlic

* Combine fish and potatoes, season to taste.
* Shape fish into cakes and sauté until brown.

Serve with your favorite dipping sauce.

Thai Fish Cakes

Dorothy~Yacht Adagio

This recipe makes 14 fish patties, enough to feed six people. Extra mixture can be formed into patties and frozen.

```
2 lb.   white fish fillets
   2    onions – diced
   2    eggs
   5    garlic cloves – crushed
 4 T    oil
 4 T    fish sauce
 2 T    ginger – minced
 2 T    hot chili sauce or fresh diced chilies
 2 t    flour
        cilantro
        S&P
```

❖ Heat 2 T of oil in a large skillet, sauté fish, onion, garlic, chili and ginger, stirring and chopping fish until just cooked.

❖ Sprinkle flour over fish and stir in.

❖ Combine remaining ingredients, add fish and mix well.

❖ Heat 1 T oil in skillet, form fish into patties and cook until brown.

Serve with sweet chili sauce or your favorite chutney.

Fish with Enchilada Sauce

```
1 lb.   fish – diced
   1    onion – diced
 2 T    olive oil
```

Sauce
```
 1 C    hot water
 1 C    tomato puree
1 can   green chilies
   1    garlic clove – crushed
 1 t    oregano
1/2 t   cumin
        S&P
```

❖ Combine sauce ingredients and simmer 10 minutes.

❖ Sauté fish and onion in olive oil, add to sauce.

Serve on rice or tortillas. with green salad.

Fish with Italian Tomato Sauce

```
   4    fish fillets
1/3 C   olive oil
```

```
1/3 C   red wine
1 can   stewed tomatoes
    4   scallions – diced
    4   garlic cloves – crushed
  3 T   capers
  1 t   oregano
        parsley
        S&P
```

❖ Sauté scallions and garlic, add wine, tomatoes, oregano and S&P, simmer 5 minutes.

❖ Taste, if sauce is bitter add some sugar, mix in capers.

❖ Add fish and simmer until cooked.

Garnish with parsley and serve with rice, pasta or couscous.

Fish with Orange Sauce

```
    4   fish fillets
```

Orange Sauce

```
1/4 C   mayonnaise
    1   orange – juice and zest
    2   garlic cloves – crushed
  2 T   yogurt
  1 T   chives – diced
```

❖ Combine sauce ingredients.

❖ Sauté fish in half sauce 4 minutes.

❖ Flip fish, add remaining sauce and cook until done.

Garnish with fresh dill and serve with potatoes and salad.

Smoked Fish with Parsley Sauce

This recipe also works well with smoked chicken. Cut smoked chicken into serving size pieces and follow the instructions below.

```
    4 C   smoked fish – flaked
1 1/2 C   milk
    2 T   butter
    2 T   flour
    2 t   parsley – chopped
          S&P
```

❖ Melt butter in pan, stir in flour and cook until frothy.

- ❖ Slowly add milk, stirring until mixture boils and thickens.
- ❖ Add fish, parsley and S&P, heat through.

Serve with potatoes and salad.

Garlic and Lemon Fish

4 salmon steaks

Lemon Sauce

1 lemon – juice and zest
3 T olive oil
3 T butter – melted
2 T garlic – diced
1 t fresh tarragon

- ❖ Combine sauce ingredients.
- ❖ Brush one side of salmon with sauce and BBQ or sauté 4 minutes.
- ❖ Flip fish and brush with remaining mixture, cook 5 minutes more.

Maple and Ginger Glazed Salmon

4 salmon fillets – skin-on
2 T maple syrup
2 T soy sauce
2 t rice vinegar
2 t grated fresh ginger
1 t fresh garlic – grated
olive oil
scallions – sliced
S&P

- ❖ Combine maple syrup, soy sauce, vinegar, ginger, garlic, 3 T olive oil.
- ❖ Brush salmon with olive oil and season with S&P.
- ❖ Sear salmon 4 minutes skin side down, flip, lower heat and cook 5 minutes until slightly opaque in center.
- ❖ Pour glaze over salmon and heat through.

Garnish with scallions.

233

Greek Baked Fish

4	fish fillets
3 C	spinach
1 C	Greek black olives
1	onion – diced
1	lemon – sliced
	basil – chopped
	olive oil
	S&P

❖ Combine olives, basil and onion.

❖ Layer spinach, fish and olives in a baking dish.

❖ Drizzle with olive oil, place a top layer of spinach and garnish with lemon slices.

❖ Bake 20 minutes or until fish is cooked.

Fish with Sun-Dried Tomato Pesto

4	fish fillets

Pesto

1/4 C	olive oil
8	garlic cloves – chopped
4 t	parsley – chopped
3 t	sun-dried tomatoes – chopped
1 t	salt

❖ Mash salt and garlic into a paste, add parsley, tomatoes and olive oil.

❖ Place pesto in fridge and let flavors develop overnight.

❖ Slice fish with length wise slits and spread with pesto.

❖ Barbecue or bake fish until done.

Cajun Blackened Fish

4	fish fillets
2 T	paprika
3 t	cumin
1 t	coriander
1 t	dried oregano
1 t	garlic powder

Fish and Seafood

1 t   onion powder
1 t   salt
1 t   ground black pepper
1/2 t cayenne pepper

❖ Combine seasoning ingredients and rub mixture on both sides of fish fillets.

❖ Add 1 T oil in pan and cook fillets until charred, about 2 minutes.

❖ Flip fish and cook other side until charred and flesh easily flakes.

Serve with a lemon wedge and coleslaw.

Fish Curry

1 lb.   fish – diced
1 T   butter
2   onions – diced
1   green capsicum – diced
1   carrot – diced
4   garlic cloves – crushed
1 lump   ginger – grated
1 T   curry powder
1 can   diced tomatoes
1 can   coconut milk
1 T   almond meal/flax meal
     *optional frozen green peas
     fresh coriander
     yogurt

❖ Sauté veggies in butter, add garlic, ginger and curry.

❖ Add fish and cook 3 minutes, add tomatoes and coconut milk.

❖ Simmer 8 minutes then add almond meal.

Garnish with coriander and serve with yogurt and rice.

Thai Fish Green Curry

4   fish fillets – cubed
2 C   coconut cream
1 C   snow peas or spinach
1 batch   *Green Curry Paste*
2   onions – sliced
2 T   oil
2 T   cilantro or basil

*you can substitute chicken for fish

❖ Sauté onions, add curry and cook 3 minutes.

❖ Add 1 1/2 C coconut cream and simmer 10 minutes.

❖ Add fish, peas and remaining coconut milk, simmer 10 minutes or until fish is cooked.

Garnish with diced basil and serve with rice.

Fish with Thai Dressing

4   fish fillets

Dressing

1/2 C   cilantro
1   red onion – diced
2 T   sherry
1 T   ginger – grated
1 T   soy sauce
2 t   brown sugar
      lemon juice
      chili of some form to taste

❖ Blend dressing ingredients together.

❖ Saute fish 4 minutes.

❖ Flip fish, add dressing and cook until done.

A Slice of Life

We'd raced across the Atlantic from England to the Caribbean on the qualifying race for the 1989 Whitbread Around the World Race – a team of girls on *Maiden*, our refitted 58-foot sloop. Having finished my rigging projects for the day I thought I'd check out the shipyard near English Harbour, Antigua, where we were moored. I entered Carib Marine, a small store with the basics and wandered aimlessly around the shelves. There was nothing in particular I needed it was just interesting to look. As I passed by a set of shelves a flash of color caught my eye. Ah ha! fishing lures.

The lures weren't rigged up, they were just a random selection of parts but they instantly reminded me how great it is to catch fish while out on the ocean. Thinking ahead to our return voyage to England I realized that as we weren't racing back maybe I could fish if conditions were right. I purchased a handful of parts with which I could create some lures and stowed them on board with my rigging kit.

Upon leaving Antigua I went to work assembling a couple of fishing lures although having never fished the Atlantic I wasn't too sure what to expect. After an hour of working with wire, hooks, skirts and resin heads I thought I'd created a couple of lures that might catch a fish so set a lure behind the boat on the nylon cord used for running halyards.

Sailing conditions were easy and our boat speed was around 10 knots with the spinnaker holding nicely in the breeze. Reggae music was playing on the stereo and I settled down in the shade of the mainsail to study my French lessons. Conversation from the on-watch drifted over. I'd never heard talk of fishing from the girls before but now everyone was an expert.

"Don't you need to been doing around five knots to catch a fish?" Louise remarked.

"There's too much line out," announced Nancy.

"Blue lures work better than green," proclaimed Marie-Claude.

"Shall I cook the fish in butter and garlic?" Jo, the optimist, asked.

These comments were all new to me but no one was asking me directly what I thought.

With the fishing lure skipping merrily behind the boat I decided to go below to rest. Later, coming up on deck ready for my watch I looked expectantly behind at our wake for the lure but there was nothing there. Checking along the deck I noticed the tail end of my halyard line still twined about its stick where I'd left is cleated off but the lure end was waving in the breeze. The on-deck conversation marched on as usual; boys, music, shore side activities but now no words of fishing.

The line had been sliced. The lure had hooked a fish alright but the on-watch had decided that fresh fish was not worth blood and death on the aft deck.

Beans anyone?

Indian Fish Tikka

4	fish fillets, you may also use chicken
1/2 C	yogurt
1/2 C	sweet chili sauce

```
  1   onion – diced
  1   lime – juice and zest
1 T   ginger – grated
2 t   coriander
2 t   soy sauce
1 t   honey
1 t   cumin
  2   garlic cloves – crushed
1/2 T ground pepper
      salt
```

❖ Combine all ingredients and marinate fish 4 hours.

❖ Barbecue, grill or sear fish in hot dry frying pan.

Garnish with lemon slices and cilantro, serve with rice and salad.

Fish with Japanese Miso Dressing

```
  4   fish fillets, preferably salmon
4 T   miso
2 T   sherry
1 T   olive oil
1 T   ginger – grated
1 t   sugar
     *2 T sesame seeds – toasted
```

❖ In a saucepan heat miso, sugar, sherry, oil and ginger.

❖ Brush fish with dressing and barbecue, grill or sauté until cooked.

Garnish with sesame seeds and serve with tossed salad and rice.

Shellfish

Clam Sauce

Cara~M/V St Elias

```
1 can clams – if using fresh clams or mussels add
            more wine and simmer until clams open
  6 T shallots – diced
  4 T olive oil
  4 T butter
  3 T white wine
    6 garlic cloves – chopped
  2 t lemon juice
```

*sun-dried tomatoes
*parsley, basil or tarragon

❖ Sauté garlic and shallots in oil and butter until soft.

❖ Add clam juice, wine and lemon juice, simmer 5 minutes.

❖ Add calms and heat through.

Serve with pasta or rice and salad.

Mussels Marinière

24 mussels – large
1 onion – diced
1/2 C water
1/2 C white wine
2 T parsley – chopped
*bacon – diced

❖ Bring onions, water, wine and parsley to a boil.

❖ Add mussels and simmer until they open, about 3 minutes.

Serve with crusty garlic bread.

Italian Mussels

Antonio~Yacht Tuiga

24 mussels – large

Sauce

1 can stewed tomatoes
1 can tomato paste
1/2 C white wine
1 onion – diced
2 T olive oil
1 T mustard
1 T parsley
2 garlic cloves – crushed
2 t flour

❖ Sauté onion, add remaining sauce ingredients and bring to a boil.

❖ Add mussels and remove as they open.

Serve with crusty herbed bread.

Fish and Seafood

Casino Oysters

6	oysters – per person, shucked
1/2 C	celery – diced
1/4 C	onion – diced
1/4 C	green pepper – diced
8	bacon strips – chopped
2 T	Worcestershire sauce
2 t	lemon juice
	hot sauce

❖ Sauté celery, onion, green pepper and bacon.

❖ Add Worcestershire sauce, hot sauce and lemon juice.

❖ Place oysters in half shell on oven tray and sprinkle with mixture.

❖ Bake 10 minutes at 400°F, or grill 10 minutes until oysters are heated through.

Serve from the shells.

Scallops in Lime

1/2 lb.	scallops
2 T	cilantro – chopped
2 T	olive oil
1 T	soy sauce
2	garlic cloves – crushed
1 t	lime juice
	pepper

❖ Heat olive oil in skillet until almost smoking.

❖ Add soy sauce and scallops, cook until browned, about 2 minutes.

❖ Flip scallops and cook until opaque, about 2 minutes.

❖ Add cilantro, garlic and lime juice, season with pepper.

Italian Fish Stew

1 lb.	fish
1 lb.	shrimp – unpeeled
1/2 lb.	calamari – cleaned and sliced
1/2 lb.	scallops
12	baby clams or cockles
12	mussels
3 C	fresh basil leaves – chopped

1 can   Italian plum tomatoes
2   onions – diced
1/4 C   white wine
1/4 C   olive oil
3   garlic cloves – crushed
1/2 t   chili flakes
S&P

- ❖ Sauté onions and garlic.
- ❖ Add pepper flakes, tomatoes and wine, simmer 5 minutes.
- ❖ Add the seafood in layers depending on individual cooking time, place squid on the bottom and firm fish next, top with scallops, shrimp, and clams last.
- ❖ Simmer until seafood is cooked, about 15 minutes.
- ❖ Add basil and season to taste.

Serve with toasted bread or couscous.

West Coast Seafood Stew

1/2 lb.   white fish – cubed
25   shrimp – shelled
20   mussels
1 can   tomatoes
1 can   clam juice
1/2 C   dry white wine
2   onions – diced
1   yellow pepper – diced
5   garlic cloves – crushed
3 T   tomato paste
3 T   parsley – chopped
2 T   flour
1 t   *Italian Herbs*
1/4 t   chili flakes
S&P

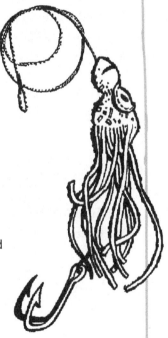

- ❖ Combine fish, shrimp, garlic and olive oil.
- ❖ Sauté onion and bell pepper until tender, stir in flour and tomato paste.
- ❖ Add clam juice and cook 3 minutes.
- ❖ Stir in tomatoes, herbs, chili flakes and S&P, simmer 8 minutes.
- ❖ Meanwhile bring wine to a boil, add mussels and steam covered until they open.

- ❖ Add shrimp and fish to sauce, simmer 5 minutes.
- ❖ Add mussels along with cooking liquid and simmer until all ingredients are cooked.

Sprinkle with parsley and serve with crusty bread and garden salad.

Calamari and Octopus

Preparing Fresh Calamari

- ❖ Carefully **pull calamari apart** by twisting and tugging head and tentacles away from the body.
- ❖ **Remove** the cuttlebone.
- ❖ **Pull off the skin** membrane covering the body and throw away.
- ❖ **Turn the calamari inside out,** rinse, and slice the body into rings.
- ❖ **Slice tentacles from the head** below the eyes and pull out the beak from the center.
- ❖ **Throw away** everything except the tentacles.
- ❖ **Slice tentacles** into rings.

Preparing Fresh Octopus

- ❖ **Turn head upside down** and sever the muscles that hold the viscera.
- ❖ **Turn head inside** out and remove dark ink sacs.
- ❖ **Beat octopus against the rocks** with a large wooden spoon or smooth piece of wood for 10 minutes, or whack the carcass against a large rock about 75 times.
- ❖ Every so often stop and **scrub the carcass** until it foams, rinse in the ocean, repeat until it stops foaming.

Marinated Giant Clam, Calamari or Octopus

1	giant clam, or equivalent calamari or octopus strips
1	onion – diced
1/4 C	soy sauce
1 T	lime juice
2	garlic cloves – crushed

2 chilies – chopped
1 t ginger – grated

❖ Boil clam meat 10 minutes.

❖ Add clam to remaining ingredients and marinate 2 hours.

❖ Cover and simmer on low 30 minutes, sirring occasionally.

Italian Calamari

1 lb. squid – sliced into rings
2 C spinach
1 C white wine
1/2 C mushrooms
1/2 C parsley – chopped
2 tomatoes
1 onion – diced
1 celery stalk – diced
1 T olive oil
1 garlic clove – crushed
chili of some form

❖ Sauté onion, garlic, chili and celery, add squid and sauté 10 minutes.

❖ Add remaining ingredients and pressure cook 15 minutes or simmer 1 hour.

Serve with crusty herb bread.

Provençal Octopus

2 lb. octopus – cleaned and tenderized
5 C red wine
2 C tomatoes – diced
1 onion – diced
2 T olive oil
1 T sugar
3 garlic cloves – chopped
3 parsley sprigs
thyme
S&P

❖ Sauté onion and octopus, add tomatoes, wine and enough water to cover octopus.

❖ Add remaining ingredients and pressure cook 20 minutes or simmer

1 hour until tender.

Serve hot or cold garnished with parsley.

Fijian Curried Octopus

2 lb.	octopus – cooked and sliced
2 C	coconut cream
1	onion – diced
1	lemon – juice and zest
2	garlic cloves – crushed
2 T	*Curry Paste*
2 t	tomato paste
1 t	ginger – grated
1 t	chilies – chopped
3 T	basil
	S&P
	*can replace octopus with shrimp

❖ Sauté onion, add garlic, ginger, chili and curry.

❖ Add tomato paste, lemon and octopus, simmer 10 minutes.

❖ Stir in coconut cream, basil and S&P, heat through.

Serve on rice with mango salsa.

Shrimp and Prawns

Boiled Shrimp

❖ Bring a pot of salt water, or 2 T salt added to fresh water to a boil.

❖ Add shrimp and boil for 3-5 minutes until shrimp turn pink, depending on the size.

❖ Do not over cook or the shrimp will be rubbery.

❖ Cool, pinch off head and tail, peel off shell.

❖ Remove dark entail tract from the back with a sharp knife, rinse.

Serve with a dip or in a salad.

Skillet Shrimp

❖ Heat skillet over medium-high and add butter or oil.

❖ Add seasoned or marinated shrimp, cook 3-6 minutes until shrimp are opaque.

Shrimps in White Wine

Jenn~Yacht Ocean Light II

2 lb.	raw shrimp
1/2 C	white wine
1/4 C	olive oil
6	garlic cloves – chopped
3	bay leaves
1 t	oregano
1 t	rosemary
	ground pepper

❖ Sauté shrimps in olive oil and herbs for 3 minutes.

❖ Reduce heat, add wine and gently cook until shrimp are done, about 3 minutes.

Serve with a dip or in a salad.

Shrimp Benedict

Theresa~Yacht Vega

1 lb.	cooked shrimp
1/2 C	cream cheese
1/2 C	mozzarella or Parmesan – grated
1/4 C	milk
1	onion – diced
1	red pepper – diced
1	zucchini – sliced
5	asparagus stalks – sliced
2 T	butter

❖ Sauté onion, pepper, zucchini and asparagus, 3 minutes.

❖ Stir in cream cheese, add cheese and milk, mix to make a sauce.

❖ Add shrimp and heat through.

Serve with pasta, rice or toasted sour dough bread.

Bahamian Shrimp

1 1/2 lb.	raw shrimp
1	green pepper – sliced
1	tomato – diced
1/2 C	cream
1/2 C	shredded coconut

<pre>
1/3 C   scallions – sliced
  4 T   butter
  2 T   rum
  1 T   Dijon mustard
        ground black pepper
</pre>

- ❖ Sauté scallions and green pepper in butter.
- ❖ Add shrimp and black pepper, cook until shrimp turn pink.
- ❖ Combine cream, mustard, coconut and tomato, add to shrimp and heat.

To serve, flambé shrimp with rum and serve with rice with salad.

Lemon Prawns

<pre>
1 lb.   raw prawns
  6 T   butter
    1   scallion – diced
    5   garlic cloves – crushed
  2 T   lemon juice
  1 T   olive oil
        lemon zest
        chili of some form
        parsley
        salt
</pre>

- ❖ Melt butter, add scallion, oil, garlic and lemon juice, cook until bubbly.
- ❖ Add prawns and cook, stirring, until prawns turn pink.
- ❖ Stir in parsley, lemon zest and chili.

Serve warm garnished with lemon wedges.

Shrimp in Cream Sauce

Dee~M/V Penguin

<pre>
1 lb.   shrimp or scallops
1 can   crushed tomatoes
1/2 C   white wine
1/2 C   cream
    8   shallots – diced
    8   scallions – sliced
  3 T   olive oil
</pre>

3 T   butter
2 T   sugar
2 T   basil – chopped
2   garlic cloves – crushed
2 t   tarragon
1/2 t thyme

- ❖ Sauté shrimp in oil and butter, set aside.
- ❖ Sauté herbs and garlic, add tomatoes and wine, cook on high heat until it thickens, about 4 minutes.
- ❖ Add cream and sugar, simmer 30 seconds.
- ❖ Add shrimp and season with S&P.
- ❖ Pour over pasta or rice.

Garnish with avocado and serve with salad.

Shrimp Curry

Jenn~Yacht Ocean Light II

1 lb.   shrimp – cooked
1 C   sour cream
1/2 C chicken broth
3   tomatoes – diced
1   avocado – diced
1   onion – diced
3 T   butter
3 T   flour
2 T   lemon juice
1/2 T curry

- ❖ Toss tomatoes and avocado with lemon juice.
- ❖ Melt butter, add curry and onion, sauté 3 minutes.
- ❖ Stir in flour and broth and bring to a boil.
- ❖ Add sour cream, fold in tomatoes and shrimp.

Serve with rice and green salad.

Cilantro Lime Shrimp

2 lb   shrimp – peeled
1 bunch cilantro – chopped
2   garlic cloves – minced

1   lime juiced
3 T   olive oil
1/2 t   salt
1 pinch   chili flakes

❖ Combine cilantro, lime, garlic, 2 T olive oil, salt, and chili. Reserve 1 T marinade.

❖ Add shrimp to remaining marinade and let sit 5 minutes.

❖ Sauté shrimp in olive oil 2-3 minutes each side or until cooked. *Serve with reserved marinade.*

The Trade Off

O cassionally it's possible to trade for local foods and gleaning a little knowledge on exactly what it is you're trading for ensures it doesn't go to waste.

Sailing through the labyrinth of Patagonia's canals we'd arrived in Puerto Eden, an isolated hamlet of 200 people south of the English Narrows. Built on a soggy island with no road access or streets just a meandering wooden boardwalk wrapping around the waterfront it appeared a bustling little place even on a rainy day.

We'd been told that the shellfish in Chile had red tide poisoning but the locals apparently ignore this warnings as I viewed piles of shells littering the foreshore and smoke wafting from small smoke houses that lined the boardwalk. The township survives on the seafood industry sending its produce to the larger towns of Puerto Mont in the north and Punta Arenas in the south.

As soon as the anchor settled a bright yellow 20-foot boat approached. A boy of about 12 years was standing up in the middle of the craft while rowing with an immensely long set of oars. In the bottom of his boat a large crab pot held various sizes of centolla crab that were eagerly crawling on top of one another. He motioned to his mouth that he wanted food and with our limited Spanish we understood that he was asking for flour and rice. I invited him on board and offered him two bags of rice and stated we were out of flour. When I opened our can locker he gasped in amazement so I gestured for him to choose some cans of his liking. As a thank you for his effort to bring us the crab I also gave him an old cap as I wished him farewell.

It was Barry's turn to cook and he proceeded to boil up the two large buckets of crabs. As the rain steadily poured down we had a grand feast around the dinning table cracking crab and recounting sailing stories although we certainly learned a lot about small centolla crab as it took us most evening to extract the meat from their spiky legs. Our expedition crew decided that next time we were offered crab we'd only accept the Big Ones!

The following day we visited the hamlet's store and noticing how bare the shelves were we then understood the young boy's wonder when he surveyed our provisions.

Crab and Lobster

Tips on Cooking Crab or Lobster

❖ Bring a large pot of **salt water** to a boil.

❖ Add crab or lobster and simmer for about 8 **minutes per pound**.

❖ Immerse cooked crab or lobster in **cold water** to arrest the cooking process.

Let cool then eat.

Crab with Black Bean Sauce

Jenn~Yacht Ocean Light II

Jenn serves fresh Dungeness crab with *Black Bean Sauce* as a dip for a healthier alternative to butter or mayonnaise.
A side dish of basmati rice completes the meal.

Stretch Lobster

Fran~Yacht Aka

Fran says she's afraid you have to use a can of cream of something in this dish but she claims that at least the lobster, fish etc. is fresh unless ....you cheat and use canned. Stretch lobster goes a long way and it's easy to increase the amount at the last minute.

1 C   cooked lobster, crab, shrimp or chicken
1 can   cream of something soup

1 can   mild chili
1 T   fresh parsley, dried herbs, or whatever you
     can get your hands on
1 t   paprika
    tarragon to taste – foo-foo according to Fran
    but it does makes the dish.

❖   Heat all ingredients together.

Serve over rice.

Chapter 14
BEEF,
LAMB AND
PORK

Pressure Cooking Times for Meat

Weight	Meat	Time	Liquid
2 lb.	beef – cubed	10 minutes	1 C
3 lb.	beef – pot roast	35 minutes	1 1/2 C
2 lb.	lamb – cubed	10 minutes	1 C
3 lb.	lamb – leg	35 minutes	1 1/2 C
2 lb.	pork – cubed	10 minutes	1 C
2 lb.	pork – ribs	20 minutes	1 1/2 C
3 lb.	pork – leg	40 minutes	1 1/2 C

Cuban Picadillo

1 lb.	ground beef
1	onion – diced
1 small	can tomato paste
1/2 C	raisins
1/2 C	dry white wine
1/3 C	olives or capers
5	garlic cloves – minced
1	green bell pepper – diced
1	red bell pepper – diced
1 t	cumin
1 t	oregano
1 t	smoked paprika
2	bay leaves

❖ Brown beef 10 minutes.

❖ Add onion and garlic, cook 2 minutes.

❖ Add remaining ingredients, cover and simmer 10 minutes.

Serve with rice and beans.

Curried Beef

Carol~Yacht Elyxir

1 lb.	beef – cubed
1 C	tomatoes – diced
1/2 C	water
1/2 C	peas
1	zucchini – sliced
1	carrot – sliced
1	onion – diced

Beef, Lamb and Pork

```
4 T    yogurt
3 T    butter
  2    garlic cloves – crushed
  2 t  Curry Paste
  1    cinnamon stick
       chili of some form
```

❖ Sauté onions, chili and garlic with curry, add beef and brown.

❖ Add tomatoes, water, cinnamon and vegetables.

❖ Pressure cook 10 minutes or simmer 45 minutes.

❖ Add yogurt just before serving.

Serve on rice with Yogurt Dressing.

Provençal Beef Stew

```
   2 lb.    beef – cubed
     3 C    red wine
   1 can    stewed tomatoes
     1 C    mushrooms – halved
   1/2 C    olives
       5    pickling onions – diced
       4    bacon strips – diced
       2    carrots – diced
       4    garlic cloves – crushed
     1 T    orange zest
     1 t    thyme
   1/4 t    rosemary
            S&P
            parsley – sprinkled on at end of cooking
```

❖ Marinate beef in wine overnight.

❖ Remove meat from marinade and brown with bacon in olive oil.

❖ Add remaining ingredients including wine and pressure cook 20 minutes or simmer 90 minutes.

Serve with rosemary new potatoes.

Sun~Dried Tomato Meat Burgundy

```
   3 lb.    beef or lamb roast
   1 can    stewed tomatoes
     1 C    burgundy wine
```

Beef, Lamb and Pork

```
1/2 C   sun-dried tomatoes
    2   carrots – diced
    2   celery stalks – diced
    1   onion – diced
    1   green pepper – diced
    3   garlic cloves – crushed
  2 T   tomato paste
  3 t   olive oil
1/2 t   thyme
        S&P
```

Pressure Cooker Instructions

❖ Brown beef on all sides, add remaining ingredients and pressure cook 20 minutes.

Oven Instructions

❖ Place all ingredients inside an oven roasting bag.

❖ Place bag on roasting dish, make slits in the top of the bag

❖ Roast 3 hours at 325°F.

Serve beef sliced with cooking ingredients and new potatoes.

Russian Beef Stroganoff

Ivana's Cafe

```
1 lb.   fillet beef – sliced into strips
  2 C   mushrooms – sliced
3/4 C   sour cream
1/4 C   white wine
    1   onion – sliced
    2   garlic cloves – crushed
  2 T   butter
  2 t   fresh tarragon
  1 T   lemon juice
1/8 t   nutmeg
        S&P
```

❖ Sauté onion and mushrooms, add meat and brown.

❖ Add remaining ingredients and simmer until beef is cooked, about 5 minutes.

Garnish with parsley and serve with egg noodles, potatoes or rice.

Beef, Lamb and Pork

Thai Beef Red Curry

Pat~Yacht Wind Haven

1 lb.	beef fillet – sliced into strips
3 C	coconut milk
1 batch	*Thai Red Curry*
1 T	fish sauce
2	lime leaves – sliced
2 t	oil
1 t	brown sugar
1	chili – minced

❖ Sauté onion, add red curry and cook 3 minutes.

❖ Add beef and brown 3 minutes.

❖ Add 2 C coconut milk and simmer until beef is cooked.

❖ Add remaining ingredients and heat through.

Garnish with basil and serve with rice.

Veal and Orange Stew

Jim~M/V Lone Ranger

2 lb.	veal – cubed
1 C	chicken broth
1 C	white wine
8	mushrooms – quartered
5	bacon rashers – sliced
3	carrots – sliced
2	onions – diced
1	orange – juice and zest
3 T	flour
2 T	vinegar
2	garlic cloves
	S&P

❖ Marinate veal in wine and garlic.

❖ Remove veal from marinade and brown with bacon and onions, stir in flour.

❖ Add remaining ingredients including marinade.

❖ Pressure cook 10 minutes or simmer 1 hour.

Garnish with parsley and orange slices and serve with new potatoes.

Beef, Lamb and Pork

Lamb and Apricot Stew

1 lb.	lamb – cubed
2	eggplants – cubed and purged
1 C	dates – pitted
1 C	chickpeas – soaked
1/2 C	dried apricots – diced
1/2 C	blanched almonds – toasted
1	onion – diced
1 t	cinnamon
1 t	sesame seeds – toasted
1/2 t	allspice
	S&P

❖ Sauté onions, add lamb and cook until brown.

❖ Add chickpeas, cover with water and bring to a boil.

❖ Add spices and pressure cook 10 minutes or simmer 30 minutes.

❖ Add remaining ingredients.

❖ Pressure cook 5 minutes or simmer 20 minutes.

Garnish with almonds and sesame seeds, serve with rice or couscous.

Lamb and Vegetable Stew

1 lb.	lamb fillet – cubed
1 can	tomato puree
1 can	tomato paste
1/2 C	water
1/2 C	raisins
2	carrots – diced
1	onion – diced
2	celery stalks – diced
2	garlic cloves – crushed
2 T	oil
	chili powder to taste
	S&P

❖ Sauté onion, chili and lamb until brown.

❖ Add carrots and celery, cook 5 minutes.

❖ Add tomato puree, tomato paste, water, raisins and S&P.

❖ Pressure cook 10 minutes or simmer 25 minutes.

Serve on couscous, rice or with potatoes.

Greek Lamb Souvlaki

1 lb.	lamb – cubed
1/4 C	lemon juice
3	garlic cloves – crushed
1 T	olive oil
2 t	oregano

❖ Kebab meat and marinate in remaining ingredients 4 hours.

❖ Barbecue or grill kebabs until lamb is done.

Serve with Greek salad.

Greek Moussaka

3 C	ground lamb
2	eggplants – sliced and purged
1 C	yogurt
1/3 C	wine
1/3 C	parsley – chopped
1/4 C	olive oil
1/4 C	Parmesan cheese – grated
1 can	tomato paste
4	tomatoes – diced
2	onions – diced
2	garlic cloves – crushed
2	egg yolks
1 T	flour
1/2 t	cinnamon, nutmeg and paprika
	S&P

❖ Sauté onion, garlic and lamb.

❖ Stir in tomato paste, tomatoes, parsley, wine and spices, simmer 15 minutes.

❖ Sauté eggplant until soft and light brown.

❖ Place 1/3 of eggplant in baking dish, spread with half lamb mixture.

❖ Repeat layers and top with eggplant.

❖ Combine egg yolks, flour and yogurt, pour over eggplant and top with Parmesan.

❖ Bake 40 minutes at 350°F until golden.

Serve with salad.

Beef, Lamb and Pork

Moroccan Lamb

1 lb.	lamb fillet – cubed
1 can	chickpeas
1 C	raisins, prunes or dates
1	apple – diced or dried apricots
1	onion – diced
3	garlic cloves – crushed
2 T	ground pepper
2 T	honey
2 T	oil
3 t	ginger – grated
2 t	cinnamon
1 t	allspice
	parsley

❖ Combine lamb, chickpeas, apple, onion, garlic, pepper, oil and ginger, add water to cover.

❖ Pressure cook 10 minutes or simmer 30 minutes.

❖ Add raisins, cinnamon, and honey, simmer 10 minutes.

Garnish with toasted almonds and parsley. Serve over couscous.

Mexican Orange Pork

Carol~Yacht Elyxir

This recipe is traditionally made with bitter oranges (*naranjas agrias*). If bitter oranges are unattainable it is possible to achieve the same citrus tartness with a blend of orange and lime juice.

1 lb.	pork – cubed
1/2 C	water
1/4 C	bitter orange juice
1/4 C	milk
1	onion – diced
3	garlic cloves – crushed
1 T	oil
1 T	lime juice
1 t	oregano

❖ Combine garlic, pork and water, simmer until the water has evaporated, about 1 1/2 hours or pressure cook 20 minutes.

❖ Add milk and orange juice, simmer uncovered until meat is brown and the liquid has evaporated, season to taste.

Serve hot with fresh tortillas and salsa.

Orange Marmalade Pork

1 lb.	pork – thinly sliced
3	potatoes – cooked and cubed
1 C	green beans
1 C	cherry tomatoes – halved
1/4 C	orange marmalade
3 T	Dijon mustard
2 T	basil – diced
1 T	olive oil

❖ Sauté pork until cooked. Add potatoes, tomatoes and green beans, sauté 3 minutes.

❖ Add marmalade and mustard, serve when marmalade is melted.

Mexican Chili Pork

1 lb.	pork – cubed
3/4 C	water
1	onion – diced
2	garlic cloves – minced
2	chilies – minced
1 t each	anise seed, oregano and cumin
1	stick cinnamon
1	bay leaf – crumbled

❖ Combine pork, onion and 1/2 C water, pressure cook 15 minutes or simmer 45 minutes.

❖ Simmer remaining ingredients in a small pan for 10 minutes, remove cinnamon stick.

❖ Add chili sauce to pork and simmer until thick.

Serve warm with fresh tortillas or tacos, and salsa.

Elephant

Fran from the yacht *Aka* is a friend I've never met. She contributed many practical recipes to this book and I included her accompanying note as it captures the spirit of food and cruising.

Thanks for inviting us to be a part of your adventure. Cooking is an adventure – just ask my husband. I've only poisoned him once; he simply got a little sick. We've been cruising since 1979 so we're on a pretty tight budget. Part of cruising for me is going to the markets and checking out what the locals eat. As it's all locally grown it's the cheapest place in town, saving me more money that I can then spend on fabric. I love getting deals and love to eat; I'll experiment with something forever. I know I've a winner when my husband says, "You guys have gotta come over to our boat; Francene makes a mean Mexican."

I look forward to your book. I'm a cookbook addict and my husband says that's why our waterline is down. He lies; it's his windsurfer.

Elephant Stew is my favorite recipe from Fran's collection and although I've never had the opportunity to prepare it myself it lends itself to a whimsical side of cooking. There's times when I find myself over my head with food and I feel like I'm Alice in Wonderland trying to decide what cake to eat. I hope this recipe gives you food for thought and if your meal planning ever becomes overwhelming take a deep breath and consider making it.

Elephant Stew

l large	elephant
	brown gravy
2	rabbits
	S&P

❖ Cut elephant into bite size pieces – this should take about 2 months.

❖ Add brown gravy to cover and season to taste.

❖ Cook over a kerosene fire for about 4 weeks at 450°F.

Makes 2,800 servings. If more guests are expected add 2 rabbits. However do so only if necessary as most people don't like hare in their stew.

Chapter 15

BREAD,
CAKES AND
COOKIES

Breads, Cakes and Cookies

Breads

Speedy Wraps

Fran~Yacht Aka

Fran claims that these wraps can be made anywhere in the world "Cheap and easy they're perfect when you run out of bread and crackers or just feel like a change. They don't require an oven as they're made in a frying pan so it's a good recipe to share with your local friends. You can wrap anything inside especially leftovers. We eat these faster than I can make them. I know you've seen recipes like this before but the hot water and baking powder makes all the difference, they'll melt in your mouth. The biggest secret is using a heavy rolling pin to roll them out as thin as possible."

```
    4 C   flour
1 1/4 C   hot water
  1/2 C   oil
    2 t   baking powder
    2 t   salt
```

❖ Sift flour, add remaining dry ingredients and mix well.

❖ Add oil and water, knead together to make a dough. Let mixture rest 15 minutes.

❖ Make dough into small balls, about walnut-shell size, roll them out as thin as possible on a floured area using a heavy rolling pin, sprinkle flour as you roll.

❖ Lay wraps on wax paper or foil, overlapping them a little.

❖ Cook each wrap in a lightly oiled pan, medium heat, when brown specks appear, flip and cook the other side.

Lesley's Crêpes

Lesley~Yacht Taitoa

```
1 C   flour
1 C   milk
  1   egg
      water
```

❖ Combine flour, milk and egg, add enough water or milk to make a runny mixture.

❖ Heat and lightly grease a frying pan with butter, pour in 1/4 C batter and roll mixture around to coat the bottom.

Bread, Cakes and Cookies

- ❖ Free edges with a spatula and flip when bubbles appear, cook other side.
- ❖ Repeat the process, greasing the pan with butter before each crêpe. *Serve hot off the pan.*

Beer Flatbread

3 C	flour
3/4 C	wheat beer
3/4 C	Greek yogurt
1 t	olive oil
1 t	baking soda
1/2 t	baking powder
pinch	salt

- ❖ Combine flour, baking soda, baking powder and salt.
- ❖ Stir in beer, yogurt and oil until dough comes together, knead 5 minutes.
- ❖ Shape into 8 balls and let rise 15 minutes.
- ❖ Press balls into 6-inch disks and cook in oiled skillet until brown, 3 minutes per side.

Flatbread

1 1/2 C	flour
1 1/2	semolina flour
1 1/2 C	warm water, more if needed
1 packet (1/4 ounce)	active dry yeast
pinch	salt
	olive oil
	coarse sea salt

- ❖ Combine flours, water, yeast and salt to form a dough.
- ❖ Divide dough into quarters, cover and let rest 1 hour.
- ❖ Using a rolling pin and lightly floured surface, roll each dough-quarter into paper-thins rounds.
- ❖ Cook in a lightly oiled skillet for 2 minutes each side or until crispy and brown.
- ❖ Brush lightly with olive oil and sprinkle with coarse salt.

Tips on Bread Making

❖ **Water temperature** should be lukewarm, 80°F, if the water is too warm, it will kill the yeast and the bread won't rise.

❖ If **bread collapses** after rising there may be too much water or the weather is warm and humid.

❖ **Let bread rise**, covered with a dishtowel, in a draft-free place.

❖ If **bread doesn't rise** maybe you forgot the yeast, the water was too hot or the bread was in a draft.

❖ To test if **bread is cooked** knock on the top, a hollow sound tells that it's done.

Beer Bread

Robin~Yacht Chinook

2 3/4 C	self-rising flour
1 can	beer
1 T	sugar
5 t	baking powder
pinch	salt
1/2 t	dried herbs

❖ Mix dry ingredients together and stir in beer.

❖ Bake 40 minutes at 355°F until done.

Italian Bread

1 1/2 C	flour
3/4 C	warm water
12	black olives – sliced
8	sun-dried tomatoes – sliced
5 T	olive oil
1 T	yeast
2	rosemary sprigs
2 t	coarse salt

❖ Combine flour, yeast, salt, tomatoes and half the olives.

❖ Add water and 3 T olive oil, mix to a soft dough and knead until smooth and elastic.

❖ Press dough into a 10" round, place on an oiled baking tray and prick with a fork.

❖ Cover with plastic wrap and let rise until double in size.

❖ Press in remaining olives and rosemary, drizzle with olive oil.

❖ Bake 20 minutes until golden.

Oatmeal Bread

Carol~Yacht Elyxir

1 C   boiling water
1 C   warm water
1 C   oats
1 C   white flour
1 C   whole wheat flour
2 T   oil
2 T   honey
2 T   yeast
2 T   sesame seeds
1 T   salt

❖ Combine boiling water, oats, oil, honey and seeds, let cool.

❖ Add warm water, flours, yeast and salt.

❖ Mix well and knead, let rise until double in size, punch down and knead again.

❖ Shape into loaf, place in bread pan and let rise 30 minutes.

❖ Bake 45 minutes until done.

Pressure Cooker Bread

Kristin~Yacht Maiden

Our replacement cook on the first leg of the Whitbread race was Kristen as Jo had broken her arm while we were on the Fastnet Race. Kristen, a professional cook, not only amazed us with great meals utilizing our freeze-dried food but also totally astounded us with delectable fresh bread when we were halfway across the Atlantic.

"Wow!" exclaimed Jeni.

On the right margin, vertical text: Bread, Cakes and Cookies

"This is the best cheese sandwich I've had all month, in fact it's the only cheese sandwich I've had all month."

When it comes to hot bread on a boat there's a basic rule – it can only be eaten once, so best get on with it.

4 C	flour
1 C	warm water
1 T	yeast
1 t	sugar
1 t	salt

❖ Dissolve sugar and yeast in warm water until it foams.

❖ Add salt to flour then yeast, knead dough for 5 minutes.

❖ Let rise 30 minutes. Punch down and knead 7 minutes.

❖ Place dough in a greased floured cake pan that fits inside pressure cooker, let rise again 15 minutes.

❖ Place lid on pressure cooker with no weight and heat 5 minutes.

❖ Place a small empty can, such as tuna, in warm pressure cooker to act as a spacer, add bread in it's pan.

❖ Bake 8 minutes on high heat, 20 minutes on half heat, and 15 minutes on low.

Salt Water Bread

4 C	flour
1 1/2 C	warm salt water
1 T	yeast
1 T	sugar

❖ Dissolve yeast and sugar in salt water.

❖ Mix in flour and knead into a soft dough.

❖ Let rise until double in size, punch down and knead again.

❖ Shape into loaf, place in bread pan and let rise another 30 minutes.

❖ Bake 45 minutes until done.

Wholemeal Bread

2 1/4 C	warm water
1 1/2 C	white flour
1 1/3 C	whole wheat flour
3/4 C	wheat germ

```
4 T    honey
3 T    oil or butter
3 T    yeast
2 t    salt
```

❖ Combine flours, wheat germ, yeast and salt.

❖ Add water, oil and honey, knead well, let rise until double in size.

❖ Punch down, place in a pan and bake until done.

Cornbread

```
  2 C    cornmeal
1 1/2 C  milk
  1      egg
  3 T    oil
  4 t    baking powder
  1 t    salt
         *sugar
```

❖ Place baking dish in oven and preheat oven to 450°F.

❖ When oven reaches temperature, remove dish and swirl oil around the inside, return to oven.

❖ Combine cornmeal, baking powder and salt.

❖ Beat milk and egg together, pour into cornmeal mixture.

❖ Mix quickly and pour batter into heated dish.

❖ Bake until golden, about 20 minutes.

Golden Cornbread

```
  1 C    cornmeal
  1 C    flour
1/2 C    vanilla soy milk
1/2 C    sweetcorn kernels
1/4 C    vegetable oil
1/4 C    applesauce
  2 T    maple syrup
  1 T    flaxseed combined with 3 T water
  1 T    baking powder
  1 t    vanilla extract
1/2 t    salt
```

❖ Combine dry ingredients.

❖ Combine wet ingredients until foamy.

❖ Combine wet ingredients with dry ingredients.

❖ Bake in greased 9x13 pan or 12-cup muffin pan 30 minutes (20 minutes for muffins) at 350°F.

Rasta Cornbread

1 C	cornmeal
1/2 C	milk
1/4 C	flour
1	egg – lightly beaten
2 T	scallions – sliced
2 T	red pepper – diced
2 T	green pepper – diced
4 t	butter – melted
1 t	baking powder
1 t	honey
pinch	salt

❖ Mix dry ingredients together.

❖ Stir in wet ingredients, add scallions and peppers.

❖ Bake 20 minutes in a greased dish at 425°F.

Bread Rolls

2 C	whole wheat flour
2 C	white flour
1 1/2 C	milk
2 T	baking powder
2 T	oil
1	egg

❖ Combine flours and baking powder.

❖ Stir in milk, egg and oil to make a sticky dough.

❖ Form into rolls and bake on a tray 15 minutes.

Herb Rolls

1 batch	*Bread Rolls* dough
1 t	dried herbs

❖ Make *Bread Rolls* dough with added herbs.
Serve with spaghetti.

Cheese and Onion Rolls

1 batch   *Bread Rolls* dough
1/2 C   grated cheese
1/2 C   onion – diced and sautéed

❖ Make *Bread Rolls* dough with added cheese and onion.
Serve with soup.

Seedy Rolls

1 batch   *Bread Rolls* dough
1/2 C   sunflower seeds
1/4 C   poppy seeds
1/4 C   sesame seeds

❖ Save 1/4 C seeds to roll buns in before baking.

❖ Make *Bread Rolls* dough with added seeds.

Serve with soup, lentils or stews.

Reading Between the Lines

Empanadas are Patagonia's equivalent to the American burger or the Kiwi meat pie. Similar to a Cornish pastie or Indian samosa, empandas are trianglar pieces of short pastry stuffed with a meat and vegetable mix, then deep fried. They're sold on most street corners, small cafés, or in bars and are best washed down with a mate tea, coffee or beer.

We'd arrived in Puerto Williams and were gleaning knowledge from the locally based expedition yachts on the logisitics of rounding Cape Horn. Jean-Paul from *Ksar* advised us to obtain weather faxes from the Argentine service in addition to the Chilean and New Zealand faxes we'd been receiving. We duly tuned into their frequency and eagerly awaited the new weather charts. When the first weather fax displayed favorable conditions we eagerly set sail for Cape Horn only to discover that our conditions were quickly deteriorating. We were forced to wait for calmer weather at Caleta Martial, an anchorage 10 miles north of Cape Horn although were not alone as *Ksar* joined us. When the next Argentine weatherfax arrived we were surprised to discover a large blob positioned at Cape Horn. Thinking we'd misread a vital weather symbol we radioed *Ksar* to ask their advice.

"Humm," replied Jean-Paul in his very French accent. "Dooes zee blob appear in zee shape of a triangle?"

With a worried look, John replied, "Yes."

"And iz zere a semi-circle to zee right?" Jean-Paul questioned.

"Seems so," remarked John.

A loud laugh came over the radio. "Zat is nothing to worry about. Zee large blob iz just where zee weatherman haz placed his morning empanada and zee circle iz hiz coffee cup, it appens quite often."

Pizzas

Pizza Crust

Vicky Witch

3 C	flour
1 C	water – very warm
1/4 C	oil
1 T	sugar
1 T	yeast
1 t	salt

❖ Mix all ingredients, except flour, until yeast is dissolved.

❖ Add 1/2 the flour and mix well.

❖ Add remaining flour and mix to a sticky dough, don't knead too much, just enough so it sticks to your fingers.

❖ Cover mixture and let rise 1 hour, punch down and spread onto a greased tray.

❖ Layer base with favorite toppings. Bake 20 minutes at 400°F.

Quick Pizza Crust

2 C	flour
2/3 C	milk

```
1/4 C   salad oil
  2 T   salad oil
  2 t   baking powder
  1 t   salt
```

❖ Heat oven to 425°F

❖ Combine flour, baking powder and salt.

❖ Add milk and 1/4 C salad oil, stir vigorously until mixture leaves side of bowl.

❖ Knead until smooth and roll into a 13" circle on lightly floured board.

❖ Place dough on a greased tray and turn up edge 1/2" and pinch in place.

❖ Brush top with 2 T salad oil and layer on pizza toppings.

❖ Bake 25 minutes at 400°F.

Easy Pizza Crust

```
2 1/2 C   flour
    1 C   warm water
    2 T   oil
    1 T   yeast
    1 t   sugar
    1 t   salt
```

❖ Stir yeast in water until dissolved, mix in sugar, let rest until it bubbles.

❖ Mix in flour and salt, let rise 20 minutes until spongy to touch, divide in half for two pizzas.

❖ Oil hand and press 1/2 the mixture onto greased tray, top with favorite toppings.

❖ Bake 20 minutes at 425°F.

Pizza Tomato Sauce

```
1 can   tomato sauce
1 can   tomato paste
    1   onion – diced
    3   garlic cloves – crushed
  1 t   chili pepper flakes
```

Italian herbs
basil – chopped

❖ Combine ingredients and spread over pizza base before adding favorite toppings and cheese.

Pizza Toppings

Pizza toppings are as varied as the base recipes and are totally up to your taste buds. Although most pizzas start with a tomato sauce topped with vegetables, meats or seafood, and cheese, others can just be a simple pesto sauce. Here's some suggestions:

❖ **Cheese:** grated Parmesan, feta, blue cheese or brie, avoid processed cheese as it won't melt.

❖ **Vegetables:** olives, mushrooms, green pepper, onion, avocado, artichoke hearts, and pineapple.

❖ **Seafood:** smoked oysters, mussels, salmon, anchovies, prawns, baby clams and baby octopus.

❖ **Meats:** salami, ham, ground beef, chorizo, Canadian bacon and pepperoni.

Scones and Muffins

Drop Biscuits

Jenn~Yacht Ocean Light II

4 C	flour
1 C	milk
1/3 C	butter
2	eggs
3 T	brown sugar
8 t	baking powder

❖ Combine all dry ingredients, cut in butter then stir in milk and eggs.

❖ Drop dollops of mixture onto a cookie tray.

❖ Bake 12 minutes at 450°F until done.

English Scones or Quick Pizza Base

3 C	flour
1 C	milk
6 T	butter
5 t	baking powder
1/8 t	salt
*2 T	sugar if serving the scones with jelly
*1/3 C	dried currants

❖ Sift together flour, salt and baking powder.

❖ Cut in butter and add milk to form a stiff mixture.

❖ Form a block 1" high, cut into 3" squares, place on floured tray with gaps between each scone.

❖ Bake 18 minutes at 350°F.

Apple Nut Muffins

1 batch	*Lesley's Muffins*
1	apple
1/2 C	nuts
1 T	orange zest
	cinnamon, ginger and nutmeg

❖ Make a batch of *Lesley's Muffin* mix.

❖ Add remaining ingredients.

❖ Bake 20 minutes at 350°F.

Banana Oat Muffins

1 batch	*Lesley's Muffins*
1 C	mashed bananas
1/2 C	oats
1/2 C	bran
1/2 C	walnuts
1 T	lemon juice
1 1/2 t	baking soda
1/2 t	nutmeg

❖ Make a batch of *Lesley's Muffin* mix minus 1/2 C flour.

❖ Add remaining ingredients.

❖ Bake 20 minutes at 350°F.

Breads, Cakes and Cookies

Chocolate Muffins

1 batch	*Lesley's Muffins*
1/2 C	orange juice
1/2 C	chocolate chips
1/4 C	cocoa
1 t	cider vinegar

❖ Make a batch of *Lesley's Muffin* mix.

❖ Add remaining ingredients.

❖ Bake 20 minutes at 350ºF.

Date Nut Muffins

Cara~M/V St. Elias

1 1/2 C	dates, prunes or dried apricots – diced
3/4 C	white flour
3/4 C	bran
3/4 C	boiling water
1/2 C	whole wheat flour
1/2 C	walnuts or pecans – chopped
1/2 C	sugar
1/4 C	oil
1/2 t	baking soda
1/2 t	vanilla or almond extract

❖ Combine dates, water, oil and extract.

❖ Mix together flours, bran, sugar and baking soda.

❖ Add date mixture and nuts.

❖ Bake 12 minutes at 350ºF.

Serve with lashings of butter.

John's Savory Muffins

For nearly every New Year's Day for the past 25 years John and I have joined a group of 30 keen cyclists for the Commitment Ride. It's a 45-minute scenic bike ride come snow, sunshine or rain which starts and the Friday Harbor post office and ends at our friends John's house for a potluck brunch complete with champagne. Everyone is welcome and this is my John's winner recipe utilizing our favorite La Morena chipotle peppers in adobo sauce.

2 1/2 C   whole wheat flour
1 C   smoked salmon – diced
3/4 C   Parmesan cheese – grated
1/2 C   medium corn meal
1/2 C   chives or green onions – chopped
1/2 C   yogurt
1/2 C   milk
1/2 C   olive oil
1/4 C   Gorgonzola cheese – crumbled
2   eggs
3 T   sun-dried tomatoes – chopped
2 T   chipotle peppers – chopped
1 T   sugar
2 t   baking powder
1 t   salt
1/2 t   baking soda

❖ Combine salmon, sun-dried tomatoes, chipotle peppers, chives, and cheeses.

❖ Combine yogurt, milk and oil until smooth. Whisk in eggs.

❖ Combine dry ingredients and add to egg mixture.

❖ Carefully fold in salmon mixture, reserving 3 T.

❖ Spoon mixture into muffin tray and top with reserved salmon mix.

❖ Bake 20 minutes at 390F°.

Lesley's Muffins

Lesley~Yacht Taitoa

2 C   flour
1 C   milk
1/4 C   oil or butter
1/4 C   sugar
2   eggs
2 t   baking powder

❖ Combine oil, sugar and eggs.

❖ Add remaining ingredients.

❖ Bake 20 minutes at 350°F.

❖ Makes 12 muffins.

Cakes and Loafs

Tips on Baking Cakes and Loafs

❖ The following cake and loaf recipes require the oven to be **pre-heated** before adding the item for cooking.

❖ The cakes are baked in a 8x11 **glass dish.**

❖ All pans are prepared by **greasing the inside** with butter.

❖ A **cake is baked** when it springs back when slightly touched.

Apple and Oat Loaf

1 1/2 C	flour
2	apples – grated
1 C	oats
1 C	brown sugar
1 C	raisins
1 C	water
1/2 C	butter
2	eggs – beaten
3 t	baking powder
1 t	baking soda
1 t	allspice
1/2 t	cinnamon

❖ Bring apples, sugar, raisins, water, butter, baking soda, allspice, and cinnamon to a boil, allow to cool.

❖ Beat in oats and eggs, sift in flour and baking powder, combine well.

❖ Bake 45 minutes at 350°F.

Apple Cake

2 C	apples – peeled and diced
1 C	sugar
1 C	flour
1/2 C	pecans – chopped
1/4 C	vegetable oil
1	egg
2 t	cinnamon
1 t	baking soda

1/2 t   salt
1/4 t   nutmeg

❖ Beat egg, add apples, sugar, oil, pecans, cinnamon, and nutmeg.

❖ Sift in flour, baking soda and salt, combine well.

❖ Bake 40 minutes at 350ºF.

Banana Loaf

1 1/4 C   flour
1 C   bananas – mashed
1/2 C   oats
1/2 C   sugar
1/3 C   butter
2   eggs
2 t   baking powder
1 t   vanilla
1/4 t   baking soda
lemon zest
pinch of salt
*grated coconut
*sultanas or raisins
*nutmeg and cinnamon
*nuts or seeds

❖ Cream sugar and butter together until fluffy, add eggs and beat well.

❖ Sift in flour, baking powder and baking soda, while adding bananas.

❖ Add remaining ingredients.

❖ Bake 1 hour at 350°F.

Banana Cake

1 3/4 C   flour
1 C   bananas – mashed
3/4 C   sugar
1/2 C   milk
1/4 C   butter
1   egg – beaten
1 t   baking soda
1 t   baking powder
1 t   vanilla

Breads, Cakes and Cookies

- ❖ Cream butter and sugar together until fluffy, add beaten egg and vanilla.
- ❖ Sift in flour, baking soda and baking powder, add milk and stir in bananas.
- ❖ Bake 45 minutes at 350ºF.

Caribbean Ginger Loaf

1 1/2 C	flour
2/3 C	coconut milk, fruit juice or milk
1/2 C	raisins or dried tropical fruit
1/2 C	honey
1/2 C	maple syrup
1/2 C	oil
1	egg
2 t	ginger
1 t	baking soda
1 t	cinnamon
1/4 t	salt

- ❖ Combine honey, syrup, oil, egg and milk.
- ❖ Sift dry ingredients, add liquid and remaining ingredients.
- ❖ Bake 70 minutes at 350ºF.

Chocolate Cake

2 C	flour
1 C	sugar
1/2 C	boiling water
1/2 C	butter
3	eggs
3 T	cocoa
1 t	baking powder

- ❖ Cream sugar and butter together until fluffy, add eggs.
- ❖ Dissolve cocoa in boiling water and add to eggs alternately with sifted flour and baking powder.
- ❖ Bake 45 minutes at 350ºF.

Ice with Chocolate Icing.

Date Loaf

2 C flour
1 C walnuts – chopped
1 C dates – chopped
1 C boiling water
1 C brown sugar
1 egg – beaten
1 T butter
1 t baking soda
1 t baking powder
1/4 t vanilla
*replace dates with dried apricots

❖ Mix together dates, water, butter and baking soda until butter melts, let rest 30 minutes.

❖ Beat sugar, egg, walnuts and vanilla into date mixture.

❖ Sift in flour and baking powder, combine well.

❖ Bake 45 minutes at 350ºF.

Ginger Cake

2 C flour
1/2 C butter
1/2 C sugar
1/2 C milk
1/4 C crystallized ginger – chopped
1/4 C walnuts – chopped
1/4 C raisins
2 eggs – beaten
3 T maple syrup
1 t baking powder
1 t ginger
1 t allspice
1 t baking soda

❖ Cream butter, sugar and syrup together until fluffy.

❖ Sift in flour, baking powder and spices, mix in eggs.

❖ Stir in ginger, walnuts and raisins.

❖ Dissolve baking soda in milk and add to mixture.

❖ Bake 45 minutes at 350ºF.

Breads, Cakes and Cookies

Hawaiian Carrot Cake

Dyan~Yacht Ascension

1 1/2 C	flour
1 1/2 C	carrot – grated
1 C	sugar
1 C	coconut – grated and toasted
1 C	macadamia nuts – chopped
1/2 C	oil
1/2 C	canned crushed pineapple – drained
2	eggs
1 t	baking soda
1 t	vanilla
1/2 t	salt
1/2 t	baking powder
1/2 t	cinnamon

❖ Sift together flour, sugar, salt, baking soda, baking powder and cinnamon.

❖ Combine oil, eggs and vanilla, stir into flour.

❖ Add remaining ingredients.

❖ Bake 1 hour at 350°F.

Ice with Cream Cheese Icing *with a little added coconut.*

Orange Poppy Seed Loaf

2 C	flour
1/2 C	sugar
1 C	oil
1/2 C	milk
1/2 C	orange juice
3	eggs
3 T	poppy seeds
1 t	vanilla
1 t	baking powder
1/2 t	salt

❖ Beat eggs, sugar, milk, oil and vanilla together.

❖ Add remaining ingredients and mix well.

❖ Bake 50 minutes at 350°F.

Ice with Lemon Icing.

Bread, Cakes and Cookies

Pumpkin Loaf

2 C	flour
1 C	pumpkin – cooked and puréed
1/4 C	hazelnuts – chopped and toasted
1/4 C	brown sugar
1/4 C	sugar
1/4 C	raisins
2	eggs
1	orange – juice and zest
1 T	butter
1 t	baking powder
1/4 t	baking soda
1/4 t	each – cinnamon, nutmeg, ginger and allspice
pinch	salt

❖ Cream sugars and butter together until fluffy.

❖ Stir in eggs, juice, zest and pumpkin.

❖ Sift in dry ingredients, add remaining ingredients.

❖ Bake in greased bread pan for 45 minutes at 350°F.

Sultana Cake

Karen~Yacht Kamaraderie

Sultana and fruitcakes have a strong tie to my sailing adventures. Summer holidays Down Under revolve around Christmas and a sailing trip wouldn't be complete without leftover Christmas cake stashed away in a locker ready to be sliced up and served with a cup of tea after a day of sailing.

When preparing for the Sydney Hobart Race one year, I was up the mast doing a rig check when a call came from dockside that someone was looking for me. Upon asking what they wanted a gentleman replied that he visiting from New Zealand and that he was a workmate of Mums. As a favor, she'd asked if he would deliver a home baked sultana cake to me. It was the best Christmas present Mum could've sent.

During the Whitbread Race when we were getting ready to depart Fremantle, Australia for New Zealand the entire town felt sorry that we'd be spending Christmas at sea. Christmas cakes came flooding down to the boat. So generous were the bakers of these cakes that we had to make a public news announcement that we couldn't possibly accept any more cakes. Even though they keep well we were also conscious of their weight on board versus freeze-dried food.

I clearly remember that one cake in particular was an incredible work of art. Its marzipan sides were woven and colored to resemble a straw basket while the entire top of the cake featured colorful miniature fruits and berries sculptured from marzipan. It was definitely far too beautiful to eat.

I owe great thanks to my Nana, Ann Searle, Christine Webb and Mum for all the memorable cakes they've baked for my sailing races as I've fond memories of sharing cake slices with fellow crew members on Whitbread, Sydney Hobart, and Kiwi Coastal Classic races.

When Mike, our first Kiwi expedition member, joined *Mahina Tiare* for the passage from Hawaii to Seattle he came toting a sultana cake his wife Karen had made for the passage. What a sport! I guess sultana cake is as symbolic to us Kiwis as brownies are to Americans.

2 1/2 C	flour
2 1/4 C	sultanas/raisins
1 1/2 C	sugar
1 C	butter – softened
3	eggs
2 t	almond extract
1 t	baking powder

❖ Boil sultanas in water, then simmer 7 minutes, strain, add butter and almond extract, then cool.

❖ Beat sugar and eggs together.

❖ Sift flour and baking powder into sultanas, add to eggs.

❖ Bake 75 minutes at 300°F.

Keeps for 1 month wrapped wax paper then newspaper.

Icings

Chocolate Icing

2 C	confectioners sugar
2 T	water
1 T	cocoa
1/4 t	butter
1/4 t	vanilla

❖ Sift sugar and cocoa, add butter and enough water to mix to a spreadable consistency, flavor with vanilla.

Cream Cheese Icing

    1 C   confectioners sugar
  1/4 C   cream cheese
    2 T   butter
    1 t   vanilla
  1/2 t   lemon zest

❖   Beat cream cheese and butter together.

❖   Add sugar, vanilla and zest, combine well.

Lemon Icing

    2 C   confectioners sugar
    2 T   lemon juice
    1 t   lemon zest
  1/4 t   butter

❖   Sift sugar, add butter and enough lemon juice to mix to a spreadable consistency, flavor with zest.

Cookies and Bars

Apricot Pecan Bars

 1 1/2 C   whole-meal flour
  1/2 C   butter
  1/2 C   apricot jam
  1/2 C   pecans – chopped
  1/3 C   brown sugar
  1/3 C   dried apricots – diced
  1/4 C   crystallized ginger – chopped

❖   Cream butter and sugar together until fluffy, add jam.

❖   Beat in flour then remaining ingredients.

❖   Press into a greased 8x8 pan and bake 15 minutes at 350°F.

Brownies

    2 C   sugar
 1 1/3 C   flour
  3/4 C   cocoa

1/2 C	boiling water
1/3 C	vegetable oil
2	eggs
1 t	vanilla
1/2 t	baking soda
1/4 t	salt

❖ Combine cocoa and baking soda, stir in oil.

❖ Stir in water, add remaining ingredients and mix well.

❖ Bake 20 minutes at 350°F.

Chocolate Almond Energy Bites

1 C	raw almonds or cashews
16	Medjool dates – pitted
6 T	cocoa powder
4 T	almond butter
	*toppings: sesame seeds cacao nibs, cocoa powder or shredded coconut

❖ Blend nuts and dates in a food processor until finely ground.

❖ Add cocoa powder and almond butter. Pulse until smooth. Mixture should stick together when pressed between your fingers.

❖ Roll dough into 1 T balls then roll in optional toppings.

Date Bars

Cowpuccino's Coffee House~Prince Rupert

2 C	oats
2 C	dates – pitted
1 1/2 C	flour
1 1/2 C	brown sugar
1 1/4 C	butter
1 1/2 t	baking soda
1 t	vanilla
1/2 t	salt

❖ Simmer dates in 2/3 C water until mushy, add vanilla.

❖ Mix dry ingredients together, cut in butter.

❖ Press 1/2 dry ingredients into a greased 8x12 pan, spread with dates and crumb remaining mixture on top.

❖ Bake 30 minutes at 350°F.

Ginger Crunch
Base

1 1/2 C	rolled oats
1 C	crystallized ginger – chopped
3/4 C	whole wheat flour
3/4 C	brown sugar
3/4 C	desiccated coconut
5 oz	butter
2 T	golden syrup
2 t	baking powder
3 t	ground ginger

❖ Melt brown sugar, butter and golden syrup over a low heat.
❖ Mix dry ingredients and pour in melted ingredients.
❖ Mix together and press mixtur into a lined 8x12 pan.
❖ Bake 20 minutes at 355°F.

Ginger Icing

2 1/2 C	confectioners sugar
1/2 C	butter
6 T	golden syrup
3 t	ground ginger

❖ Melt butter and golden syrup, beat in ginger and icing sugar.
❖ Pour over still-warm base.

Louise Squares

Tessa~Yacht Kiwi Lass

1 1/4 C	flour
1/2 C	desiccated coconut
1/2 C	sugar
1/3 C	butter
1/4 C	raspberry jam
2	eggs – separated
2 T	sugar
1 t	baking powder

❖ Cream butter and 2 T sugar together until fluffy, beat in egg yolks.
❖ Sift flour and baking powder together and stir into creamed mixture.
❖ Press mixture into a greased 8x12 pan and spread with jam.
❖ Beat egg whites until stiff but not dry, mix in 1/2 C sugar and coconut, spread meringue over jam.

Breads, Cakes and Cookies

❖ Bake 30 minutes at 350°F or until meringue is dry and lightly colored.

Cut into squares while warm.

Macadamia Butter Cookies

2 1/2 C	flour
1 1/3 C	salted macadamia nuts – chopped
1 1/4 C	sugar
1 C	butter
1	egg
1 t	baking soda
1 t	vanilla
	*chocolate chips

❖ Cream butter and sugar together until fluffy, beat in egg and vanilla.

❖ Mix in flour, baking soda and nuts.

❖ Drop 1 T balls on tray and press flat with a fork dipped in sugar.

❖ Press a chunk of nut into the center of each cookie.

❖ Bake 15 minutes at 375°F.

Oatmeal Chocolate Chip Cookies

Jenn~Yacht Ocean Light II

2 1/2 C	oats
2 C	flour
1 1/2 C	sugar – white and brown mix
1 C	butter
1 C	chocolate chips
1/2 C	pecans – chopped
2	eggs
1 t	vanilla
1 t	baking soda
1 t	baking powder
pinch	salt

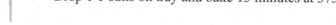

❖ Cream butter and sugar together until fluffy, mix in eggs and vanilla.

❖ Add combined flour, baking soda and salt, stir in oats, nuts and chocolate.

❖ Drop 1 T balls on tray and bake 15 minutes at 375°F.

Oatmeal Raisin Cookies

Pat~Yacht Danzante

3 1/2 C	oats
1 1/2 C	flour
1 C	raisins*
1 C	butter
3/4 C	brown sugar
2	eggs
1 t	vanilla
1 t	cinnamon
1/4 t	salt

*substitute dried cranberries, pecans or yogurt covered sultanas for variation.

❖ Cream butter and sugar together until fluffy, beat in eggs and vanilla.

❖ Mix in remaining ingredients.

❖ Drop 1 T balls on tray and bake 15 minutes at 375°F.

No-Bake Granola Bar

Mary-Ann~Yacht Highland Queen

1 C	shredded coconut
1 C	dried apricots – sliced
3/4 C	rolled oats
1/2 C	dried cranberries
1/2 C	butter
1/2 C	honey
1/2 C	pumpkin seeds
1/4 C	sesame seeds
1/4 C	brown sugar

❖ Combine oats, coconut, dried fruit and seeds.

❖ Heat butter, honey and sugar, while stirring, until sugar dissolves, 3 minutes.

❖ Bring to a boil, reduce heat and simmer, without stirring, 8 minutes until caramelized.

❖ Pour over dry ingredients and stir to combine.

❖ Press into a greased and lined 7x10 pan.

❖ Chill until firm then slice into bars.

Secret Granola Bars

Cowpuccino's Coffee House~Prince Rupert

1 1/2 C	oats
1/2 C	chocolate chips
1/2 C	raisins
1/2 C	sunflower seeds
1/2 C	rice krispies
1/2 C	sweetened condensed milk
1/3 C	butter – melted

❖ Mix all ingredients together.

❖ Press into a greased 8x12 pan.

❖ Bake 25 minutes for 325°F until golden.

Chapter 16

DESSERTS

Desserts

Desert Crêpes ~ Lesley's

Yacht Taitoa

❖ Make a batch of *Lesley Crêpes*.

Serve hot sprinkled with Banana Flambé, Warm Mango Sauce *or sprinkled with sugar and lemon.*

Fruit Deserts

Apple Cobbler

3	apples – sliced
1 C	oats
1/2 C	flour
1/2 C	walnuts – chopped
1/4 C	sugar
1/4 C	brown sugar
1/4 C	butter
1	lemon – juice and zest
1/2 t	cinnamon
1/8 t	nutmeg
pinch	salt

❖ Combine oats, flour, sugars, lemon zest and spices.

❖ Rub in butter and add nuts.

❖ Mix apples and juice together.

Oven Option

❖ Place apples in a buttered dish, top with oatmeal mixture.

❖ Bake 45 minutes at 325°F.

Pressure Cooker Option

❖ Place apples in a buttered 6 C soufflé dish and top with oatmeal mixture.

❖ Cover with buttered foil and place in drainer basket.

❖ Pour 1 1/2 C water into pressure cooker and place basket inside.

❖ Pressure cook 20 minutes.

Serve with ice cream, whipped cream or custard.

Banana or Pineapple Flambé

This quick favorite one-pan desert of my Mum's results in a sure way to use up ripe bananas. It looks impressive when set alight and the rum makes it an instant hit. You can also use both bananas and pineapple.

```
4   bananas – 1 per person and/or
    fresh pineapple – sliced into rings
1/4 C  butter
1/4 C  brown sugar
1/4 C  rum
```

❖ Melt butter in skillet, add sugar and heat.

❖ Add fruit and stir until butter and sugar caramelizes.

❖ Pour rum into pan and set alight.

Serve immediately.

Baked Papaya

```
2   ripe papaya – peeled and sliced
2 T  brown sugar
2 T  lemon juice
2 T  brandy
```

❖ Place papaya in a buttered baking dish.

❖ Sprinkle with sugar, lemon juice and brandy.

❖ Bake 30 minutes at 350ºF.

Serve with ice cream, whipped cream or custard.

Canned Fruit Cobbler

Dee~M/V Penguin

```
1 can  peaches, apples, berries or apricots
1 C   flour
1/2 C  brown sugar
1/4 C  white sugar
1/2 C  milk
1/4 C  butter
1   egg
2 T  lime juice
    tapioca or cornstarch
1 t  cinnamon
```

Desserts

❖ Place drained fruit in a baking dish and add lime juice.

❖ Heat half the canned fruit juice in a pan, add enough tapioca to thicken, pour over the fruit.

❖ Combine remaining ingredients and place on top of fruit.

❖ Bake 20 minutes at 375ºF.

Peaches Drowned in Red Wine

6	peaches – sliced
7 T	sugar
2	whole cloves
1	cinnamon stick
	red wine – preferably Chianti

❖ Sprinkle peaches with sugar.

❖ Add spices and cover with red wine.

Refrigerate overnight and serve cold.

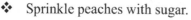

Fruit Compote with Merlot

2	apples – peeled cut into wedges
1	orange – zest and juice
1 C	dried apricots
1 C	dried cranberries
1/2 C	raisins
1/2 C	fruity red wine, such as Merlot
1/2 C	light brown sugar
1	cinnamon stick
5	cloves
2 T	rum

❖ Add water to orange juice to measure 1/2 C.

❖ Wrap cinnamon and cloves into a cheese cloth sachet.

❖ In pressure cooker combine juice, zest, dried fruit, wine, sugar and spices.

❖ Cover dried fruit with apple and pressure cook 1 minute or simmer 15 minutes.

❖ Remove fruit to a bowl and boil cooking liquid until reduced by half, about 5 minutes.

❖   Add rum and pour over fruit.

Serve warm or chilled with ice cream or sorbet. Also goes well with pork.

Strawberry Dip

I first had this dessert when I was fifteen at the St. Francis Yacht Club. We'd sailed from Hawaii into San Francisco and Henry, the gentleman on the yacht beside us in Sausalito, invited us to dinner at the club. When I entered the dinning room I was in awe as I'd never seen such elegance before. A huge table with a carved ice statue of King Neptune and his dancing dolphins took center stage. When this dessert arrived it appeared rather simple but what a joy it was to leisurely dip and devour each decadent strawberry.

<blockquote>
6   strawberries per person – rinsed, but not hulled
1 C   sour cream
1 C   brown sugar
      *quartered apricots can substitute for strawberries
</blockquote>

For each person the St. Francis Yacht Club served two small pots: one of sour cream and the other of brown sugar, along with the strawberries in a dish, though this presentation is a little impractical on a yacht.

A simpler option is to place a bowl of each ingredient in the center of the table and each person first dips a strawberry in the sour cream then the brown sugar.

Tropical Fruit Cobbler
Filling

<blockquote>
3   bananas – sliced
3   mangoes – diced
3   pineapple slices – diced
1/3 C   brown sugar
1/3 C   orange juice
1   lemon – juiced
</blockquote>

Topping
1 1/2 C	flour
3/4 C	rolled oats
3/4 C	brown sugar
1/2 C	shredded coconut
1/3 C	butter
1/2 t	cinnamon

❖ Mix filling ingredients together in a buttered baking dish.

❖ Rub topping ingredients together using fingers, spread over fruit.

❖ Bake 20 minutes at 375°F.

Serve with ice cream, whipped cream or custard.

Puddings and Pies

Coconut Chia Seed Pudding
1 C	almond milk
1 C	coconut milk
5 T	chia seeds
2 T	shredded coconut
1 T	honey
1	diced mango or berries

❖ Soak chia seeds in both milks, coconut and honey for at least 1 hour, stirring occasionally until it thickens.

❖ Serve in glass cups/jars topped with mango.

Fruit Sponge
1 C	flour
1 can	fruit
1/2 C	butter
1/2 C	brown sugar
2 T	milk
2	eggs
2 t	baking powder
1 t	vanilla

❖ Cream butter, sugar and vanilla together, beat in eggs.

❖ Sift in flour and baking powder, add milk and mix well.

❖ Place fruit in bottom of baking dish, spoon in mixture.

❖ Bake 40 minutes at 350°F until sponge springs back when touched lightly.

Bread Pudding ~ Jamaican

3 C	milk
8	bread slices – buttered and sliced into strips
1/3 C	honey and/or brown sugar
1/2 C	dried mixed tropical fruit: pineapple, papaya, citrus peel, dates and/or shredded coconut
1/4 C	raisins
1/4 C	rum
3	bananas
2	eggs
1 T	lemon juice
1 t	vanilla
1/4 t	each – nutmeg, cinnamon and ginger

❖ Slice bananas and mix with lemon juice.

❖ Layer bread in buttered baking dish, followed with bananas and fruit.

❖ Continue layering bread and fruit, ending with bread.

❖ Beat milk, honey, rum, eggs, vanilla and spices together, pour over bread.

❖ Bake 45 minutes at 325°F until egg has set.

Serve hot or cold.

Lemon Meringue Pie

Lorena~Cape Horn

Base

2 C	flour
1/3 C	butter
1/4 C	sugar
3	eggs – yolks
1 t	baking powder

❖ Rub flour and butter together, mix in sugar and baking powder, add egg yolks.

Desserts

❖ Press mixture into buttered pan and poke with a fork.

❖ Bake 15 minutes until golden.

Filling

    1 can   condensed milk
    1/2 C   lemon juice
      2 t   lemon zest
    1/4 t   vanilla

❖ Whip filling ingredients together and pour into base.

❖ Bake until set, about 5 minutes.

Meringue Topping

    1/4 C   confectioners sugar
      3   egg whites
    1/4 t   vanilla

❖ Beat egg whites until stiff, beat in sugar 1T at a time until thick and glossy, stir in vanilla.

❖ Top pie with meringue and bake 10 minutes until golden.

Mango Cream Pie

Base

      2 C   plain cookies – crushed
      1 C   desiccated coconut
    1/2 C   brown sugar
    1/3 C   melted butter
      1 t   cinnamon

❖ Combine cookie crumbs, coconut, sugar and cinnamon, mix in melted butter.

❖ Press mixture into a baking dish.

Filling

    1 1/2 C   mango – mashed
        3   eggs – separated
      1 can   condensed milk
      1/2 C   lime juice
              lemon zest
              *can replace mango with papaya, pineapple, or guava

❖ Combine egg yolks, condensed milk, lime juice and zest.

Desserts

* Beat egg whites until stiff and fold into fruit, pour into dish.
* Bake 1 hour at 300°F.
Serve hot or cold.

Microwave Mexican Flan

Dee~M/V Penguin

1 can	evaporated milk
1 can	sweetened condensed milk
2/3 C	sugar
4	eggs
1 t	vanilla

* Beat milk, condensed milk, eggs and vanilla together until fluffy.
* Prepare a shallow dish of warm water in which a large bowl can easily sit.
* Melt sugar in frying pan until it caramelizes, don't burn.
* Pour caramel into bowl and swirl around to evenly coat the base and sides.
* Pour beaten mixture inside caramel coated bowl, cover with plastic wrap.
* Microwave on high for 12 minutes.
Chill and flip out onto a plate before serving.

Rice Pudding

3 1/2 C	milk
1 C	rice
1/4 C	brown sugar
1/4 C	raisins – soaked in rum
1/4 C	nuts – chopped
2 T	lemon zest
2 T	butter
2 t	vanilla
	cinnamon and nutmeg

* Sauté rice in butter until rice is coated, stir in remaining ingredients.
* Pressure cook 10 minutes or simmer 25 minutes until rice is tender.
Serve garnished with chopped nuts.

Desserts

Indonesian Rice Pudding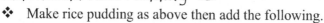

❖ Make rice pudding as above then add the following.

    1 C coconut milk
    2 T lemon zest
  1/4 t cardamom
        *crushed pineapple

❖ Heat milk and ingredients until just about to boil.

❖ Leave for 5 minutes then pour onto rice pudding.

Serve warm or cold.

Dessert Sauces

Caramel Sauce ~ Quick

    3/4 C evaporated milk or 2/3 milk and 1/3 cream
    1/3 C brown sugar
      2 T butter
  3 drops vanilla extract
        *melted chocolate for chocolate sauce

❖ Combine all ingredients and cook gently while stirring for 7 minutes.

❖ Remove from heat and beat till glossy.

Serve hot or cold.

Mango Sauce

     2 mangoes – diced
  1/3 C sugar
  1/4 C water
   1 T lemon juice

❖ Combine half of the mangoes with sugar, water and lemon juice.

❖ Bring to a boil and simmer 3 minutes.

❖ Purée mixture until smooth, add remaining mango and heat through.

Serve hot with Lesley Crepe's, *ice cream, or cold with* Mango Cream Pie.

Maple Syrup ~ Mock

Fran~Yacht Aka

A very good substitute when you're out of the real thing.

    1 C   brown sugar
    1/2 C water
    1 t   vanilla

❖ Boil water and sugar until sugar dissolves.

❖ Cool and add vanilla.

Chapter 17

CHUTNEYS, RELISHES AND JAMS

Cabbage Kimchi

While at the gym John got chatting with Charles, our Korean friend who owns several restaurants in Friday Harbor. When John mentioned that I was keen on kimchi, Charles instantly volunteered to show us how to make it, adding that he eats kimchi with nearly every meal plus serves it at his restaurant, China Pearl. The next morning we gathered in the restaurants extensive kitchen and as a foreign sci-fi movie played on a big screen Charles rapidly wielded a large cleaver with amazing dexterity and passion to create this kimchi, making it look so easy.

1	napa cabbage – quartered and cut into 2-inch pieces
12 C	filtered water
1/4 C	kosher salt
2	green onion – sliced
1 C	daikon radish – julienned
1/2 C	carrot – julienned
1/4 C	ground Korean chili powder
6	garlic cloves – minced
3 T	Asian fish sauce
1 1/2 t	minced fresh ginger
1 t	sugar

❖ Mix salt with water. Add cabbage and let soak 2 hours.

❖ Drain cabbage, rinse then squeeze out excess water.

❖ Add remaining ingredients and stir to combine using gloved hands.

❖ Pack kimchi into a jar and lock the lid.

❖ Let sit at room temperature for 2 days. When bubbles appear, it's fermented.

❖ Store in the refrigerator for up to 4 months.

Chutneys

Green Papaya Chutney

1	green papaya – grated
1/4 C	lemon juice or vinegar
1 t	salt
1 t	ginger
	ground pepper to taste
	*cucumber or tomatoes with crushed garlic may be substituted for the papaya.

❖ Combine all ingredients and test for flavor.
Serve with curry and fish dishes.

Banana Chutney

4 C	bananas – mashed
2 1/2 C	malt vinegar
2 C	raisins
1 1/2 C	brown sugar
2	garlic cloves – crushed
2 T	ginger – grated
1 T	chili sauce
1 t	*Garam Masala*
1/2 t	cinnamon
1/4 t	cloves

❖ Purée raisins with 1 C vinegar, ginger, garlic and chili.

❖ Combine all ingredients simmer until thick, 1 hour,

❖ Pack into sterile jars.

Cranberry Chutney

2 C	cranberries
1/2 C	onion – diced
1/2 C	water
1/4 C	currants
1/4 C	sugar
1	apple – peeled and diced
1	orange – juice and zest
6 T	cider vinegar
5 T	brown sugar
1/2 t	ginger – grated
1/4 t	salt
1/4 t	nutmeg
1/4 t	curry

❖ Simmer onion, sugar and water 20 minutes.

❖ Add vinegar, apple, spices and zest, simmer 30 minutes.

❖ Stir in remaining ingredients, simmer until cranberries pop.

❖ Let cool, cover and refrigerate.

Chutneys, Jams and Relishes

Mango Chutney

5 C	mangoes – diced
2 1/2 C	cider vinegar
2 C	brown sugar
2 C	raisins
3/4 C	onion – diced
1/4 C	ginger – chopped
1/2 T	chili peppers
1 t	salt

❖ Combine all ingredients and bring to a boil.

❖ Simmer 30 minutes or until mixture is thick.

❖ Cool 15 minutes, stir well and bottle.

Makes 12 cups.

Tomato Chutney

Nina~Musket Cove

1/2 C	cider vinegar
1/2 C	brown sugar
1/4 C	raisins
1/4 C	nuts
5	tomatoes – diced
2	onions – diced
2	apples – diced
2	celery stalks – diced
1	green pepper – diced
1	red pepper – diced
	citrus peel
	ginger – grated
	S&P

❖ Combine all ingredients and bring to a boil.

❖ Simmer 30 minutes or until the mixture is thick.

❖ Cool 15 minutes, stir well and bottle.

Makes 12 cups.

Relishes

Asian Relish

1/4 C	sesame seeds
3	scallions – diced
1	garlic clove – crushed
2 T	soy sauce
2 t	ginger – diced
1 t	rice vinegar
1 t	sesame oil
1/4 t	sugar
	salt

❖ Blend all ingredients together.

Serve with Asian Marinated Fish.

Tomato and Cucumber Relish

This refreshing relish goes well with fish, chili dishes and curries.

1/2 C	tomato – diced
1/2 C	cucumber – diced
1/3 C	yogurt
	fresh mint
	S&P

❖ Combine ingredients, chill and serve.

Nana's Tomato Relish

This tangy relish was a staple item on Nana's condiment shelf. I've fond summer memories of sandwiches liberally spread with relish containing slabs of Sunday's cold cut roast beef and tasty cheddar cheese.

6 C	tomatoes – diced
2 1/2 C	vinegar
2 C	brown sugar
4	onions – diced
1	apple – diced
3	chilies – chopped
1 T	mustard
2 t	salt
1 t	curry

❖ Simmer tomatoes, onions, apple, chilies and 2 1/4 C vinegar for 1 1/2 hours.

❖ Mix remaining ingredients into a smooth paste and add to relish.

❖ Boil 5 minutes to thicken, pack into sterile jars.

Makes 6 cups.

Pink Onion Relish

Juan~Acapulco Yacht Club

2 C	water
1	red onion – sliced thin
1 T	salad oil
3 t	vinegar
1 1/2 t	vinegar
1/2 t	mustard seed
1/4 t	cumin seed
	salt

❖ Bring water and half the vinegar to a boil.

❖ Add onion and simmer 3 minutes, drain and cool.

❖ Add remaining ingredients and season to taste.

Serve with bean chili.

Jams and Jellies

Tips on Jam Making

❖ Select fruit that is in **good condition** and not overripe.

❖ A stainless steel **pressure cooker** is ideal for jam making.

❖ **Towards the end of the cooking** time watch and test jam frequently as it can easily burn.

Three Methods for Testing if Jam Will Set

❖ Dip wooden spoon into jam allowing mixture to drip; when two drops merge on the end of the spoon the jam will set.

❖ Place a little jam on a cold plate from the fridge, let

cool, when mixture is pressed a finger a wrinkle should form.

❖ Place a little jam on a plate, draw a channel through the jam with a knife; the gap should remain open and not cave in.

Sterilizing Jars

Sterilize jars and lids by cleaning them thoroughly in hot soapy water, then follow one of these procedures.

❖ Place jars in an oven for 30 minutes at 250°F.

❖ Cover jars with water and boil for 15 minutes.

Blackberry or Raspberry Jam

> 2 C crushed blackberries
> 2 C sugar
> 2 t lemon juice

❖ Combine ingredients, bring to a boil and simmer 5 minutes.

❖ Reduce to medium heat and cook 12 minutes.

❖ Skim the foam off and store in a heat-proof container.

❖ Jam will thicken as it cools.

Mango Jam

> 4 C ripe mangoes – diced
> 3 C sugar
> 1/2 C water
> 1/4 C lemon juice

❖ Combine mangoes, water and lemon juice, bring to boil and simmer covered 15 minutes until mango is tender.

❖ Add sugar, stirring until dissolved, then boil uncovered without stirring until jam sets.

❖ Bottle in hot sterilized jars and cover when cool.

Orange Marmalade

> 2 lbs oranges

8 C   water
6 C   sugar
2   lemons – juiced

❖ Cut oranges in half and squeeze out juice, scrape out pulp and discard seeds.

❖ Thinly slice orange skins and simmer with water until peel is tender, about 20 minutes.

❖ Add remaining ingredients and gently heat, stirring until sugar dissolves.

❖ Boil uncovered, without stirring, until marmalade sets, about 25 minutes.

❖ Bottle in hot sterilized jars and cover when cool.

Pineapple Jam

6 C   pineapple – diced
4 C   sugar
2 1/2 C   water
4   lemons – juice and zest

❖ Combine all ingredients and refrigerate overnight.

❖ Simmer 1 hour uncovered, stirring only at the end of cooking.

❖ Bottle in hot sterilized jars and cover when cool.

Chapter 18

WATER

MANAGEMENT

Water Management

Water Capacity

❖ Carry a minimum of **1.5 gallons of water** per person, per day, for offshore passages.

❖ Consider carrying **extra water** in rigid plastic jugs for emergencies.

❖ For transporting water by dinghy it's a good idea to have at least four 5-gallon **collapsible jugs.**

Water Catchement Ideas

❖ Consider rigging a **water catchment** system utilizing your sun awning or a separate foredeck awning.

❖ **While sailing**, rainwater can be caught in a bucket or canvas catcher hanging at the gooseneck.

❖ To **obtain water in a downpour** an option is to place a towel across the deck to dam and direct water into the deck fill after the rain has thoroughly washed the decks.

Hints on Galley Water Consumption

❖ Use a **foot pump** instead of pressure water.

❖ Installing a **saltwater** foot pump in the galley may reduce water consumption by 50%.

❖ **Dishwashing**:

    ❖ Provide each crewmember with their own **drinking mug** so that it only needs to be rinsed after each use.

    ❖ Use **small dinner plates** rather than large as there's less surface area to wash.

    ❖ A **paper towel** might be better than a sponge for wiping up messy jobs, as it doesn't require rinsing.

    ❖ **Avoid stacking dirty plates** after a meal so you don't have to scrub the bottom of each plate.

    ❖ **Heated water** is more efficient for washing dishes than cold.

    ❖ Use **salt water** for washing dishes and then rinse them with fresh.

    ❖ Choose **biodegradable** soap that lathers well in salt water for seawater dishwashing.

❖ Cooking with **salt water**:

    Beans: soak in 100% salt water
    Eggs, hard boiled: 100% salt water

Whole potatoes and carrots: 50% salt water
Rice: 50% salt water
Oats: 25% salt water

Warnings About Contaminated Water

❖ **In the tropics**, drinking water may be scarce and expensive. Supplies may come from rain catchment, slightly brackish wells, expensive desalination plants or may be transported to small islands by barges. The water on high islands comes from springs, natural rain catchment reservoirs and rivers. Any of these may be contaminated although generally water coming from deep wells and springs is potable.

❖ When **obtaining water from shore**, ask around about the quality, especially from other yachties, as the locals build up resistance to bad water. Check sanitation: Does the water flow from a river with a village upstream? Is it clear rather than turbid?

❖ **Avoid contaminated water** by catching your own rainwater or using a watermaker.

❖ **Babies and children** are more susceptible to serious diarrhea from contaminated water than are adults. For cruising babies and young children always boil contaminated water for at least three minutes or filter using a high-quality water filter system.

❖ **Ice and containers** in contact with contaminated water should also be considered unsafe. It's safer to drink directly from a can or bottle but water on the outside may be contaminated and should be wiped off.

❖ **Carbonated beverages** are safe as a result of the acidity caused by the carbonation. Some noncarbonated "bottled" water may simply represent recycled packaging with contaminated water.

❖ **Hot drinks or coconut milk** straight from the nut are not contaminated but do not drink from coconuts that have been opened for more than 30 minutes as they may cause food poisoning.

❖ **Ice cream** made with contaminated water or milk is a risk.

Water Management

Water Treatment

❖ The most effective way to treat drinking water is to **bring it to a vigorous boil** for several minutes and then allow it to cool. Boiling destroys all the diarrhea producing organisms but some single-celled parasites such as *Entamaeba histolytica*, which causes amoebic dysentery, may take longer to destroy.

❖ The best way to **treat tank water** is with iodine. Purifying tablets are available from pharmacies, REI, or sporting goods stores. Two-percent tincture of iodine from the first aid chest can also be used. In addition you can get iodine crystals, add water periodically, and thus have a continuous supply of iodine solution. Five drops per liter or quart are needed for clear water and ten drops for cloudy water. If the water is extremely cold it needs to be heated for the chemical reaction to take place. After adding iodine, allow the water to stand at least 30 minutes. Adding a squeeze of citrus juice will mask any after taste caused by purification.

❖ **Chlorine** may also be used for treating water, though it's not quite as effective as iodine.

Chlorine Strengths	Clear Water	Cold or Cloudy Water
1%	2 drops per gallon	4 drops per gallon
4-6%	4 drops per gallon	8 drops per gallon
7-11%	8 drops per gallon	16 drops per gallon or 1 teaspoon per 10 gallons of Clorox household bleach

Water Filtration

❖ **Pre-filter shore water** before putting it in you tank by running it through an in-line water filter that rids the water of chlorine, sediment and minerals.

❖ Install, at a minimum, a permanently mounted **water filter** that utilizes replaceable cartridges.

❖ For a **pressured system** consider installing a Seagull IV Water Purifier. www.general-ecology.com

❖ **UV water sterilizers** are more complicated and expensive than the above options.

❖ If you plan on extensive hiking ashore in less developed areas, consider carrying a **hand-operated water purifier.**

Treating Water Tanks

❖ **Bacteria** grows inside water tanks in the tropics, resulting in a foul taste in your water. You may think your water and tanks are wonderfully clean and clear until you start sailing to windward, when the sediment and bacteria that has collected and settled in the bottom of the tank gets shaken up.

❖ **Sanitize your water tank** and hoses once or twice a year by mixing 1/4 cup of liquid dishwashing detergent and 1/8 cup of household bleach. After the solution is dissolved, pour it into your boats empty tank. Add 10 gallons of warm water and rock the boat to ensure the solution is well mixed in the tank. Then open each tap including the showers until the sanitizing solution appears at the faucets. Let the solution remain in the tank and lines for at least an hour to enable complete disinfecting. Next, open all taps and allow all the solution to run out. Follow this with at least two full rinses of the tank to ensure that all the sanitizing solution is flushed out.

❖ To **treat water in your water tanks** (as long as they aren't aluminum), use 1 teaspoon of household bleach per 10 gallons of water. Increase the amount of bleach if the water is cloudy.

❖ Treat **water stored in jugs** with chlorine or iodine.

Care of Aluminum Water Tanks

❖ **Chlorine**, contained in many large city water supplies and **bleach** should be avoided in aluminum water tanks. These chemicals react with the aluminum causing aluminum chloride; a white pasty oxidation that occurs in your tanks and thus clogs your filters.

Watermakers

❖ Consider carrying a small **hand-operated watermaker** for emergencies. The PUR Survivor 06 is small enough to fit into most abandon-ship bags.

❖ **High output watermakers** generally require AC power necessitating a diesel generator.

❖ **DC watermakers** run off the vessel's batteries. They range from the Katadyn PowerSurvivor 40E to the more efficient Spectra models which make up to 380 gallons per day.

❖ It's important to follow the watermaker directions explicitly on **installation and on biociding** the membrane when the unit is not in use.

❖ Seawater in commercial harbors generally contains **pollutants** which will damage the watermaker membrane.

❖ Running the watermaker **at anchor** frequently leads to increased wear and early failure of the watermaker seals and o-rings due to the microscopic sand particles in the seawater.

❖ You'll find that only running the watermaker **offshore** will greatly lengthen the time between pump rebuilds and membrane replacements.

❖ When **arriving in a harbor** where we know that clean water is going to be difficult to obtain, we'll purposefully run the watermaker offshore to fill the tanks.

Chapter 19

FOREIGN PROVISIONING

World Provisioning Guide

Worldwide provisioning is becoming far less difficult as foreign trade and manufacturing expand.

Mainland provisioning ports may have large supermarkets that are clean and temperature-controlled, with a high turnover providing excellent selection with moderate prices. The variety of goods will never rival that of a North American store but you'll not want for much. Plan large provisioning shops in accordance with the areas you intend to cruise or before crossing large expanses of ocean. Most often these are areas in which you'll be spending hurricane season such as Australia, New Zealand, Europe, Venezuela and South Africa.

Small Island Nations have less selection than mainland countries, and the governing body for the islands determines the overall selection. The main port for entry and customs clearance generally contains the largest stores and often a thriving local produce market.

For example French Polynesia, is funnily enough, rather French complete with baguettes, croissants and macarons. In 1988, Continent superstore opened in the main port Papeete totally cleaning up all the local stores. Now it's Carrefour and it's incredibly well stocked with products from Europe, Chile, New Zealand and the U.S. Basic items are a great value but you'll have to splurge for airfreighted Washington cherries and gourmet potatoes shipped from France buried in crates of French soil.

Cruising through the other South Pacific islands will be a matter of hit-and-miss as to what's available. The Cook Islands, Samoa and Fiji have a New Zealand influence, while American Samoa relies on supplies from the U.S. There's only a few super bulk-buy stores in the entire South Pacific and they mainly cater to the local hotels and restaurants.

Outside the main ports, small village stores contain basic supplies of long-lasting goods. Fresh produce is often harder to find and if excess is not sold on roadside stands you may have to ask around. Fresh meat, poultry and fish may be out of the question as most stores don't contain refrigeration.

Remote Cruising lends itself to being resourceful and relying on the provisions you have. For a couple cruising, this is not too difficult as you're basically forced to make-do with what you have, so it's rather like being at sea. Hopefully, you provisioned wisely in your last major port of call although you may be able to supplement your diet with items you trade for, are able to purchase or perhaps discover.

I once met a cruising boat that had taken a local lad aboard as they cruised through the Society Islands, offering to pay his ferry ride home from their last port of call. He proved to be most helpful in his skills of diving and fishing, scaling coconut trees and preparing local recipes. In return, he really enjoyed the sailing and the opportunity to share his knowledge.

Arrival and Food Quarantine

❖ Many countries have strict **quarantine laws** applicable to agricultural products. These products may contain diseases that are a risk to the country's environment and generally require inspection if not confiscation.

❖ For **current infromation** on provisioning and the latest on agricultural restrictions for foreign ports visit www.noonsite.com.

❖ As master of a vessel you are responsible for ensuring that your crew is aware of **quarantine restrictions** applicable to the country you are entering.

❖ An example of strict quarantine is **New Zealand's agricultural clearance requirements**. www.biosecurity.govt.nz. Though few countries are as stringent.

> **All meat** must be declared: beef, lamb, pork, poultry and venison, but not fish. This includes canned, fresh, frozen, dehydrated, vacuum packed and freeze-dried meat products.

> **Fresh provisions** such as vegetables and fruits may not be landed and will be confiscated.

> **Anything that can sprout**: popcorn, sprouts, seeds and beans will also be taken away.

> **Honey** is not allowed as it may be contaminated with a virus that kills bees.

> **Eggs and egg cartons** will be confiscated.

Stored products will be inspected, assessed and depending on the disease risk released or destroyed.

Live plants may not be bought into the country.

Garbage from meat, eggs, fruit and vegetables must be disposed of in special bins as directed by the quarantine officer.

❖ **Before arriving** into port I undertake a clean out of the fresh food storage areas while making an inventory of the items I have left. Knowing the country's agriculture restrictions beforehand helps in using up supplies that are likely to be confiscated. If I've over provisioned I feel guilty wasting good produce so I work at utilizing as much fresh produce as possible the last few days at sea. On the up side it's great to be able to see the bottom of the fridge and I always look forward to discovering what's in season in each new port.

Where to Provision in Foreign Ports

❖ **Local markets** vary in quality worldwide but they're generally colorful, cheap and contain the best selection of fresh local produce.

❖ If available, do your bulk purchasing in a **large air-conditioned supermarket** with a guaranteed high turnover of products as this generally ensures your purchases are as fresh as possible and free from weevils.

❖ Some supermarkets **discount** for large orders.

❖ **Hiring a taxi** driver for bulk items and busy trips to the market or town help make the excursion less daunting.

Guides for Foreign Shopping

❖ Have a good knowledge of both the **metric and imperial systems**.

❖ At the least, learn **hello and thank you** in the local language of the country you are visiting. A few words and pleasant smile go a long way in aiding communication.

- If you are unfamiliar with the language carry a **translation dictionary**.
- Take your own **canvas tote bags** for carrying home your purchases.
- **Arrive early** at public markets for the freshest foods and best selection.
- In the local markets the **produce changes daily**. If you see an item that you need it's best to buy it there and then rather than wait.
- **Educate yourself** about local food, recipes, diseases, and endangered species.
- I carry **snapshots** of our boat when shopping and when I encounter a storekeeper or market stall owner who has good produce I'll introduce myself and give them one. This makes future provisioning a little easier as I can then request produce to my liking such as slighty ripe bananas instead of green or over ripe.
- Many supermarkets **don't have people to help pack your groceries** so you need to take someone with you to give you a hand. They can help push the cart, unload it, reduce the packaging and sort your groceries into their designated bags. It also helps avoid a queue of customers behind you.
- In many countries, the locals shop every day so goods are packaged in small quantities. If this is the case I'll ask the deli section to pack my items in **larger quantaties** and double wrap them.
- **Budget** for a meal or two out at a local restaurant. This way, you'll get a feel of what's available as you scan the menus.
- Take a cue from the locals and **dress accordingly**. Don't wear fancy jewelry or revealing clothes.
- **Be considerate**. Don't draw attention to yourself by being loud and demanding.
- If **security** is an issue, always go shopping with someone else. We sometimes hire a taxi driver instead of renting a car or taking the bus if we're unsure of the lay of the land.
- Ask before **picking or gathering** fresh produce that you see lying about, as they may be someone's property. The same also goes for inshore fishing, be it the area or type of seafood you're gathering.

Food Items Readily Available Worldwide

Bread – white
Butter
Cheese – processed or long life
Cookies – very plain and or rather sweet
Cooking oil
Cake mix
Hot dogs – canned
Corned beef – canned
Flour – white
Fruit – canned
Mayonnaise
Milk powder
Pasta – white spaghetti noodles
Pulses – beans, lentils
Rice – white
Sugar – white
Soft drinks
Spam
Tomato suces
Tuna – canned
Vegetables – canned
2-minute noodles

Items Hard to Find or Expensive in Remote Loctions

❖ **Antibacterial soap.**

❖ **Baking mixes:** pancake, muffin, bread, waffle, bread, brownie, and cookie are most often available in American ports and large bulk buy stores that import goods.

❖ **Beans and seeds** for sprouting.

❖ **Breakfast cereal:** variety may be hard to find but basic brands such as corn flakes and rice crispies are frequently available and not too expensive.

❖ **Biodegradable soap.**

❖ **Cans** of whole chickens, chilies, pie filling, boneless chicken, ham, turkey, roast beef and ready-to-go meals.

❖ **Chicken breasts** either frozen or fresh are often expensive or unavailable. Boneless, skinless, and iced glazed breasts are available throughout the world at Costco Warehouse stores. Although they take up more space than freezing fresh breasts they're often a good buy.

❖ **Chocolate chips** may be difficult to find or in the tropics may come melted together. An option is to cut up dark chocolate bars.

❖ **Condiments** including peanut butter, bacon bits, maple syrup plus American brand ketchup, hot sauces and mayonaise.

❖ **Dish soaps** vary in quality. Some local brands may not suds up well and may not be biodegradable.

❖ **Ethnic ingredients** such as bamboo shoots, baby corn, water chestnuts, curries and herbs.

❖ **Fruit juice** concentrate without large amounts of sugar may be unavailable.

❖ **Grains** like farro, quinoa, wild rice, cracked wheat, etc.

❖ **Health bars** and other nutritious individually wrapped snacks.

❖ **Ham slices** and cold cuts for sandwiches may be of poor quality and expensive.

❖ **Ice cube bags:** disposable plastic pocketed bags that make ice cubes for drinks.

❖ **Hot drinks:** herbal teas, hot chocolate, ground coffee and assorted black teas may be of various quality and expensive.

❖ **Nuts and seeds** are generally only available in small packets and are expensive.

❖ **Pastas** of any specialty such as lasagna, spinach or whole wheat.

❖ **Paper towel rolls** vary in size throughout the world, so consider installing a holder with a center bar that goes through the roll. The quality of paper also varies with some falling apart as soon as they're wet while others act like grease proof paper.

❖ **Raisins** and other dried fruit and berries.

Cruising the Aisles

We cleared into Chile in the city of Puerto Montt and spent a week outfitting at Marina Del Sur before sailing south on expeditions to Cape Horn, Argentina and Antarctica. Eighteen months later we returned in order to prepare for an eight-week passage, with four expedition crew, to the Marquesas via Easter Island and Pitcairn, knowing that our next major provisioning port would be Hawaii several months later.

Over the past year I'd acquired many shopping skills so provisioning the second time around in this bustling town was far less daunting than when we'd first arrived. The biggest improvement was being able to speak and understand more of the language. I'd only a basic knowledge of Spanish when we first arrived and was rather shy about using it. Chileans are most friendly and though most don't speak English they go out of their way to encourage communication, always with a big smile. At first, when I was out and about, I constantly referred to a small pocket Spanish dictionary I carrried but as my confidence and vocabulary grew I found that I didn't need to rely on it as much.

To provision for a passage my first visit to town is taken rather casually. I'm like a submarine with its periscope up as I'm surveying the scene while compiling a mental inventory of what's available and the prices. Before heading into town, I've already asked fellow cruisers and the marina office what's the best supermarket to shop at. Puerto Montt is easy to navigate. The bus from the marina takes you along the port waterfront to downtown where the two largest supermarkets are situated next to each other and a colorful thriving local produce market fills the surrounding streets and plaza.

Supermarcado is the largest store and I cruise its aisles with a slightly glazed look, absorbing and plotting, while preparing for my second excursion through its islands of shelves in a few days. This shopping mission is small; one bag of items that we'll consume over the next few days. I wander through the local market where wheelbarrows overflow with bananas, cherries and grapes. Parcels of cilantro and piles of tomatoes form colorful displays among heads of cabbage and lettuce. In between the stands of fruit and vegetables are other stalls with mounds of smoked shellfish looking interesting and inviting but we've been warned to avoid them as they may be affected by red tide.

Under a gaily colored umbrella a man calls out from behind a bench with a large chopping board. He reaches beneath the table and produces a gigantic salmon from an iced tub and then skillfully fillets the fish according to the customers instructions. A glass cabinet nearby displays smoked trout and salmon fillets wrapped in plastic ready for purchase. They share shelves with curling-stone-sized local cheeses sealed in bright waxes and large jars of cloudy local honey.

A slight pause in front of the cabinet produces an excited response from the vendor, who eagerly asks if I would care to try a small sample. With a flourish, he cuts a slice of cheese and passes it to me on the blade, next is a sliver of salmon, followed by a wooden stick dipped in honey. I purchase a salmon fillet knowing that this is one stand I'll return to.

Two days later, I again catch the bus to town. I'm now carrying eight canvas carry bags and two large duffels. I exit the bus and tour the market stands introducing myself to a stall keeper whose produce looks the healthiest. I mention that I'm off a sailboat and will be leaving for Easter Island in a few days. Together we discuss the items I'll require, their state of ripeness and the quantities. We arrange to meet again on Saturday and I hand over a picture our yacht sailing in Tahiti. With a toothless smile, he shakes my hand and introduces himself as Luis.

I enter the supermarket and exchange my jacket and bags at the baggage counter for a numbered disk. Collecting a shopping cart, I steer down the rows of shelves, loading the cart with non-perishable items. Canned goods are easy to choose as their labels contain brightly colored pictures of the contents. Condiments are my next selection: mayonnaise, mustard, ketchup and imported salad dressings, followed by olive oil and vinegar.

Toilet paper is cheap but paper towels are more expensive than in North America. In the health food section I select local herbal teas and

Foreign Provisioning

small expensive packets of raisins, dried fruit and nuts. Nestle has a high market share of goods producing inexpensive two-minute noodles, cookies, hot chocolate and breakfast cereals. Beans, rice and pasta are easily found and added to the cart which is then topped up with flour, sugar and cleaning supplies.

As I approach the checkout I produce my credit card and wait patiently as a separate counter is opened up to process it. Two young boys appear and they're very efficient at packing items for long-distance travel as the supermarket supplies many isolated estancias (ranches) and salmon farms. Boxes and balls of twine are at the ready waiting to truss up my purchases, complete with handles.

I politely refuse the boxes and hand over my baggage claim number explaining that I'd like the items packed into my own bags. To eliminate any unnecessary packaging on board, I request that they remove breakfast cereal packs from their boxes. The boys grin and tear the boxes apart with relish. It's a delight to have help as in some countries – such as Argentina and French Polynesia – I've discovered that I'm on my own in the checkout department.

Ten minutes later my stuffed bags are loaded into a waiting taxi and I leap in after them to be whisked away through town back to the boat. Below it's a hectic couple of hours as I gain access to stowage spaces under the floorboards and bunks plus behind the main saloon settee. I'm also busy transferring bulk items into small handy squeeze-bottles or smaller containers if it's kept in the galley. The remaining supplies are stored in large plastic sealed containers or Ziploc bags.

Saturday I meet a welcoming Luis at his market stall and we review my order plus select more fruits and vegetables that are unavailable in the supermarket. He adds up the amount and gives a 10 percent discount for such a large order. I load the produce into canvas bags and leave them beneath his counter for later collection. I call by the salmon stand and choose a smoked salmon fillet plus a large block of farmers cheese from the northern Lake District.

It's now time for the final supermarket showdown and I enter ready for action. I'm purchasing perishable goods and start at the deli department where I ask the assistant to slice ham and cheese into 2 kg. packages. This took me a while to figure out. When I provisioned for Cape Horn the deli packs of ham and cheese only had six slices on a plastic-wrapped polystyrene tray. This resulted in a more rubbish and took up a fair share of fridge space.

Quickly, I grab an empanada for lunch which I'll eat it on the taxi ride home. I collect four roasted chickens that smell divine and proceed to the in-house bakery section which emits delicious aromas and where I smartly sweep up loaves of hot sliced wheat bread. Next I carefully deposit seven cartons of brown eggs into the cart having checked them for breakages. I gather up items from the dairy section – yogurt, butter cheese and bacon from the open fridge. From the large freezers I choose pastry for quiches, frozen vegetables, imported shrimp, flash-frozen Chilean fish fillets and chicken. We don't eat much red meat but it's readily available and best purchased fresh in the meat department.

I blaze through the checkout, pile into a taxi, swing by the market to collect my bags saying farewell to Luis and then head back to the marina. Loading the fridge and freezer takes planning. Three hours later the fridge containers are packed, labeled and stacked, and the freezer is loaded with layers of quart Ziploc bags containing diced chicken, fish, meat and vegetables. I slump down on the settee, three roasted chickens sitting before me and proceed to pull off the meat and place it into quart Ziploc bags for freezing. Next, five dozen eggs each get a light coating of Vaseline before being stowed in a galley locker.

I'm done and greatful to have saved some roast chicken to eat with a fresh salad for dinner. Thank goodness we're leaving on Monday giving me Sunday to scan my provisions and meal plans to ensure we've got all we need.

Food and Waterborne Illnesses

Amoebic Dysentery

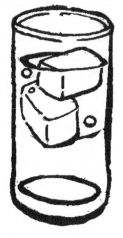

If cruising in areas where amoebic dysentery from contaminated water and vegetables is known to occur, laboratory stool exams should be carried out annually or at least upon return to your home country. Have your stools checked if you experience chronic diarrhea or cramping, particularly with fever. If amoebiasis goes untreated it can cause dangerous liver problems. Giardia from contaminated water, another less severe form of amoebic infection, should also be treated. It can cause cramping, nausea, gas and loose stools but not blood in the stool or fever.

Botulism - Canned Food Poisoning

Botulism is a highly dangerous food poisoning from improperly canned foods. It can be acquired not only from ingestion of toxic food but from touch and inhalation of toxic fumes. Even if there is no odor, gas, or signs of food spoilage, botulism can still be present in food. The toxins affect the nervous system and progress to paralysis and respiratory failure. Prevention is essential. These measures include: meticulous sterilizing technique for canning goods, careful can storage to prevent rust and punctures of cans and prudent inspection of cans before opening for signs of spoilage, i.e., bulging ends. Hissing or exploding contents upon opening is definitive of spoilage. Suspect metal cans will start to bulge, due to the gas production from bacterial growth, and should be discarded.

Home-canned foods are best boiled for 10 minutes before eating, allowing the high temperatures to destroy the botulism toxin.

Honey from any source or country should not be given to infants younger than one year due to a risk of developing an infantile variety of botulism.

Cholera

Cholera is acquired from contaminated food and water and is a severe infectious diarrhea that occurs in epidemics, particularly in Asia and Africa. However, the infection may also be mild and self-limiting for two to seven days. Alternatively, it may be a massive diarrhea that can be fatal.

In areas where cholera is common, special preventive measures should be taken. Some endemic regions require cholera vaccinations; refer to *Health Information for the International Traveler* for a list. Recent studies using an oral vaccination have been promising. The cholera organism is easily destroyed by chlorination and heating of water. Avoid eating uncooked vegetables and drinking contaminated water.

Symptoms: diarrhea stools from cholera have the appearance of "rice water" and may also be associated with vomiting, fever and abdominal cramps. If fluids and electrolyte levels in the body can't be maintained, severe dehydration progressing to shock and death may occur quite rapidly, otherwise recovery is easily achieved. Treatment includes replacing body fluids and electrolytes at the same rate of loss using oral rehydration solution. In severe situations, intravenous fluid replacement is necessary, and medical assistance required. Don't use Lomotil or Imodium in cases of severe watery diarrhea. Treatment with Tetracycline or another antibiotic kills the bacteria and usually stops the diarrhea in 48 hours.

Hepatitis A

Hepatitis A is a viral infection of the liver acquired from contaminated food, water, and shellfish in areas of poor sanitation. Cruisers in tropical regions and in developing countries who don't travel the usual tourist routes may be at greater risk for infectious hepatitis. People visiting areas with high incidences of hepatitis A and B should consider protection with a preventive vaccine named Havrix. Prevention for infectious hepatitis requires avoiding contaminated foods and shellfish taken from contaminated or suspect water. Water should be considered contaminated and possibly harboring hepatitis in areas with poor sanitation, for example if there is a village or animals upstream.

Symptoms of the illness begin with mild flu-like symptoms: anorexia, malaise, fever, nausea, vomiting and headache. It's during the initial 14 days of hepatitis that it is most contagious. The infection can be transmitted by direct contact, using the same dishes, poor hygiene

Foreign Provisioning

and sanitation, lack of hand washing and from kissing.

Jaundice doesn't always occur with hepatitis. If jaundice occurs, the yellow eyes and skin appear 3-10 days after the flu-like symptoms, and may be associated with dark urine, light colored stools and itchy skin. Affected persons are no longer infectious once the jaundice is obvious. The jaundice peaks in 1-2 weeks and the patient will start to feel better despite the worsening color.

Positive diagnosis of hepatitis involves blood tests. Antibiotics will not help hepatitis. Debilitating convalescence with listlessness, depression, and poor appetite may last from several weeks to four months. Care should be taken to ensure adequate rest during this time to promote healing and prevent lasting liver damage. In severe cases, with significant fluid loss from diarrhea and with reduced fluid intake, one could become seriously ill. Encourage the patient to drink small amounts at frequent intervals especially in hot weather. If significant dehydration should occur, medical help should be sought for intravenous fluid and electrolyte replacement. This can usually be accomplished even in poorly equipped medical facilities.

Hepatitis A virus is excreted in the urine, stool, and saliva for the first two to three weeks. Appropriate isolation measures should be taken to prevent others from contacting infected material.

The compromised liver function associated with hepatitis can be minimized by abstinence from drugs that are metabolized in the liver and from alcohol, for up to one year. A low fat diet is recommended

with hepatitis because the liver is involved with digestion. Aspirin preparations should be avoided with hepatitis because of the possibilities of increased bleeding tendencies.

Salmonella

Salmonella bacteria occur in infected meat, poultry, raw milk, eggs and egg products. Salmonella infection causes gastrointestinal upset 12 to 48 hours after ingesting infected food.

Symptoms are nausea, abdominal cramp, diarrhea, fever, and sometimes vomiting. The upset lasts 1 to 4 days and is usually mild. Treatment involves plenty of fluids and a bland diet. Salmonella occurs on the shell of freshly-laid eggs. When using unwashed eggs don't use cracked eggs and ensure that the shell does not come into contact with the contents. Never let foods containing uncooked eggs remain at warm temperatures for more than an hour. Salmonella reproduces in food held at temperatures 40° to 140° and is killed when food temperatures reach 140°. To avoid salmonella contamination in raw chicken, clean all equipment, surfaces and containers used in preparation with hot soapy water.

Staphylococcal

Staphylococcal food poisoning occurs from eating food contaminated with staphylococci bacteria and results in diarrhea and vomiting. Food becomes contaminated when people with staphylococcal skin infections, such as boils, handle food that is then left at room temperature, allowing the bacteria to grow. Foods likely to become contaminated are custard, cream-filled pastry, milk, processed meats and fish.

Symptoms of nausea, vomiting, abdominal cramp, diarrhea, headache, and fever last less than twelve hours. Treatment consists of drinking adequate fluids with electrolyte replacement and complete recovery is usually ensured.

Worms

Intestinal worms are common in some less-developed communities and are easily acquired from eating inadequately cooked pork, beef, fish, and from water. They are relatively harmless and treatment can usually wait until the next port.

Symptoms may be vague and go unnoticed. Drug therapy for pinworm, which causes rectal itching among children, and roundworm, which can be seen in the stool as large, earthworm size creatures is Pyrantel-Pamoate (Antiminth) or Vermox (Mebendazole), usually available worldwide in pharmacies.

Poisonous Animals

Ciguatera - Fish Poisoning

Ciguatera , which occurs between the latitudes of 35°N and 35°S, is food born illness caused by eating reef fish whose flesh is contaminated with certain toxins. Outbreaks are usually localized and its occurrence is unpredictable and patchy both in distribution and time.

Cooking will not destroy the toxins. Some island cultures test fish for ciguatera by first feeding it to a cat. The toxin is cumulative so larger reef fish like barracuda and red snapper that are higher on the food chain are more poisonous. Pelagic (ocean going) fish such as tuna and mahi mahi, are least likely to be affected.

Eating a small portion of the affected fish may not produce symptoms but eating more at a second meal could increase the toxin levels enough to produce poisoning.

Ciguatera poisoning affects the nerves and gastrointestinal system. It's fatal in three percent of cases in the Pacific but rarely in the Caribbean.

Symptoms can start immediately or up to 30 hours later. Severe cases may occur earlier and milder cases may be precipitated by alcohol ingestion.

Clinical Features Include:

General weakness: tingling and numbness, especially of face, hands and feet, respiratory failure in severe cases.

Reversal of temperature perception: hot feels cold and cold feels hot.

Red itchy rash and sometimes hives.

Varying degrees of gastrointestinal symptoms: nausea, vomiting, diarrhea and/or abdominal cramps.

Uncomplicated episodes usually subside in 24 hours, but residual weaknesses, numbness and temperature perception reversal may last for many months. Flare-ups may occur with ingestion of alcohol or more ciguatera toxic fish.

Prevention:

Check with knowledgeable locals on types and location of safe reef fish.

Eat only smaller reef fish, testing with a small portion first.

Avoid ingesting fish organs as these have higher levels of toxin than flesh.

Avoid eating barracuda and tropical moray eels at they have a high incidence of ciguatera.

Test the fish on an animal or adult, as children are more susceptible to ciguatera poisoning.

Treatment:

Induce vomiting and use laxatives to remove any remaining unabsorbed toxins.

Bed rest and reassurance.

Resuscitation in extremely severe cases.

Medical assistance and hospitalization for observation of all but mild episode.

Paralytic Shellfish Poisoning

Paralytic shellfish poisoning (PSP) or red tide is caused by consuming a toxin produced in blooming red algae that accumulates in crabs, clams, lobsters, mussels, oysters, scallops and whelks. PSP occurs even after food has been cooked and attacks the nerves. The algae blooms occur in both the Pacific and Atlantic oceans above 30°N and below 30°S.

Symptoms start as a tingling and numbness around the lips and mouth that spreads to the face and neck beginning 5 to 30 minutes after eating. Nausea, vomiting and cramps follow. 25 percent of affected people develop muscle weakness which may progress to paralysis.

High levels of PSP can result in severe illness and death.

Puffer Fish Poisoning

Puffer fish are highly toxic if eaten. Fortunately, they're easy to identify by their ability to inflate themselves with water or air. All varieties throughout the world contain tetraodon poisoning, including porcupine and ocean sunfishes. Although the Japanese consider these a delicacy preparation by anyone other than an expert is not advised.

Symptoms of poisoning are similar to ciguatera.

Endangered Food to Avoid

❖ **Triton Shells** are the only natural predator of the crown-of-thorns starfish, which can destroy coral reefs rapidly if the natural balance is thrown off.

❖ **Lobster** take several years to reproduce and have been overfished in many areas by locals and cruisers.

❖ **Turtle**. All seven species of marine turtles are considered threatened, yet it continues to be legal to hunt sea turtles in 42 countries and territories worldwide.

❖ **Whale meat**. Politely refuse any offers of whale meat.

Chapter 20

PELAGIC
FISHING

"Fishing with Big Poppa Gus"

While canning conjures up memories of my Nana (grandmother) fishing brings my grandfather to life. My poppa Gus was a colorful character, always enjoying the simple pleasures of life like working in the garden, a local Saturday rugby match, and fishing. A favorite photo shows him casually leaning on the swing clothesline, a slow smile on his lips, sparkling eyes. While one hand is hanging on a clothesline wire the other holds a 25-lb. red snapper, a result of a quiet morning spent out on the bay in his boat away from Nana's chatting.

Nana and Poppa would join us in autumn as we cruised around the Northland coast. We'd go hiking with Nana, listening to her stories throughout the day as we marched up bush clad peaks and swam in cold stoney rivers, Dad always hoped that the fast pace he set would tire her out so maybe she'd be quiet for awhile.

Pop would stay aboard, a fishing line lazily dangling in the water. Locals would swing by and call out, "There's nothing left in the bay mate, we've been cleaned out this summer." He'd listen, smile and ask if they'd heard a cricket match score, changing the subject as he nonchalantly reeled in his line with another beauty of a snapper on the hook. We'd sail through a flock of working birds, their frantic diving a sign that kahawai fish were also around. Pop and I would stand on the aft deck each with a line in hand. As the fish bit and we hauled them in hand-over-hand Pop would quietly mention that he'd give me 50 cents for every fish I caught over his. Dad would cut donuts through the birds and time after time we'd haul in our lines, remove the active fish from the hook, then toss the line back out behind us. My heart would pound with excitement as I'd try to beat Pop, mindless of the blood splattering about from the caught fish flapping around our ankles.

Now when I haul in my line, a large pelagic fish fighting for it's life, I say a prayer to poppa Gus. Each fish has his name on it, a silent tribute to a wonderful man. It's not the 50 cents that come to mind but an appreciation for the fishing skills he taught me along with the importance of giving thanks for marvelous gifts from nature.

Fish You Can Catch

Tuna ~ Yellow Fin, Big-Eye, Bonito, Skipjack and Albacore

Tuna are the most common fish to catch on ocean passages. When caught on a meat line they're not so large as to be out of control once landed. Tuna can survive in depths up to 1,000 ft and as they're red-blooded, once landed they need to be bled to rid the meat of blood. They're tubby, shaped like a rugby ball, ranging from one to three feet in length and they hit hard on the lure and tend to dive deep. Tuna carry a lot of meat and a single fish can provide several meals. The best meat comes from around the tummy and you need to fillet around the dark red meat that runs the length of the side bones as well as the meat that contains the strings of white tough muscle. Yellow fin tuna, easily identified by its yellow crescent tail and fins, are the most delicious of the tunas with firm rose-colored meat. Black skipjack and big eye tuna's meat tends to be quite red and bloody, containing many strips of white sinuous tissue.

Mackerel ~ Spanish, Pacific, Wahoo

Wahoo is my favorite fish. I rarely catch them in the middle of the ocean but as we get closer to land I'm more likely to hook one. It's a long blue, black, and white-striped fish resembling a barracuda with a smiling face. It's easily handled once caught and requires little bleeding. Wahoo's white flesh is firm and it cooks, barbecues, marinates and freezes well. It's particularly good in ceviche and *Poisson-Cru*.

Mahi Mahi or Dorado

Considered the prince and princess of the tropics, mahi mahi have two dazzling color costumes. While swimming, their display is cobalt spots on an indigo back with pearl sides. When excited, their back becomes an iridescent emerald, their sides turn golden with fluorescent blue spots and their fins turn azure. Mahi are surface dwellers, they like to linger around floating debris and can sometimes be viewed swimming alongside the boat. Tahitian fisherman chase down mahi in a speedboat with a joy stick control in the bow. When they draw alongside a tired fish, they then spear it to bring it aboard. This requires great skill as mahi have exceptional eyesight and attain speeds of 40 mph. Reaching full length at six months, they're a long, lean, compressed fish. The male is easily distinguished from the female by it's higher rounded forehead. It's sad to watch them die for they rapidly flash through their wardrobe of colors, paling to a spotty milky white. They don't require bleeding and their flesh is lean, soft and juicy.

Billfish ~ Black, Blue, and Striped Marlin, Swordfish, and Sailfish

With billfish populations on the decline globally, I refrain from catching these fish. If we hook a billfish or shark we bring it along side so I can hopefully save the lure by sliding it up the line, away from the hook and fish, before cutting the leader with wire cutters.

Lures, Lines and Equipment

This following details the equipment I use for basic trolling otherwise called meat fishing. I think "meat fishing" sounds like I'm out to catch a great white shark so I prefer to call it trolling. You can create your own lures and I've heard many fish tales from people catching fish by dragging almost anything covering a hook. I'm not going to offer instructions on how to make lures from scratch but I'll share what's worked for me. To learn what lures are catching fish ask around, talk to fellow cruisers, local fishermen, and visit shops that carry lures.

Carry a selection of lures for if you haven't caught a fish you can try switching them out. Catching a fish is not an instant event, you need patience.

Line

Use a 120 ft. length of 200 lb. monofilament line terminated with a sturdy stainless swivel and closed hooked catch to attach lure leaders.

Reel

We use a round 12-inch plastic reel that the line gets wound around by hand. Previously I used a 8" x 12" piece of plywood with a V cut out at each end to hold a wrapped line.

A more user-friendly option is having a winding reel mounted on the rail.

Leader

For the leader, attaching the lure to the fishing line, I rig a 6' length of 200 lb. stainless steel wire. An end loop, in the leader, allows you to easily change out lures from the attachement hook in your monofilament line. Made of wire so that the fish don't bite through it, the leader also needs to be long so the fish don't notice the attachment swivel, and to provide enough length to save the lure if you catch billfish or shark.

Crimper and Sleeves

If you're serious about catching fish invest in a hand-crimping tool and appropriate sleeve sizes for both your leader wires and monofilament line. John bought me a cripmer as a birthday present after he'd repeatedly witnessed my distress when my squish job with pliers would fail and I'd lose both fish and lure. Now making lures is fun and it's easy to replace the hooks when they get broken or straightened out by a big fish.

Wire Cutters

This tool gives you a nice clean cut through your leader wire, making it easier to thread on the sleeves.

Lures

There are two main types of lures suitable for ocean trolling and both aim to mimic the food fish eat.

❖ A **flying fish** lure is most commonly a 6" Rapala painted metallic blue and silver to resemble a small fish. Rapalas come fitted with two small triple hooks that soon rust, one situated on the belly and the other at the tail. They have a spoon protruding above the fish lure's mouth to make it ride better. I've had reasonable success catching wahoo with a Rapala when close to land and around reefs but not out in the ocean. Wahoo tend to swallow the lure and hook good and hard so take care when removing the hook.

❖ If you're keen you can rig your own flying fish lures. "Louie the Fish", a keen fisherman and bone carver from American Samoa, ensures me that the best lure is using the real thing: Collect a flying fish that lands on deck. Insert a wire leader inside the flying fish's mouth and exit out the underside of the belly. Attach a large single hook and insert it into the belly so that just the curved hook is showing. You may need to wire the hook in place. Connect the lure to your line and troll it behind.

❖ **Squid** are also eaten by big fish and sometimes when I've opened a fish stomach I've found them inside. As squid have the ability to turn many colors, thus attracting fish, squid lures give you a creative license to asssemble your own designs by choosing your materials and colors.

At the top end of the market: production designer resin cast heads with wiggle eyes and a double neck to attach two squid skirts with whipping. Zuker are my favorite brand of resin heads with the overall head size being about 2¼" and the color a deep blue. I generally whip on two 8-inch squid skirts of different colors.

A cheaper version of a squid lure is a simple rugby ball-shaped lead weight with a hole down the length. The lead gets inserted inside an 8" plastic squid skirt then threaded with a wire leader and hook. I find this lure a little heavy so it tends to troll deep and the squid skirt don't last as long as when they're attached to resin heads.

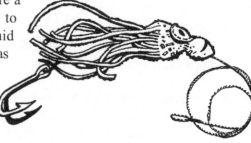

When I troll a second line and lure, with

a cheaper smaller squid of a different color to the main line, the Zuker lure gets the most strikes.

If you're whipping skirts onto your lures you need to carry a good supply as the fish's sharp teeth rip them up.

Lure Colors

It's totally up to you what colors you choose for your lures. You need to experiment, keeping in mind the species of fish you're targeting. I usually open up the stomach of the fish I catch to see what they've been feeding on. Note what the common food source is in the area you're fishing. Shades of metallic pink and gold resemble the color of squid when they flash and these colors have worked well for me. Green, blue and silver mimic the colors of small bait fish and if you're in an area of pelagic algae or seaweed try matching its green to amber colors. Fish scrutinize the ocean's surface for food so choose a color opposite from the weather conditions to create a distinction. If it's bright and sunny choose dark purples, deep blues and maroons for your lures. On cloudy days, try lighter shades of color such a pink, orange and sliver.

Fish Hooks

I use a double 2 ½" barbed stainless steel hook with my lures. They're more expensive than steel but are stronger, last longer, don't rust or stain anything, and it's easy to keep a sharp point on the hook with a small file. Rig the hook so that the bend of the hook protrudes slightly from the base of the skirt. Small plastic beads threaded on the leader wire help space the distance from the hook to the lure. You can also place crimps on the wire to keep the hook at a set distance.

Setting the Line

Trolling Distance

There are many different theories as to how much line to let out. I'm pretty much a set-and-forget person while others say adjust the line throughout the day, especially if you're not having any luck, the shortest distance being a boat length.

I pay out 100' of line, run it over the middle rail of the aft stanchion, and then cleat it off on the aft deck cleat. There's a better chance of catching a fish if you run out two lines.

Pelagic Fishing

Speed

Boat speed is not too critical, though the general consensus is the faster the better. Our average speed is 6 to 8 knots and this works well. I've talked with many boats that average faster speeds than us and they too catch fish.

Clip and Rubber

To set the hook in the fish's mouth and avoid your line breaking when a fish strikes you can rig a shock absorber in the line.

- ❖ The simplest method is to clip up a loop of line with a **clothespin**. When the fish takes the line it trips the clothespin and has a few feet of line to run with allowing it to swallow the hook.

- ❖ Another option is to install a **rubber link** in the line. The rubber is tied into the line so that it takes some to the shock of the fish hitting the line.

Alarm

You can rig a bell on the line so that it rings when you have a fish in tow.

Remember:

- ❖ **Announce to the crew** that the fishing lines are out and mention that they can no longer turn the boat around in a hurry in case they run over the lines and foul the propeller or rudder.

- ❖ **Never leave the lines in the water** if you're in little wind or making no way through the water as the lines may foul your propeller or rudder.

- ❖ Remember to **look aft to check** if you've caught a fish. On a recent passage one of our expedition crew set the lines after we'd not been fishing for a few days due to bad weather. At the end of his watch Jimbo pulled in a line and discovered a battered fish head on the hook. Oops, we'd dragged the poor fish for his entire watch as no one remembered to see if we'd caught anything.

- ❖ I generally don't rig an alarm as I try and train our crew to frequently scan aft to see if we've caught anything. Sometimes we incidentally gather flotsam or **seaweed on the hook.**

Catching a Fish

Time

The best time for catching fish is at sunset. For us this is rather an inconvenient time as I'm generally in the middle of preparing the evening meal having already defrosted something to eat. However, fresh fish is always welcome! Sunset is not always a guaranteed time catch time as I've caught fish in all hours of the day and in conditions ranging from bright sunshine to gray skies.

Flotsam and Jetsam

Fish hang around flotsam, so swing off course to trail your lures beside floating matter. In the fishing world flotsam is defined as anything found floating in the sea - a common log, a discarded wooden pallet, nets, ropes or rafts of sargassum weed. No matter what the floater is made up of, it represents a unique opportunity for life to take hold and form its own ecosystem, which in turn attracts fish.

Currents

Fish follow the warmer ocean currents so keep an eye on the seawater temperature.

Landfall

Within a day or so of making landfall is a good time to be fishing. Even if you don't need the fish, someone ashore will be grateful for it.

Birds

A flock of feeding, diving birds is an indication that bigger fish are driving smaller fish to the surface in a feeding frenzy. It's more likely this will occur closer to land as these feeding birds roost ashore each night. If fishing, consider altering course to cruise through the middle of the diving flock. A good idea is to start the engine and continue doing runs through the working birds.

Nighttime

For safety's sake it's wise to pull fishing lines in at dusk. I heard from Crystal on the Irish yacht *Turn-nah-nog* that they caught a wicked creature one night. With bulging eyes, spiky fins and razor sharp teeth there was no way they wanted it aboard, even to save their lure, so they cut it away.

Have I Caught a Fish?

Once you set the lure you need to study how much tension is on the line and the direction it leads due to swell and wind. When a fish strikes, the line will go taut, the alarm will sound, and the fish will either break to the surface or swim. A fish can easily swim the same speed as the boat, fooling you into thinking it got away. Slowly pull in the line until the fish breaks the surface and starts to tire. Sometimes you might miss the alarm and not notice the fish until it's being dragged behind which is very obvious due to the disturbed water.

Landing the Catch

When a fish is on the hook, it's best to start reeling it in as soon as possible so that it doesn't get away. Towing the fish tires it out and brings it to the surface, making it easier to pull in. Fresh air also starts to kill the fish. You need to be quick if you're in an area of sharks, as your fishy may soon become chomped.

While one person is reeling in the fish, John and I set about assembling all the necessary processing equipment: gaff hook, rum, sail tie, cutting board, knife, bucket, dish soap, scrub brush, and container. As a fish catching event is rather messy, I'll change into and old swimsuit though it's not overly glamorous for the finale catch photo.

1. When the fish is alongside **gaff** it through the gills. Our gaff hook is extendable and can reach the water while standing on the deck.

2. We're now a total of three people to land one fish; one on the line, John on the gaff hook, and someone to pour **rum** down the gullet of the fish as it's lifted out of the water. Rum, you may well ask, but it works wonders to sedate the fish and saves a lot of the bloodshed and violence other methods produce. Any cheap alcohol will do and as we generally have an overzealous crew in the alcohol pouring department it may require a fair amount.

3. Now that the fish is quiet, don't think you've got it under control. Next slip an old webbing **sail tie,** with a loop, over the tail of the fish so both the gaffer and sail tie holder can lift the fish aboard. Then tie the fish down with the sail tie.

   Another option is to place the fish in a **garbage bag**. Once its eyes are covered it will slowy beome quiet. You can then fillet the fish inside the bag thus reducing the amount of clean up.

4. If you've caught a **red blooded fish** such as tuna, and you're not planning on filleting it right away, you'll need to bleed the fish so that the meat is not rich in blood. I generally make an incision behind the head and using a sail tie I'll hang the fish by the tail over the side for about 5 minutes.

5. I then position the fish over our a large **plastic cutting board** and proceed to fillet it with a sharp knife.

6. John is the cleanup crew and stands by with **bucket, scrub brush, and dish soap**. It pays to keep your filleting area damp with salt water so the fish blood doesn't dry and stain.

7. Once the fish is filleted, place the fillets in a **container** and pass them below to the chef.

8. **Clean up** begins with a scrub down of myself before I go below to change. The scrub bucket brigade follows, cleaning all the equipment and deck.

Cookie Cutter Shark

If you land a fish and it has a two-inch or smaller disc of meat removed from the flesh, don't throw it back thinking it has an ulcer. This hole is caused by the cookie cutter shark; an amazing little fellow who flashes his body bright colors to attract fish. The fish then think it's a squid and approaches the shark who then flips back its head, opens its jaws wide, bites the fish then executes a tail spin, thus removing a perfect circle of flesh from the fish.

Marks made by cookiecutter sharks have been found on marine mammals, fishes, as wall as on submarines, undersea cables, and even human bodies.

Filleting a Fish

Filleting a large fish for the first time can be daunting so it helps to have the right equipment. My knife is an 8" stainless steel fillet knife with a protective sheath made by Dexter Russell and available from West Marine or any commercial fishing supplier in the U.S. It gets sharpened after each catch with a good quality knife sharpener.

Filleting a Small Fish
Mackerel and Mahi Mahi

1. On a cutting board, place the fish on its side with the belly towards you.

2. Cut through the skin behind the head and slice halfway through the fish as if you were cutting off the top quarter of its head. Work your way along the spine and across the belly avoiding the stomach as shown in the diagram.

3. Turn the fish around.

4. Insert the knife, held horizontal at the tail, and slice your way up the length of the fish's back along the dorsal fin. Keep the knife blade horizontal along the dorsal fin and the tip of the blade just hitting the spine. Stop when you reach the cut you made to the head.

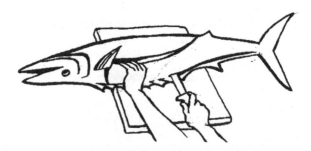

5. Turn the fish around and starting at the tail, slice up the other side as you did in step 4, until you reach the stomach.

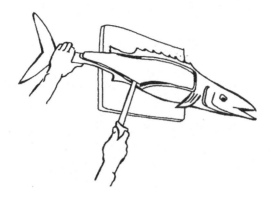

6. Starting at the tail lift up the fillet and with the knife held horizontal slice up the spine to release the fillet from the backbone. If the fish is a mahi you will need to work up and over each vertebrae. Skirt around the stomach.

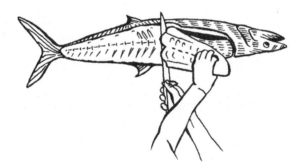

7. Turn the fish over and repeat on the other side.

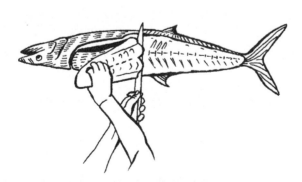

8. You're now done with the carcass.

9. By now your knife has lost its sharp edge which is ideal as you don't want a knife that is too sharp to remove the skin.

10. Place a fillet on cutting board with the skin side down. Insert the knife at the tail end, and while keeping the knife horizontal to the board, hold the tail skin flat as cut along the length of fillet removing the skin.

11. Repeat with the other fillet.

11. For each fillet cut away the rib cage, any dark meat or unwanted bones.

13. Keep fillets in a container.

Filleting a Large Fish

Tuna

Filleting a large tuna requires more slicing than the previous steps as the fish is tubby with a quartered bone structure whereas the mahi and wahoo have a flatter stronger spine. You'll be filleting this fish in four sections.

1. On a cutting board place the fish on its side with the belly towards you.

2. Cut through the skin behind the head and slice halfway through the fish as if you were cutting off the top quarter of its head. Work your way vertically along the spine and across the belly, avoiding the stomach as shown in the diagram for mahi and wahoo.

3. Insert the knife, held horizontal at the tail, and work your way up the length of the fish's back along the dorsal fin. Keep the knife blade horizontal along the dorsal fin and the tip of the blade just hitting the spine. Stop when you reach the cut you made to the head.

4. Lift the fillet up and cut it away from the rib cage.

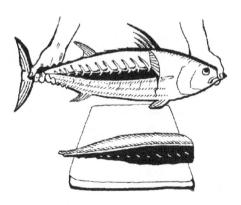

5.   Turn the fish around and starting at the tail, again cut through the other side as you did in step 3, until you reach the stomach. Once again lift up the fillet and remove it from the rib cage.

6.   Turn the fish over and repeat on the other side. You're now done with the carcass.

7.   Place a fillet on cutting board with the skin side down. Insert the knife at the tail end, and while keeping the knife horizontal to the board, hold the tail skin flat as cut along the length of fillet removing the skin.

8.   Remove any bones, dark meat, and sinuous veins.

9.   Repeat for the other fillets.

10.   Place fillets in a container.

Preserving Fish

Fresh Fish

I cut up the choicest fillets to use for dinner either that night or the following day, and keep them in the fridge. At dinner I usually cook up extra fillets for the following days lunchtime meal, either salad or sandwiches, unless the fish is a firm white flesh then I'll make *Poisson-Cru*. With tuna, lunch options include *Sushi, Poke* or sashimi.

Freezing Fish

Depending on the condition and size of the fillets I'll prepare extra fillets for freezing. The bigger the fillets, the longer they'll keep in the freezer. I place large fillets into gallon Ziploc bags, remove the air, and place them in another Ziploc for double protection. Small fillets get cut into bite size cubes and packed into quart Ziploc bags ready for meals such as *Fish Taco*s or *Fish Curry*.

Canning Fish

See Chapter 2.

Pickling Fish

Fish pickled in sterile jars will keep for several weeks.

4	fish fillets
3 C	vinegar
1 C	olive oil
3	garlic cloves – chopped
10	peppercorns
2 t	red pepper flakes

❖ Sauté fish fillets with garlic and red pepper 3 minutes each side, let cool.

❖ Pack fish into sterile jars with a few peppercorns and fill with 3/4 vinegar and 1/4 oil.

❖ Cover jars tightly.

❖ To use: drain fish and mix into a salad, rice dishes or pasta sauces.

Smoking Fish

See Chapter 2.

Resources

❖ *The Cruiser's Handbook of Fishing*, by Scott and Wendy Bannerot. International Marine ISBN 0-07-134560-4. This book is a fantastic reference covering all you need to know on how to fish, shrimp, crab, spearfish and cast nets.

Chapter 21

SEASICKNESS

Turning Green

Occasionally I'm asked if I've ever poisoned anyone. I can truthfully say that I don't think I have. Some folks aren't satisfied with that answer so they than ask if I've ever served a meal that was a disaster. The answer to this question is, yes! It was not so much the meal as the circumstances.

At 19 I'd volunteered to be the cook on a 10-day coastal voyage aboard New Zealand's youth sail-training 105' square-rigged ship, *The Spirit of Adventure*. The passage I chose was a rugged one from the town of New Plymouth, on the West Coast of the North Island, to the Manukau Harbour further north along the coast. Two years earlier, I'd been a trainee on *Spirit* and at 18 I'd returned as a watch leader. The next opportunity for me to sail on *Spirit* was when I turned 21 as then I could sail as a mate. Being disappointed that it would be three years before I could return, I asked if the cook's position had an age limit.

"No," was the reply.

"Great, sign me up!"

It was not until I was in the galley stowing supplies to feed six crew and 25 trainees, who were 17-year-old boys, that I started to have self-doubts. Walking into the freezer, I was overwhelmed by the quantity of food I was responsible for. Would there be enough of everything? Did I have all the necessary ingredients? Then there was a slight panic when I realized I'd been a vegetarian for over a year and wondered if I still remembered how to cook meat. I doubted if many of the trainees would welcome vegetarian meals.

On meeting with the captain, I was advised that we were to spend the first evening in port then depart first thing in the morning. I'd not chosen the provisions; they were the standard fare and they'd been loaded aboard before I arrived. After reading through the stores list I decided on corned beef for dinner. It had always been one of my least favorite meals so I thought it best to get it over with, in the hope that the meals would only get better.

The instructions for creating the meal seemed easy: boil the three-pound chunks of meat in water for over an hour, until tender, then serve the corned beef sliced with mashed potatoes and peas. I was on schedule, with the beef simmering away, when the captain came into the galley. He stated that the weather conditions were deteriorating as a cold front was coming our way. As New Plymouth was not a very sheltered harbor for *Spirit* and we were moored in the berth for the tender to the Maui natural gas platform it was best that that we put to sea.

We departed and dinner was served while we pounded our way north in a moderate swell. The trainees sat around the dining tables, a jovial group eagerly sounding out each other and rather smug that their adventure was under way. Apple pie and ice cream followed the main course and I breathed a sigh of relief that my first meal was a success.

As the seas began to build the trainees started turning green while coming to the realization that they were about to be seasick. When darkness fell a decision was made, for safety reasons, to assemble the trainees in the saloon rather than at their deck stations or in their bunks. Soon came the cry, "Get me a bucket, I'm going to be sick." Others quickly joined in and before long all five small buckets were occupied with seasick heads. The trainees were dropping like flies; those tough guys who had sat around the dinner table making jokes were now quiet and grey. I dashed down to the galley returning with six 5-gallon buckets used for swabbing the decks and vegetable preparation. I thought it best to place a bucket at each table.

The scene in the dining room was now comical – 25 lads slouched around the saloon floor with a wayward hand clutching one of the six buckets. Every few minutes a head would duck into a bucket, generally followed by a few others. In another scenario, you'd think they were bobbing for apples. This situation continued throughout the night as none of the trainees dared to go forward to their bunk; they felt safer in numbers.

By morning conditions had improved and after a hearty breakfast of porridge, dolphins appeared surfing on the bow waves raising everyones spirits. On future expeditions, I never again served boiled corned beef. My secret disguise for it was to chop it up and bake it with barbecue sauce as I never wanted a repeat of 25 green trainees.

Dehydration

* **Your body is about 70% water** and you've got to top it up to keep yourself bright-eyed and bushy-tailed! In the tropics you need to drink more water than usual, a minimum of 2-3 liters a day.

* **Breathing depletes one liter per day** and sweating depletes up to one liter per hour. When a breeze cools your skin you'll be unaware of losing fluid as your clothes aren't becoming damp and sweaty. The hotter it is plus the more you exercise and perspire, the more you'll need to drink.

❖ You need to have a way of **measuring your water intake**. It's your responsibility to avoid dehydration.

❖ **Once dehydrated**, you become a liability on board, not an asset. You can't rely on thirst to tell you when you need water, as you can become seriously dehydrated, to the point of going into shock, without becoming thirsty.

❖ **Diuretics** (fluids that cause your body to lose an equal amount of water) include coffee, black tea, cola and beer.

❖ **Water shortages**, contaminated shore water, and unappealing tank taste pose problems when the cruiser needs to be drinking ample water.

Symptoms of Dehydration

❖ **Symptoms of dehydration** are similar to food poisoning or flu - it's the body slowly going into shock due to the lack of moisture in the cells, including the brain.

❖ **Lack of hydration** can cause or affect the following: anxiety, constipation, cystitis, depression, diarrhea, drowsiness, excessive sleeping, strokes, headaches, heat stroke, irritability, liver damage, lack of concentration, loss of motivation, kidney stones, seasickness, and yawning.

❖ Dehydration is the **most common and serious medical problem** we encounter during our sailing expeditions.

Seasickness

❖ Motion sickness is a **physical disorder caused by sensory conflict** between the inner-ear balance center and visual perception.

Who Gets Seasick

❖ **Rare is the sailor who never gets seasick!**

❖ Those **most prone to motion sickness** are the very old, very young, and women. Women more susceptible to seasickness before and during menstruation and during pregnancy.

❖ People who've experienced **ruptured eardrums** either as a result of an infection or diving/surfing incident frequently suffer from seasickness.

❖ Seasickness is primarily a **hereditary condition**, with 20% of the population resistant, 20% extremely susceptible, and the rest somewhere in between.

Symptoms of Seasickness

❖ **Motion sickness begins with** skin pallor, cold sweating, drowsiness, yawning, and increased salivation. It may progress to symptoms of dizziness, headache, drowsiness, malaise, severe depression, and even reduced survival instincts. Gut symptoms of queasiness, nausea, vomiting and dry heaves follow.

Cautions and Care of the Seasick Sailor

Motion sickness can be seriously debilitating, causing physical safety problems on board as well as serious dehydration.

❖ Look after your seasick shipmates; they **may be weak, dizzy,** and unable to concentrate, making them incapable of looking after themselves. Their body temperature and blood pressure might be low and they may be at risk of hypothermia, even in the tropics. They may lack the motivation and energy to put on more clothing, so help them with warmer garments. Conversely, they may be frying in the sun, unable to move and protect themselves.

❖ Never assume seasick crew are capable of maintaining **a safe watch.**

❖ **Use a 1.5 liter** plastic container with tight fitting lid to vomit into. You can use the container above and below decks.

❖ **Don't lean over the side** to vomit use a container.

❖ Ensure seasick crew on deck are wearing a **safety harness**.

❖ Taking the self-steering vane or autopilot off and **hand-steering** might help avoid or cure seasickness.

❖ After vomiting, the seasick person's loss of body fluids and electrolytes (salts), low blood pressure, and increased blood viscosity can lead to serious problems. Encourage them to **take small amounts of fluids with electrolytes** every 15 minutes. Glucose and electrolyte fluids (such as oral rehydration salts, Gatorade, or Pedialyte) should be given, and they may also tolerate eating dry crackers. A mixture of one quart of water, 1 teaspoon salt and 1/2 teaspoon baking soda with lemon flavoring will also replace lost electrolytes.

❖ If the patient is **unable to take oral fluids** and is in progressive dehydration, fluids may be administered rectally or parentally by needle under the skin.

❖ **Rehydration** is critical to overcoming seasickness.

Prevention of Seasickness

Tips to Avoid And Reduce Seasickness

❖ Refrain from **eating fatty and spicy foods** the day before starting a passage.

❖ **Eliminate coffee and alcohol** at least 48 hours before starting, and during ocean passages.

❖ **Increase your water** intake to 2 to 3 liters/quarts per day.

❖ **Start medications** 12 hours before casting off especially if you have a history of seasickness.

❖ **Once seasickness nausea has begun,** it may be too late to take oral preparations. Keep a variety of preparations onboard, including rectal suppositories.

❖ The **result of taking seasickness medication** varies for each person, therefore, it may be necessary to try more than one remedy at different times.

❖ Continue the intake of fluids **or if shaky drink Gatorade, ORS** (oral rehydration salts) or some other electrolyte replacement.

❖ **Eat some food** in small amounts – such as crackers, cookies, crystallized ginger, canned fruit (this really works), and bananas.

❖ **Being on deck** and looking at a stationary point on the horizon reduces the sensory conflict.

❖ **Diversional activities**, especially steering the boat (but not reading), may reduce symptoms.

❖ If not steering, position yourself where there is **least motion** – from amidships to the stern. Preferably out in the fresh air, tethered in the cockpit and in a comfortable shady place.

❖ **Look at a fixed place** on the horizon. If you can't keep your eyes on a fixed object, keep them closed to reduce sensory conflict between the inner ear balance center and visual perception.

❖ Keep away from **odors**.

❖ A **cool wet cloth** placed on the back of the neck and forehead may help.

❖ **Lie on your back**, with head supported and still. Lying down prevents histamine from reaching the brain, decreasing nausea. If you're not on watch lie down in your bunk.

❖ When going below, first take your **foulies** off in the cockpit rather than below decks to reduce the time you spend below.

❖ When possible **minimize the time** you spend moving or working below. The faster you either get back on deck or lie down the better you'll feel.

❖ Avoid lying down in your **foulies** for an extended period of time to lessen the chance of hypothermia.

❖ **If sailing close-hauled,** it may be better to drop off a few degrees to a close reach and take an extra day or change your destination to another landfall for a more comfortable trip.

❖ Fortunately, motion sickness is usually only experienced the **first day or two** of a passage.

Alternative Remedies for Seasickness

These have the advantage of no noxious side effects, and help many but not all seasickness sufferers.

❖ **Ginger Powder Capsules**: Two taken every 4-6 hours may alleviate nausea symptoms. Ginger snap cookies and crystallized ginger are an old fishermen's prevention. A few slices of ginger root in hot water is also refreshing and worth trying, as is ginger ale.

❖ **Acupressure Wristbands**: These are straps with pressure nodules worn strategically around the wrist to exert pressure on specific acupressure points that prevent nausea. Conflicting reports exist about their effectiveness but if they work for you they offer the strong advantage of no drug side effects.

Medication for Seasickness

❖ **Nonprescription antihistamines:** include: Dramamine (chemical name Dimenhydrinate; brand names outside the U.S., Nauseatol, Andrumin), Marezine, Antivert, Bonine (Cyclizine, Meclizine, Meclozine, Ancoloxin, Bonamine, Ancolan). Dramamine causes the most drowsiness, Bonine is the longest acting, and Marezine causes the least drowsiness.

❖ **Outside the U.S.**, other medications such as Sturgeron may be available.

❖ The above antihistamines are for **mild seasickness** sensitivity and need to be taken prior to departure before any nausea symptoms begin. They take at least 4 hours to be fully effective and should be taken every 6 hours. Take at least 2 doses before departing, (e.g., 8 hours and 2 hours before departure). This allows adaptation to the drug and its side effects.

❖ Most antihistamines do have a noticeable **side effect** of drowsiness, which may be hazardous if the person is also responsible for keeping watch.

Prescription Drugs For Seasickness

❖ **Compazine Suppositories**: a good choice once nausea and vomiting have begun. They last at least 8 hours and may have some associated drowsiness but generally much less than with antihistamines. In rare cases, Compazine may cause an involuntary muscular rigidity (extrapyramidal syndrome), which is quickly overcome by taking an antihistamine such as Benadryl.

❖ **Transderm-Scopolamine**: These small drug-impregnated skin patches are placed behind the ear. The drug is absorbed through the skin into the blood stream. These are used mainly for prophylaxis and should be applied the night before departure. Each patch lasts for 72 hours. Caution should be taken not to get any of the drug in the eyes, otherwise blurring or loss of short-range vision due to pupillary dilation may occur, making it impossible to read the compass or chart. Wash hands well after applying. These patches have a few unpleasant side effects and may cause some drowsiness and blurring of vision, psychosis, and hallucination in some cases, increased sweating, bladder retention, and possibly decreased heart rate.

Chapter 22

WASTE
MANAGEMENT

Waste Responsibility

Whenever we travel it's our responsibility as visitors to be aware of the impact we have. By following guidelines we can lesson our impact on the environment and discover ways to make a positive contribution to the communities and places we visit.

MARPOL V International Treaty was created to reduce and eliminate the amount of ship generated garbage discharged into the ocean and applies to U.S. flag vessels anywhere in the world and to foreign flag vessels within the 200-mile Exclusive Economic Zone of the U.S. All vessels 26' and over are required to prominently display a durable placard of at least 4" x 9" in size notifying passengers and crew of MARPOL V discharge restrictions and penalties. In addition, vessels 40' and over are required to have a written waste-management plan describing the procedures used for collecting, processing, storing and discharging the vessel's garbage and listing the person in charge of the vessel's waste management.

Waste Reduction

❖ Consider alternatives to **plastic cling wrap**: reusable containers, silicone lids, reusable cloth covers or wax wrap.

❖ **Paper towels** are made white by bleaching with chlorine, the by product is dioxin which is one of the most carcinogenic chemical known to science. Instead use 100% recycled dioxin-free paper towels or alternatives such as dish towels, microfiber cloths or eco-friendly sponges.

❖ Another avoidable source of dioxin is **white-bleached paper coffee filters**. Alternatives are nylon filters, cotton or unbleached paper filters.

❖ Bring aboard as little **disposable plastic** as possible.

❖ Snip/break each of the rings of **plastic six-pack can holders** then if they accidentally fall overboard they won't get tangled in or strangle birds and marine animals.

❖ When you have an option, buy **supplies packaged in glass or metal**. We pull socks over glass jars and bottles to prevent them from rattling.

❖ We use **sponges and rolled up newspapers** to fill the spaces in lockers with items that rattle or move about.

❖ When arriving in a new port we're always on the lookout for **recycling bins.**

❖ When cruising in **less-developed countries**, we've found that villagers are sometimes happy to receive our used clean jars with lids.

❖ Make a point of saving **aluminum cans**, compressing them, and taking them to recycling bins.

❖ Many large motor yachts and sailing yachts have **trash compactors** in the galley. Most crews enthusiastically endorsed this product as a great way to reduce on board waste.

Waste Disposal on Ocean Passages

❖ At sea, we place **two plastic bags** in our galley garbage bin – one for plastic waste and the other for overboard waste

❖ When our **galley rubbish** is full or starts to smell we compact it before placing it inside a large sturdy garbage bag. We can choose the anchor, gas, or aft deck locker to store the trash bag in for intelligent and responsible disposal once we reach a major port.

❖ **Organic waste** from the galley gets thrown overboard at sea. I generally wrap galley scraps in newspaper and toss the entire package overboard.

❖ Unwanted **glass and cans** can be filled with salt water and dropped overboard only if you lack sufficient storage to hold them until your next port.

❖ **Plastic, batteries** and items detrimental to the environment should not be thrown overboard.

Tossing It All Away

D isposal of food wastes at sea can be challenging and the following incident compelled us to devise a better method for waste management.

We were on passage to Tahiti from New Zealand and it had been boisterous for a good week. The crew's seasick stomachs were slowly settling down and I'd made spaghetti for dinner although it was a struggle for some to finish their entire serving. Plates were returned to the galley and I scraped the leftovers onto a large dish. Ready to start the dishwashing, I handed the leftovers dish on deck, asking if someone on watch would dispose of the scraps overboard.

Suddenly the entire dish was sailing through the air. In an attempt to dislodge it's contents, the plate had been thrown like a frisbee except the plate was released along with the food. Double trouble had occurred as the food contents had also scattered about the deck. Now I use paper bags for food scraps or wrap them in newspaper so that the entire package can be tossed overboard with ease.

My mum has also told me a cautionary tale on washing dishes or laundry in a bucket. Before throwing away the sudsy water be sure to check the bottom of the bucket as many a item has been lost to Davy Jones's locker when the fouled water has been tossed overboard with an item hiding in its depths.

Waste in Port

❖ When arriving in port you need to **do your research** as to the correct procedure and place for your garbage disposal. Don't arrive at an anchorage and expect the locals to take responsibility for your waste. I once went ashore in a small village to do some provisioning and dispose of our rubbish. I was greeted by a group of eager children so I explained that I was looking for a trash bin. One of the girls stepped forward with a big smile and stated that she'd take my rubbish to the bin. I handed over our trash and headed into town. After completing my shopping I was half way back to the dinghy when, to my dismay, I spotted our garbage strewn about the roadside. It was obvious that it had been searched for anything interesting.

❖ I've been to some locations where garbage is tossed into the sea as the locals have a **"disposable"** attitude about material products. In the past items like coconut shell bowls, wooden spoons and woven fiber baskets would biodegrade, now however, goods made of plastic don't. They break down in the ocean to very small bits that may last forever.

❖ Our oceans have a lot of plastic floating in them. I'm often saddened by the sheer amount of **plastic garbage** littering the shoresides worldwide. Sometimes I'll choose a theme item, such as toothbrushes, shoes, disposable lighters or toys, to see how many I can collect in 5 minutes. I've created 3' long rainbows from lighters and I once titled a gathered toy figurine scenario "Toy Soldier Meets Godzilla on the Farm". Please be thoughtful on your trash disposal.

❖ If you can't wait until a major port for garbage disposal an option is to take your **"burnables"** ashore, dig a hole below the high tide line, burn them, then bury the ashes.

Freon Gas

Don't vent freon into the atmosphere when recharging your refrigeration system. Newer refrigeration systems use a freon replacement gas that's not harmful for the ozone. Ozone depletion is a major environmental problem as it increases the amount of ultraviolet radiation that reaches Earth's surface, which in turn increases the rate of skin cancer, eye cataracts, and genetic and immune system damage. Other sources of CFC (chlorofluorocarbon) pollution include halon extinguishers, aerosol spray cans, styrofoam and foam-fitting packaging.

RESOURCES
AND INDEX

Resources

Recommended Books

❖ **Cooking under Pressure** ~ Lorna Sass ~ an updated timeless classic with pressure cooker tips and recipes.

❖ **Good Boatkeeping** ~ Zora and David Aiken ~ ideas to make your boat safer, tidier, and homey.

❖ **Keeping Food Fresh** ~ Janet Bailey ~ practical advice on selecting and storing provisions.

❖ **Sailing the Farm** ~ by Ken Neumeyer ~ a guide to homesteading on the ocean.

❖ **The Cruiser's Handbook of Fishing** ~ Scott and Wendy Bannerot ~ an excellent reference.

❖ **The Joy of Cooking** ~ great all-round food reference and cookbook.

❖ **The Top One Hundred Pasta Sauces** ~ Dianne Seed ~ superb recipes for pasta lovers.

❖ **The Voyager's Handbook** ~ Beth Leonard ~ valuable and essential information for the offshore cruiser.

Manufactures of Long Lasting Food

❖ **Alpine Aire** ~ www.alpineairefoods.com ~ quality individual freeze-dried meals using wholesome ingredients.

❖ **Backpacker's Pantry** ~ www.backpackerspantry.com ~ a wide range of great freeze-dried meals and food.

❖ **Mountain House** ~ www.mountainhouse.com ~ a wide variety of freeze-dried food and meals ranging from individual servings to 1-gallon cans that serve ten.

❖ **Eggs** ~ www.amazon.com ~ powered, whites, yolks and scrambled.

❖ **Washington State University Creamery** ~ creamery.wsu.edu ~ 30oz cans of natural cheddar cheese.

Galley Supplies

- ❖ **Plastic Storage Containers** ~ www. consolidatedplastic.com ~ wide mouth square containers with plastic screw caps.

- ❖ **Plastic Bags** ~ www.bradleybag.com ~ different sizes and thicknesses of zipper plastic bags.

- ❖ **Seagull IV Water Purification System** ~ www.gernaral-ecology. com ~ General Ecology, H_2O Purification

Marine Stores

- ❖ **Downwind Marine** ~ www.downwindmarine.com ~ located in San Deigo they offer a broad range of cruising gear.

- ❖ **Fisheries Supply Seattle** ~ www.fisheriessupply.com ~ based in Seattle, Fisheries carries over 100,000 products and ship worldwide.

- ❖ **West Marine** ~ www.westmarine.com ~ over 250 stores nationwide and ships equipment to cruisers worldwide. An excellent source for galley supplies, including stoves, barbecues, cookware, non-skid dinnerware and Scoot-Gard.

Foreign Provisioning Information

- ❖ **Noonsite.com** ~ the ultimate cruisers resource.
- ❖ **Seven Seas Cruising Association**. (SSCA) ~ www.ssca.org

Index

Resources and Index

Additional Titles From
Mahina Offshore Services

Offshore Cruising Companion
by John Neal & Amanda Swan Neal

An indispensable guide for preparing yourself and your sailboat for safe coastal and offshore adventures, as well as the textbook for the Offshore Cruising Seminars. We offer unbiased sage advice on over 36 topics including: Boat Selection, Priority and Optional Equipment, Seamanship, Anchoring, Storm Tactics, Communications, Insurance and Managing Your Escape. Updated annually, this comprehensive book also contains multiple checklists and resources allowing you to fast-track your cruising dreams into reality. 270 pages, $60.00

The Expedition Companion
by Amanda Swan Neal and John Neal

This manual covers most topics taught on our sail-training expeditions. If you're considering and expedition with us, this book will help you evaluate our offshore instruction program. 98 pages, $20.00

Marine Diesel Engine Essentials –
A Learning and Coloring Book
by Amanda Swan Neal

This 20-page coloring book takes you on an exploratory adventure to help you understand the six systems that make a marine diesel engine work. As you color, notes, labels, and whimsical sea-themed friends help you identify the individual components of each system. Illustrated by sailing artist Andrea England and endorsed by diesel engine expert Nigel Calder. $10

Selecting & Purchasing an Ocean Cruising Boat
by John Neal   www.mahina.com/book.pdf

This free book enables you to select an offshore cruising boat with confidence and pride, knowing that the listed boats are tried and tested. Chapters include: 20 Qualities of an Ideal Cruising Boat, Evolution of Yacht Design, Why Some Boats More Expensive than Others, Negative Design and Construction Aspects to be Avoided, and 400 Specific Recommended Boats.

Storm Survival Tactics

by John and Amanda Swan Neal

This 25-page booklet accompanies our one-hour Mastering Storm Survival and Avoidance Seminar. Topics include: Selecting Your Boat and Equipment, Sail Reduction Guide, Understanding Weather, Ten Storm Procedures and Tactics, Seasickness, and Dealing with Anxiety and Fears. $10

Also Available

Mahina Offshore Cruising Seminar

Our eight-hour seminar is presented annually in mulitple locations throughout North America and is packed with current information. Each of the eighteen topics have a dedicated PowerPoint presentation that closely follow the *Offshore Cruising Companion* ensuring you'll understand and retain crucial information needed for your cruising adventures.

Mahina Offshore Sail-Training Expeditions

Consider joining us for a unique hands-on experience. Expeditions are one to three weeks long, providing the opportunity for you to increase your confidence and safety level. Daily instruction with documentation and testing ensures that you become totally competent in all aspects of operating, navigating, and maintaining a modern cruising boat.

Mahina Boat Purchase Consultation

If you're searching for a boat for offshore voyaging and want to avoid costly mistakes and time-consuming errors, we can help you. $750

P.O Box 1596, Friday Harbor, WA 98250, USA

phone 360.378.6161   sailing@mahina.com

www.mahina.com

About the Author

Amanda Swan Neal grew up in a boat building and sailing family in New Zealand and has been traveling the world under sail, covering 345,000 miles since she was 11 years old. Her first professional cooking experience was at 19 aboard the 105' *Spirit of Adventure*, one of New Zealand's sail-training tall ships, and later she helped design the galley and sailed as an officer aboard the 150' *Spirit of New Zealand*. Amanda has also worked in some of Auckland's and Sydney's finest restaurants and as chef aboard the classic 76' Fife yacht *Tuiga* for a voyage through the Mediterranean.

Amanda is a qualified sailmaker and was the rigger aboard *Maiden,* the first all-women entry in the 1989-90 Whitbread Around the World Race. *Maiden* won two strenuous Southern Ocean legs in their class, finishing second in their division.

Joining John Neal aboard *Mahina Tiare II* in 1994 Amanda has co-conducted over 203 offshore sail-training expeditions in locations from Antarctica to Alaska and Svalbard to Australia. She has lectured extensively in Europe, North America and New Zealand and contributes to numerous sailing magazines. Since 2005 Amanda has written the monthly Galley Essentials column in *48 North Magazine* and she is the author of *Marine Diesel Engine Essentials – A Learning and Coloring Book.*

Amanda annually spends seven months at sea on sail-training expeditions with her husband, John Neal aboard their Hallberg-Rassy 46, *Mahina Tiare III*. When not at sea they live on San Juan Island, Washington.

Made in the USA
Monee, IL
29 July 2020